About Entrepreneurship

About Entrepreneurship

Björn Bjerke
Linnaeus University, Sweden

Edward Elgar
Cheltenham, UK • Northampton, MA, USA

Published by
Edward Elgar Publishing Limited
The Lypiatts
15 Lansdown Road
Cheltenham
Glos GL50 2JA
UK

Edward Elgar Publishing, Inc.
William Pratt House
9 Dewey Court
Northampton
Massachusetts 01060
USA

A catalogue record for this book
is available from the British Library

Library of Congress Control Number: 2013932986

978 1 78254 538 5 (cased)
978 1 78254 539 2 (paperback)
978 1 78254 540 8 (eBook)

Typeset by Servis Filmsetting Ltd, Stockport, Cheshire
Printed and bound in Great Britain by T.J. International Ltd, Padstow

Contents in brief

Full contents

Introduction:
A book about, for or in
entrepreneurship?

Why this book?

There are many books published on the subject of entrepreneurship and more are on their way at a great rate. Entrepreneurship has truly become a popular subject. In this wave of literature, readers may ask themselves why I, as a researcher and author, found a reason for writing one more book. There are many ways to justify this. Two such motives (which are not directly to do with me personally) could be, first, that the subject of entrepreneurship today has become so wide that there is always knowledge space to fill and, second, that the subject is developing so fast that what is already written in the subject quick becomes outdated. Both of these general reasons have had some influence on my decision to write this book.

There are, however, as I see it, two more specific reasons behind the writing of this book, above all behind its content and wording. Both have to do with how I experience most books and what else that has been written or is on its way to be written discussing entrepreneurship:

1. It is my opinion that very little entrepreneurship text clarifies whether it is *about* entrepreneurship, *for* entrepreneurship or *in* entrepreneurship.
2. I claim that much of what is written discussing entrepreneurship covers more aspects of the subject than what I would call *purely entrepreneurial aspects*.

Let me clarify what I mean by these two statements.

What books discussing entrepreneurship can cover

I will present a more extensive picture of the history of the academic subject of entrepreneurship in the next chapter, but let me here, in order to give a further perspective on how to look at this book, put some light on what has been stressed when discussing entrepreneurship from a theoretical perspective during the years. The subject is (academically) about 300 years old and during the first 250 years or so (that is, until the middle of the twentieth century), only economists were involved in discussing it (Hébert and Link, 1982; Casson, 1982; Barreto, 1989). Books (and other texts) discussing entrepreneurship were about *the role and the function that entrepreneurship plays in an economy* (it may be worth pointing out that very few economists were interested in the entrepreneurship phenomenon). Aspects like, for instance, how entrepreneurship influences growth and revitalization of an economy, the amount and importance of entrepreneurship in different economic cycles, or which types of businesses and industries that dominated specific historical periods, were discussed. Scholars were, however, never interested in, for instance, what kind of people entrepreneurs were physically, mentally or culturally, nor in what business start-ups look like, how they are shaped or how they develop, when they are successful.

What scientific field the person discussing entrepreneurship belongs to will, of course, influence which focus he or she has and which theories he or she is using or developing (Landström and Löwegren, 2009, p. 20). It was, however, not until the second half of the twentieth century that researchers other than economists started to be interested in the subject of entrepreneurship. It was then mainly behavioural scientists such as psychologists, sociologists and anthropologists, whose approach was gradually combined with those views of different kinds of business scholars, who led the development (Filion, 1997; Grant, 1998; Scott et al., 1998; Tornikoski, 1999; Alberti, 1999; Landström 2005; Bjerke, 2007). Other aspects of entrepreneurship then entered the subject, like the psychological profile of entrepreneurs, their behavioural pattern, their networking, management and marketing of new business ventures, government support of entrepreneurship and entrepreneurship education. During the latest 10–15 years or so, other types of entrepreneurs than the purely economic ones have been added, that is, social entrepreneurs (Brinckerhoff, 2000; Borzaga and Defourney, 2001; Nicholls, 2006; Wei-Skillern et al., 2007; Gawell et al., 2009; Ziegler, 2009; Bjerke and Karlsson, 2013) and, among others, entrepreneurs with different ethnic backgrounds (Light and Gold, 2000; Ram et al., 2006) academic entrepreneurship (Nordfors et al., 2003; Bengtsson, 2006) and entrepreneurship in a gender perspective (Ahl, 2002; Holmquist and Sundin, 2002; Campbell,

2004; Carter and Bennett, 2006). This book is written by a business scholar, which the reader should keep in mind when reading it.

At the same time as the development of entrepreneurship theories has taken place, there has been a methodical development of how to study this phenomenon (Fayolle et al., 2005). The methodical issue of science at large is, of course, older than the issue of entrepreneurship, but of interest to the entrepreneurship subject (even if the influences were seen much later in the development of this subject), heated discussions about which methods that should govern science took place within historical sciences in the nineteenth century (Böhm-Bawerk, 1890–91). According to von Wright (1971) and Apel (1984), the historical scientist Johann Gustav Droysen (1808–84) was a prominent figure here. In his work *Grundrisse der Historik* (1858 [1897]), he formulated three possible scientific ambitions: to speculate, to explain and to understand. Explanations aim at objectivities while understanding (and speculations, of course) allows subjectivities. It is possible to see Ludwig von Mises (1933 [1981]) as one of the first contributions to the subjective idea within entrepreneurship research. Von Mises called his approach a praxeology, the science of purposeful human actions (Buchanan, 1982; Rizzo, 1982).

The differences between 'explaining' and 'understanding' are decisive to understanding the differences between Chapters 4 and 5 in this book, that is, the differences between what could be called the narrow and the broad views of entrepreneurship, which are related to the state of opposition between the analytical dominance in scientific thinking in the United States – for instance, within entrepreneurship research with its economic roots – and some more interpretive currents in Europe (I will present a more philosophical and theoretical discussion of the differences between 'to explain' and 'to understand' in Chapter 11). This is also related to the earlier mentioned transition from when only economists studied entrepreneurship (economists are generally very explanatory oriented) to when more behavioural human approaches were used to study this subject. One consequence of the same transition is that a number of qualitative research approaches have appeared besides those quantitative research approaches that dominated before (Stevenson and Harmeling, 1990; MacMillan and Katz, 1992; Choi, 1993; Hill and Wright, 2001; Neergaard and Ulhøi, 2007).

Let me, with this background, go over to my two previously mentioned opinions about and experiences of many existing books in the subject of entrepreneurship, what I see as their lack of precision, that is, that they rarely say whether they are about, for or in entrepreneurship, and that they often go beyond what I see as what entrepreneurship is all about and should be about.

The entrepreneurial orientation of this book

It is possible, as I see it, to have three alternative orientations when writing a book discussing entrepreneurship, orientations that I think are very difficult to combine in one and the same book:

- *About entrepreneurship*. This a book about what you *think you know about the subject*, directed at readers who may want to get a comprehensive knowledge of what entrepreneurship consists of as an academic subject. Such a book may, for instance, be used as a textbook for students at a university, who want to get an overview of what the subject is about and what the researchers think they know about the subject at present. The same type of book can also be directed at people, who want to get a basic general knowledge of what entrepreneurship means in a modern per-spective without looking at it as part of a formal education.
- *For entrepreneurship*. This is a book written for people who would *want to become* entrepreneurs. There are several differences between what you are looking for in knowledge *about* and *for* entrepreneurship, that is, dif-ferences between, on one hand, a compilation of what you should know about a subject after having studied it in all important variations and, on the other hand, a description what a person should know *before* he or she enters an entrepreneurial career. It is so, for instance, that when reading about entrepreneurship the point may be to take part of the findings that entrepreneurs are active networkers, that successful entrepreneurs *after the fact* may look like they have followed a clear plan, that they have used opportunities at hand and that they are good at marketing in the wide sense of the term, all of it specified in some kind of theoretical terms. Persons *who intend to become entrepreneurs* may possibly rather consider whether they have the persistence, the powers of persuasion and the right contacts without putting this in any theoretical framework. To think too much may even be an obstacle to starting something new!
- *In entrepreneurship*. This is a book for people who are *already on* an entre-preneurial track, who have problems and/or want to become better in that orientation in life. What they need is completely dependent on the situation in which they are. It may, for instance, be a better plan, appro-priate banks to talk to or contacts with people who can join them to sup-plement those skills that may be needed for their business operations to succeed better and to move forward.

This book is meant to be a book *about* entrepreneurship and it is based on my collected theoretical and practical experiences of the subject for more than 30 years.

The other 'criticism' that I mentioned is that I find that books about entrepreneurship contain more than just entrepreneurship. Such a statement is, of course, dependent on my opinion of what the subject of entrepreneurship is about and what it is not about. Let me clarify this issue before I, at the end of this introductory chapter, summarize my conceptualization of what I think entrepreneurship is and provide an overview of how the book is laid out as it goes on.

Enterprising, entrepreneurship, small business and management

Books presenting themselves as being about entrepreneurship do not always make a distinction between enterprising, entrepreneurship and small business, which I think should be done. As the reader will see soon, I *associate* entrepreneurship with being *enterprising*, which small (and even big) businesses not always are (even if they may once have been so). If you put an *equals sign* between enterprising and entrepreneurship and between entrepreneurship and small business there is a risk that you are a victim of what Wood (2005) refers to as *the fallacy of misplaced concretization*, that is, to confuse a concept with a way in which this concept may express itself (Lindgren, 2009, p. 216). As mentioned, all small businesses may not be entrepreneurial, as I see it, and even big businesses can be entrepreneurial. Entrepreneurship in established business firms (small or big) is sometimes called *intrapreneurship*. All enterprising is, as I see it, not entrepreneurial. Only some enterprising is (see further in this chapter). I want to present it as in Figure I.1., which is based on Bridge et al. (2009, p. 1).

Figure I.1
Enterprising,
entrepreneurship and
small business

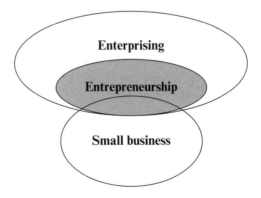

Enterprising is used in a number of situations with a number of different meanings. There is a narrow view of enterprising in the limited sense of entrepreneurship specifically concerning business firms and there is a broader view that has a more general human meaning (see further in Chapters 2, 4 and 5).

The reason why an equals sign is often placed between enterprising and entrepreneurship and between entrepreneurship and small business is that 'enterprising' sounds like 'entrepreneurship' and that businesses are, practically speaking, always starting small and that, because the subject of entrepreneurship, due to its popularity, has been allowed to contain ever more, even if the mentioned narrow view still is completely dominating. With this view it is claimed that entrepreneurship, above all, has several positive economic consequences like new jobs and economic development and that most new jobs are created by small firms (when they grow).

I mean that, in order to get a better focus on what you are talking about, a distinction should be made between enterprising, entrepreneurship and small business (which specific differences I refer to more specifically will come up as we move on in this introductory chapter). To express it more distinctly: businesses are not always enterprising and business leaders are not always leaders!

Some opinions about enterprising (Bridge et al., 2009, pp. 143–6):

- Enterprising is a relative concept
- Enterprising is a good thing
- Enterprising is necessary for the development of the society
- Enterprising has strong political and social consequences

Enterprising is a relative concept

Some societies are considered to be more enterprising (at least in the narrow business sense of the term) during some periods compared with other periods. Societies in South East Asia (so-called tiger economies) are often brought up as an example of this and they were, during the latest 30 years or so, thought to be more enterprising than those societies that were placed in the East European bloc. Whether the Western world can be thought of as enterprising or not depends on what you compare it with (I will be back discussing business entrepreneurship in different cultures in Chapter 10).

Individuals can be thought of as being enterprising or not in a broader, not just economic, sense, which indicates some kind of relative judgement as well. In practice, you then compare an individual with another individual or with some kind of 'standard level' of an enterprising individual, even if this standard may vary over time and between different places and situations. It is so, however, that even in enterprising societies not everybody is enterprising, even if the society at large could be thought of as enterprising. On the other hand, the more people that are enterprising in a society, the more you can say that the society as a whole is enterprising.

In short, there are no objective marks of what constitutes a high, low or normal enterprising level.

Enterprising is a good thing

More enterprising is normally preferred to less enterprising. The assumption is based on things such as that a more enterprising individual influences his or her environment, for instance, by creating more utilities and/or jobs, more pleasure and/or welfare and/or citizenship compared with a less enterprising individual. This is so at a national as well as a local level of a society. Why this is so is not always clear, but it seems to be associated with the view that enterprising leads to a higher quality of life or to a better ability to control one's own future. Enterprising individuals and enterprising societies have truly become synonymous with successful individuals and successful societies.

To associate a successful society with enterprising may, of course, have its unpleasant sides. It may mean, for instance, that you believe that the society stands or falls with entrepreneurship. The relationships in a society are never so one-dimensional in my opinion.

Enterprising is necessary for the development of the society

Enterprise may lead to more happiness or a better situation, but those means or that process by which this takes place is rarely particularly clear. It is somewhat simpler to discuss enterprising in a pure business sense. It seems to be, as has already been mentioned, that it will lead to more job opportunities and economic growth. Whether this means more happiness is, however, a different issue, which is beyond the scope of this book to clarify. Less clear (or possibly more complicated) is what the consequences are of entrepreneurship in a more social (not only economic) meaning. I have, however, problems in seeing any negative consequences of more enterprising. It could possibly be that stressing this could, perhaps, lead to neglect of basic social problems like quality, justice and morality.

Enterprising has strong political and social consequences

The term enterprising is applied and used, as mentioned, concerning aspects with a broader cultural orientation as well as to describe the way in which single individuals can act. Let me here just keep to the former; in this book, to discuss political and social consequences of individual enterprising in any detail would lead too far. In Europe, during a major part of the twentieth century, the government configuration in the eastern and central parts has been communistic. The economies in these countries were centrally planned unlike those market economies that existed in the rest of Europe. The latter, together with some countries (for instance, the United States), were often characterized as countries with 'free enterprise' and this way 'enterprise' got a political connotation. Such references to enterprise provide an image of freedom, liberalism, market dominance and free individual choices, which have many political and social associations.

Different sizes of business

The European Commission coined the presently widely recognized term 'small and medium enterprises' (SMEs) and defined this in 1996 by classifying businesses as follows:

Microbusiness	0–9 employees
Small business	10–49 employees
Middle-sized business	50–249 employees
Big business	250 employees or more

Highest levels for turnover and budget volume were also given when talking about a business as an SME. In other parts of the world the classification looks different. In the United States, for instance, having 500 employees or more is needed to be referred to as big business.

Many commentators assert, however, that small business is not only based on numbers but also on more qualitative circumstances such as the following three criteria:

1. *Market influence.* In economic terms a small business firm has a small part of the market. It is therefore normally not big enough to be able to influence the prices and the national quantities of those goods and/or services they provide. Many successful business firms, which are small as far as number of employees is concerned, may however operate in a market segment where they can influence the prices as well as the quantities that are offered, at least locally.

2. *Independence.* The small business firm is independent in the sense that it is not part of a larger business firm and that its owners and senior managers are formally independent of control from outside and they can make their own decisions.
3. *Personal influence.* The small business firm is led in a personal way and not by mediation of a larger business firm in a formal leadership structure. The person at the top of the small business firm (often the owner) is involved in all possible aspects of his or her firm.

Small business is interesting if for no other reason than in most societies, the majority of business firms are small. This book is, however, not about small business as such but about entrepreneurship (which, sometimes, may be the same).

Entrepreneurship, innovation and self-employment

How is the concept of entrepreneurship related to the concepts of innovation and self-employment? As in the case of entrepreneurship, enterprise and small business, these three concepts are often seen as approximately the same. The equality between entrepreneurship and innovation can be traced back to Schumpeter (1934, p. 74), who defined entrepreneurs as individuals who come up with new combinations in the economic value chain of the society, which is one way to look at innovations. Schumpeter separated four roles in the innovation process: the inventor, who comes up with a new idea; the entrepreneur, who commercializes this new idea; the capitalist, who provides the financial resources to the entrepreneur; and the manager, who takes care of the daily routines in the company, realizing the innovation. These roles are usually played by different individuals (Kenney, 1986). The entrepreneurship literature can see in the narrow view of the concept some variations of the entrepreneurial, which, however, in all cases have at least implicitly an economically positive connotation. If the entrepreneurs are defined as those persons who are ingenious and creative in finding a way to extend their own assets, power and prestige (Baumol, 1990), it could be expected that their activities will not always provide any major contribution to the society at large (Murphy et al., 1991). There are also other reasons why many entrepreneurs do not directly contribute to the increase of the gross national product in economic terms: some types of entrepreneurship, of a social entrepreneurial type, are, for instance, rather characterized as a non-profit seeking activity (Benz, 2006).

More independence and self-fulfilment are often mentioned as important prime motivators to becoming self-employed (EOS Gallup, 2004).

Empirical studies show that the (average) start in self-employment, however, has a negative effect on a person's monetary income (Hamilton, 2000; Parker, 2004). To be an entrepreneur can, however, be favourable over and above just being self-employed because it may lead to non-monetary merits like more independence, broader use of one's own skills and the possibility of implementing one's own ideas, that is, more freedom (Sen, 1999). These far-reaching effects of entrepreneurship are seen behind the broad view of entrepreneurship, that is, everything from growth of employment, lower unemployment, flexibility in the economy and degree of innovation in the economy to individual development, emancipation of women and integration of immigrants into the new society.

There are lots of definitions of entrepreneurship (Hébert and Link, 1989; Thurik and Van Dijk, 1998). There is really no single answer to the question of what the entrepreneurial phenomenon 'really' is or what it is all about 'more exactly'. Rather than looking for some essential 'really true' definition of entrepreneurship, people often prefer to study different varieties and functions of entrepreneurship. If we bring together all business-oriented entrepreneurial definitions, they show in rough outlines two relatively distinct (but overlapping) phenomena (compare Davidsson, 2004). The first of these is the phenomenon that some people, instead of working for somebody else in an employment contract, break out on their own and become self-employed. This often means some degree of innovation at the start-up (at least for the entrepreneur) and probably often requires some degree of innovative ability in order to survive. However, innovation must not be substantial in this context. There are many examples of self-employment, for instance, when a person educated in law starts a lawyer's firm, when a doctor participates in opening a private clinic or when somebody opens a shop or a restaurant, which may not have any notable innovation content.

The second phenomenon means a clearer renewal and development of a society, market, economy or organization based on actors at a micro level taking the initiative and having the perseverance to make things happen in a new way. 'Entrepreneurship' means here the creation of new stand-alone economic activities and organizations ('independent entrepreneurship') as well the transformation of those economic operations that exist already ('intrapreneurship').

My conceptualization of entrepreneurship is more focused on the second phenomenon. Some self-employed are innovative, but most of them are not and I am interested in innovative enterprising. In order to get some limitations on my discussion, however, I suggest that entrepreneurship should be looked at as a market change (in the business entrepreneurial case) or a new social arrangement in some way (in the social entrepreneurial case). The change of market or the new arrangement in society normally means some kind of new value to the user (hopefully higher) or new ways to provide or deliver existing values. This means, in my understanding of entrepreneurship, excluding some varieties of being one's own (like non-innovative self-employment) and part of the innovative phenomenon, even if I mean that all entrepreneurship contains some aspects of acting innovatively, at least periodically. See Figure I.2, which is based on Stam and Nooteboom (2011, p. 424).

I exclude from my meaning of entrepreneurship, for instance, activities like specific changes of contract (for example, from employed to self-employed) plus internal, administrative or organizational changes which do not influence the market or the rest of society at all. I also exclude considerations of new ideas or completely unsuccessful attempts which also do not influence the market or the rest of the society. Consequently, I do not include all news or all creativity within all human behavioural areas in my entrepreneurship concept. We should finally bear in mind that much of entrepreneurship takes place part-time, that is, many people combine it with being employed somewhere else or employed in other ways. This complicates the picture a bit.

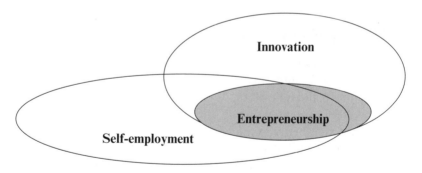

Figure I.2 Entrepreneurship, innovation and self-employment

It is possible to formulate four necessary conditions for entrepreneurship, the way I see it:

● Entrepreneurship is not only the result of the fact that entrepreneurial opportunities (changes in the environment: technological, political/regulatory, social/demographic) have come up, which is a common opinion about entrepreneurship (Shane, 2003; see further in Chapter 2 of this book) but can also be a result of the existence of entrepreneurial ambitions *which do not* arise from entrepreneurial opportunities, but simply from a person's interest in acting innovatively and achieving something new for himself or herself and for others.

- There are differences between people in their willingness and ability to perceive and act on an opportunity or in their entrepreneurial orientation without any apparent entrepreneurial opportunities.
- Organization of entrepreneurial activities (can be a reaction to an entrepreneurial opportunity existing in society, but can also be a consequence of a person's entrepreneurial interests without the existence of such an opportunity) can take place either by creating a new business operation or renewing an old one or by developing some other kind of social activities.
- Entrepreneurship means innovation, a combination of resources (in a limited economic sense or in a wider sense) in a new shape which is not a perfect imitation of what exists already, and which users in the society (could be, for instance, consumers, clients or citizens) perceive as a change and something new.

At the same time, however, entrepreneurship is incredibly full of variations and very contextual, in my opinion. I will come back to this several times in this book.

Entrepreneurship and management

A distinction is not always made (which I do) between enterprise, entrepreneurship and small business or between self-employment, entrepreneurship and innovation. It is also possible to see no important differences between entrepreneurship and management. Everybody does not make a distinction between the two. There are many who assert, especially in the narrow view of entrepreneurship, that entrepreneurship is a kind of management. In my opinion, as a representative of the broad view of entrepreneurship, management and entrepreneurship are based on different logic and thinking.

> I make use of an analysis of entrepreneurship as distinct from management, the latter being focused on efficient stewardship of existing resources and social control, while the former is animated primarily by creativity, desire, playfulness and the passion for actualizing what could come into being. (Hjorth, 2009, p. 207)

Management can be seen, which I do, as primarily a profession, a profession where the point is to handle a more or less given situation (compare the relationship between the words 'management' and 'manual', that is, something that has to with your hands = handle). In order to handle what is needed as a manager, you need technical skills in the wide sense of the term (like reading an organization diagram, coming up with a budget, closing the books, etc.). As manager, you relate to the company where you are employed or the organization where you work and whether you are successful or not is judged by this employer or place of work. Entrepreneurship is more of an attitude, a view of life, being interested in coming up with something new. To be able to do this, mental skills are needed first of all. You relate to the user of what you have come up with; whether you are successful or not is judged by this person.

I will come back to similarities and differences between management and entrepreneurship later.

What this book is about and what it is not about

Let me present what this book is about and what it is not about as points:

- It is possible to say that management and marketing can be done in a more entrepreneurial way. Entrepreneurial marketing is, for instance, an established concept (Bjerke and Hultman, 2002). But none is necessary for a company to be able to grow (it may, however, be needed for a business firm to survive). It is probably crucial to having a good formula and a successful way to work and implement this in management as well as in marketing at a larger scale than before (more of the same, so to say) in order to grow.
  So, I do not deny that there are aspects of business that could be called entrepreneurial management and entrepreneurial marketing (or entrepreneurial financing to take an example from another business function), but I hardly discuss them at all in this book. It would be to go too far to do so.
- This also means that I am not particularly interested in growth issues in this book. Growth has more to do with management and marketing than with entrepreneurship, as I see it.
- Nor am I particularly interested in issues of strategy in this book. It is my conviction and experience that entrepreneurs rarely think strategically in the meaning in which that subject is normally treated in the business literature.
- There is a huge number of different kinds of entrepreneurs and the number and specialties of the phenomenon seem to grow all the time

(for instance, e-entrepreneurs, student entrepreneurs, technology entrepreneurs or barefoot entrepreneurs). I discuss these 'special types' very little in this book with two exceptions: social entrepreneurs (a rapidly growing category) in Chapter 6 and women as entrepreneurs (which concerns half of humankind) in Chapter 9.

- Entrepreneurs also appear in a number of different situations. To give one, which I see as interesting, view of this, I discuss entrepreneurs in different 'national' cultures in Chapter 10.
- This book is about entrepreneurship, which I do not see as the same as enterprise, small business, self-employment or innovation, even if there are connections between entrepreneurship and all these concepts.
- Regional development is a popular subject today. This subject, however, contains much more than entrepreneurship, for instance, economics, politics, geography and history. But I claim that local development is very dependent on different kinds of entrepreneurs. I discuss this in Chapter 7.
- In spite of the fact that creativity is intimately related to entrepreneurship (above all in the broad view of the subject; see below), I enter very little into a discussion about creativity in this book. I refer the interested reader to special literature discussing creativity more thoroughly.
- In the same way, innovation is closely related to enterprising business, that is, entrepreneurship (I mean that all entrepreneurship contains some aspect of innovation), but, as mentioned already, I do not discuss this subject specifically. Here also, I refer the interested reader to special literature.
- The book is practically exclusively about the very start of a business or another social activity, which did not exist in exactly the same form before and I am not particularly interested in what comes after this start in this book (where these activities often stop being entrepreneurial anyway). I discuss, to some extent, entrepreneurship in existing businesses, that is, intrapreneurship, in Chapter 8.
- I have put together more profound philosophical and theoretical discussions in a chapter of their own (Chapter 11) for those that may be especially interested in these topics.
- At the end of every chapter, there are a number of 'Think' exercises and a case study from practice, which may be of some use when studying the subject alone or when teaching it.

My conceptualization of 'entrepreneurship': a summary

It is necessary to be enterprising when a situation is (Bridge et al., 2009, p. 58):

⇨ non-routine
⇨ somewhat complex
⇨ goal-directed

when the goals are

⇨ demanding but attainable

and when the task is

⇨ tackled in an adventurous manner
⇨ approached in a determined and dynamic manner
⇨ accomplishing the set goals (or comes near to doing so)

Enterprising is often seen as the same as entrepreneurship, which has been mentioned already, but this must not, as I see it, be the case. In order to set some limits on a phenomenon that can easily (and in many cases already has) exceeded all borders (there are many, who warn against allowing entrepreneurship to mean almost anything and that the concept has been watered down that way, for instance, Jones and Spicer, 2009), I want to conceptualize entrepreneurship to such enterprises that lead to results which *have some kind of news value, at least in some respect, and which are used by somebody who is not (only) the entrepreneur him- or herself.* This somebody could be called the user (the entrepreneur could also be a user, of course). Whether entrepreneurial results may come up outside the limits of the law or possibly be forced to happen by some kind of dictator, I do not take any stand for or against here.

In order to leave some doors open, I rather want to talk about *conceptualizations* (from the Latin *concipere* = summarize) than about *definitions* (from the Latin *definire* = put limits to). Most American definitions of 'entrepreneurship' tend to limit it to specific behaviour and to specific thinking. Some examples:

> Entrepreneurship is the process by which individuals pursue opportunities without regard to resources they currently control. The essence of entrepreneurial behavior is identifying opportunities and putting useful ideas into practice. The tasks called for by this behavior can be accomplished by either an individual or a group and typically require creativity, drive, and a willingness to take risks. (Barringer and Ireland, 2006, p. 5)

> Entrepreneurship, as a field of business, seeks to understand how opportunities to create something new arise and are discovered or created by specific individuals,

who then use various means to exploit or develop them, thus producing a wide range of effects. (Baron and Shane, 2008, p. 5)

An entrepreneur is one who creates a new business in the face of risk and uncertainty for the purpose of achieving profit and growth by identifying opportunities and assembling the necessary resources to capitalize on those opportunities. (Scarborough et al., 2009, p. 21)

Entrepreneurship is a mindset or way of thinking that is opportunity-focused, innovative, and growth-oriented. Entrepreneurship is also a set of behaviors. Entrepreneurs recognize opportunity, gather the resources required to act on the opportunity, and drive the opportunity to completion. (Allen, 2010, p. 3)

I do not want to put such limits of entrepreneurs by characterizing them in terms of separate features, behaviours or acts. It is my opinion, for instance, that entrepreneurs, in order to succeed, must not have a specified general behaviour set-up (the hope and belief in finding a specified general set of character traits associated with entrepreneurs only, most researchers have given up on long time ago), nor that they must be growth-oriented, which is common in the American type of definitions (see above). It is even so that most business firms do not grow after having been started (or are even interested in growing) over and above a certain level (Davidsson, 1989; Wiklund, 1998). Social entrepreneurial ventures are often more useful if they are locally connected and do not become too big (Nicholls, 2006, p. 226).

To be involved over and above the usual

I am of the general opinion that entrepreneurs, maybe social entrepreneurs in particular, should be seen with the use of one's 'acting' eyes, not by one's 'behaviour' eyes (the differences between 'behaviour' and 'acts' are discussed more thoroughly in Chapter 11). I have found it useful to discuss entrepreneurs using two metaphors:

1. Entrepreneurship means 'not just to be' and to 'act as if'.
2. Entrepreneurs are involved with more parts of their body than just their brains.

To be an entrepreneur means basically, as I see it, 'not just to be', for instance, not just to be employed, not just to be a business manager, or not just to be a citizen, to take some examples. It is also necessary to be involved over and above just to be any of this in order to come up with *new* methods to satisfy users' demands or needs to be worthy of the epithet 'entrepreneur'. These demands or needs may in turn be old or new. This indicates that people are often entrepreneurs only periodically, which in turn indicates that many entrepreneurial activities take place part-time. It is also possible to see it such that to be entrepreneurial means not to be restricted in your actions by those resources that exist (and are expected to come) but to act in such an interesting way to others (among others, potential users of what you come up with) that new resources are generated, not only in terms of money but also in terms of voluntary help, time, cooperation and joy. It is the same as the difference that some make, a difference which I have already mentioned, between *management behaviour* (administrative and bureaucratic behaviour) and *entrepreneurial action*. The former means to operate within those resources you have and expect to get, the latter means to operate such that new resources will be created or *as if* new resources already are there.

To act 'as if' does not, however, only mean to act as if you already have necessary resources. It can also be seen as:

- To act 'as if' you can forecast the future better than others.
- To act 'as if' you already are on the road of success, even though you may not have got there yet.

Gartner et al. (1992) express it such that entrepreneurship always has to do with something which is going on, never with something which is finished.

I have found another interesting metaphor to discuss all kinds of entrepreneurs, which is that they, in order to be successful, should involve four different parts of their body, which are:

- The *brain* (in order to know)
- The *heart* (in order to be willing)
- The *stomach* (in order to dare)
- The *limbs* (in order to do things)

All these parts must be there. If any of the four is missing, the actual entrepreneurial attempt will not succeed. If you do not 'know', you will fumble blindly. If you are not 'willing', it will become an action against yourself. If you do not 'dare', something constructive will hardly come out of it. The fourth, that is the 'limbs', means that you must *do things*, that is, act. This is another example of *the necessity to act, not behave, if you are an entrepreneurial person.*

These two metaphors should not be taken to mean that I believe that I, better than others, have been able to come with a formula for what must be going on when you want to succeed as an entrepreneur. The metaphors should rather be seen as examples of as a special way to work with pictures, what Max Weber calls *ideal types*. He also refers to them as *pure types*. One of his famous examples of ideal types is the distinction between traditional leadership, charismatic leadership and bureaucratic leadership. Weber asserts that you rarely find these ideal or pure types in reality, but that combinations and deformed varieties of all three exist (Weber, 1975).

Weber points out that ideal types are a kind of utopian image that stresses specific characteristics in reality in order to make this more understandable. He says further that they should not be seen as averages or representations of reality. He asserts that they should be seen, not as goals, but as means in the research process (Ljungbo, 2010, p. 411).

The layout of the rest of this book

This book contains 11 more chapters:

- In Chapter 1, I provide the theoretical history of the subject of entrepreneurship.
- In Chapter 2, I present my version of our modern society, a society that has consequences for the scope and orientation of entrepreneurship today.
- In Chapter 3, I point out the variety of the entrepreneurial phenomenon, stressing those varieties that I will discuss as I go on.
- In Chapter 4, I present the so-called narrow view of entrepreneurship.
- In Chapter 5, I present the so-called broad view of entrepreneurship.
- In Chapter 6, I look at social entrepreneurship.
- In Chapter 7, I look at the relationships between entrepreneurship and local development.
- In Chapter 8, I look closer at the start of entrepreneurial activities.
- In Chapter 9, I discuss women as entrepreneurs.
- In Chapter 10, I look at entrepreneurs in different national cultures.
- In Chapter 11, I put some philosophical and theoretical foundations in the book.

At the end come references and an index.

The layout of the rest of the book can be seen in Figure I.3.

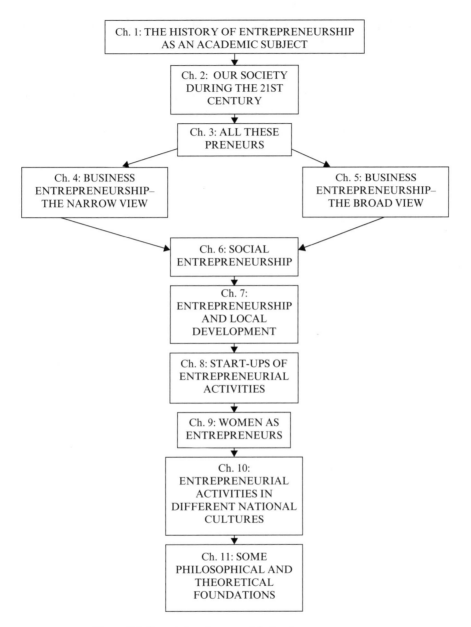

Figure I.3 Remaining chapters of the book

Think I.1   What main differences do you see between *about, for* and *in* entrepreneurship? Give examples of knowledge that might be found in one of them but not in the other two.

Think I.2   If *you* start a business, which knowledge would you need in your opinion?

Think I.3   What shortage in terms of knowledge do you think often exists among those who fail to start a business successfully?

Think I.4   Give examples of what a person 'not just is' and when he or she 'acts as if' and when an entrepreneur can be said to be involved with the whole body, not only with the brain.

INTRODUCTION – CASE STUDY

Start CZ

(Adapted from Hatten, 2003, pp. 66–7)

Karin Genton-L'Epée was between management jobs when she learned of a new and exciting business opportunity in Prague, the capital of the Czech Republic. She had moved there from Paris, attracted by a job in a recruitment ad placed by *Agency Start*, the Prague franchise of *Start Holland*, an executive search agency. A native of France, Karin was fluent in English, proficient in German and had a basic knowledge of Czech. She was 40 years old, single, with a background in wholesaling, retail sales and general management. Before going to Prague, she had worked as a consultant in international distribution and marketing in Paris and New York.

In Prague, Karin first worked for an Italian caterer and then became general manager for *Macadam*, a clothing retailer, where she had no trouble working with and managing Czech employees. Karin's administrative assistant, Barbara, acted as interpreter and office manager. Although Karin helped open three new stores, she disagreed with the retailer's strategic diversion and resigned. Shortly afterwards, she met Frans Hoekman, *Agency Start*'s owner.

New business idea. Frans had an idea for opening a temporary-employment agency for blue-collar workers. He had clients who were interested in temporary factory workers, but had been unable to find them through *Agency Start*. Frans believed that the best way was to establish a separate agency that specialized in temporary work contracts. However, he was not in a position to invest either the time or money necessary to open another business.

Frans envisioned a service that would 'help both those companies in financial trouble who want to lay off workers and those who wish to hire them' by shifting workers between companies as demand warranted. 'Production highs and lows in different firms do not coincide', he observed. Frans saw a market for a service that could match excess workers at one company with production demand in another.

Although she knew nothing about temporary employment, Karin was intrigued by Frans' idea. She began to collect information about the Czech labour market, then she and Frans approached *Start Holland*. The corporation supplied a grant to develop a business plan. Two months after Karin submitted the plan, *Start* approved the proposal to open offices in each of the Republic's seven regions, aiming for 15 to 19 within 3 years. Karin set a deadline for opening the first office in Kladno, an industrial city near Prague.

Laying the foundation. Karin hired Barbara, 20, her assistant at *Macadam*, and Angela, 22, to set up the central Prague office. Both part-timers were fluent in English and Czech. Meanwhile, Frans hired Martin, 26, as financial director. Martin was Czech, but had grown up in Canada, had worked for a year in cost analysis for *Philip Morris*, and then served for 3 months as assistant financial controller for *Train Air Conditioning*. Karin expected Martin to set up the financial and accounting procedures, take the lead in preparing the employment contracts and supervise Barbara and Angela in the day-to-day office administration.

INTRODUCTION – CASE STUDY *(continued)*

Karin hired Richard, 25, to manage the *Start Temps* office in Kladno. Richard had tried to start a recruitment agency in Prague with three friends, but had sold his share over disagreements involving software design and office management. Richard understood employment issues in the Czech Republic and wanted to design his own operation, but had no experience with legal contracts. He thought Karin and Martin would handle the legal issues.

While the Czech Labour Code did not recognize temporary employment as such, the Czech Parliament had recently expanded the definition of 'employer' for income tax withholding purposes. By doing so, the government acknowledged the right to hire employees to work for a third party, a common practice among construction contractors. Nevertheless, Czech workers, used to guaranteed positions with well-defined job descriptions, found temporary employment a foreign concept. For their part, Czech managers were used to following well-established norms and working within familiar bureaucratic systems.

Karin knew that contracts for client companies and employees would have to be carefully worded to operate within the evolving legal system, a challenge complicated by legally mandated health benefits and retirement accounting. 'Anyone can set up an individual placement office and match a few people with a few companies and make money', said Karin. 'Small guys can make it, but we want to expand. Kladno will be our blueprint. We can't do each contract from scratch. We need a system.'

The deadline nears. As her self-imposed deadline for operating the Kladno office approached, Karin saw several issues. She was the only one who seemed to feel the need for clear and precise documents. Barbara and Angela did what they were told, but did not understand what else needed to be done. Martin was trying to understand the accounting system, but was not delegating adequately. There seemed to be some question whether the Kladno office would open or not.

? DISCUSSION QUESTION

How much of entrepreneurship do you see in *Start CZ*?

To access the teacher's manual that accompanies this book, please use the following link:

http://goo.gl/DXQas.

1

The history of entrepreneurship as an academic subject

Introduction

In this chapter the academic history of the subject of entrepreneurship is presented broadly. I concentrate on its present position. The past is touched upon only when it has any influence and importance for how we look at the subject today.

It started in economics

Entrepreneurship has, as an academic subject, existed for about 300 years. During the first 250 years or so, only economists were interested in the subject. Entrepreneurship has, however, never been part of the mainstream of economics.

It might be of some interest in this book to bring up four classical research- ers from that time when only economists were interested in entrepreneur- ship and to present their ideas of what entrepreneurship is all about. They are Richard Cantillon (1680–1734), Jean Baptiste Say (1767–1832), Carl Menger (1840–1921) and Joseph Schumpeter (1883–1950).

Richard Cantillon, an Irish banker, who worked in Paris most of the time, was the first to give the concept of entrepreneurship an analytical content. In his book *Essai sur la nature du commerce en general*, which was published posthumously in 1755, the entrepreneur was given an acknowledged role in economic development. It can be said that Cantillon coined the concept 'entrepreneur' or, at least, gave it an economic meaning. So, the concept comes from the French verb *entreprendre*, which literally means to 'go in between', that is, in Cantillon's time, to be a middleman between, on one hand, the person who has the financial means and who wants a mission to be done and, on the other hand, those production resources which are necessary for this mission to be done. Richard Cantillon, like most economists after him, was mainly interested in the entrepreneurial function and not so much in the entrepreneur as a person. Cantillon included trade and agricultural work in his view on entrepreneurship and as the entrepreneur is often not sure of what price is obtainable when selling the results of what has been achieved, he saw the entrepreneurial function to *take risks*, in the sense that the entrepreneurs buy at given prices without knowing which prices will prevail later when sales are to be done.

The content of the concept of entrepreneur widened as time went on. The nineteenth century was fertile ground for entrepreneurship with the breakthrough of the industrial revolution, which led to lots of innovations and inventions. Even if researchers still did not study what these behaviours consisted of, during this century the idea that the entrepreneur was not the only person to take risks was developed (there were other people in the society who took risks as well) but also that entrepreneurs were not capitalists and therefore had a separate function to fulfil in the economy (the same difference is noted today between the venture capitalist and the person favoured by the venture capitalist). The French economist Jean Baptiste Say (1855), who brought together much of the knowledge that existed on entrepreneurship at his time, made a distinction between three economic activities in a society: (1) research that generates new knowledge, (2) entrepreneurship that applies this new knowledge and (3) workers that are involved in production. Say claimed that entrepreneurs bring production factors together and organize business firms. Say saw the entrepreneurial function to *build production units*. The reward for this was the entrepreneur's profit, which he saw as different from the return of the capitalist's financial investments.

Carl Menger is seen as one of the founders of the so-called Austrian school. He established what is sometimes called 'the subjectivistic perspective in economics' with his book *Principles of Economics* (1871). According to Menger, economic changes do not depend on circumstances in themselves, but on specific individuals' awareness and understanding of these circumstances. The entrepreneur therefore becomes a change agent who transforms resources to value-added goods and services and who often creates those circumstances leading to economic growth. Menger visualized a causal chain of events where resources not having any direct use in fulfilling human needs are transformed to highly valuable products that fulfil these needs directly, that is, a classic production theory. Menger saw the entrepreneur as *a clever individual* who could imagine this transformation and create those means that were necessary for this to happen.

So, Say saw no difference between the entrepreneur and the business leader. Menger did, and at the beginning of the 1900s it became more distinctly expressed that the function the entrepreneur fulfils in the economy is somewhat different than that of the business leader. The person who is often seen as the most influential classical scholar of them all within entrepreneurship theory is Joseph Schumpeter. Schumpeter was born in Austria but worked his last 20 years at University of Harvard in the United States. To Schumpeter the critical function of the entrepreneur was *innovation* – to introduce new products, processes or organizational units (see, for instance, Schumpeter, 1934). Schumpeter's intellect included many areas: apart from economics, he was familiar with classical history, law, history of arts and sociology. He contributed many new ideas to the theory of entrepreneurship, among others:

- He claimed that the main mechanism in economic development is *creative destruction*, that is, entrepreneurs in their interest in what is new will, more or less voluntarily, destroy existing market mechanisms and market shares in order to build new ones.
- He also claimed that people stop being entrepreneurs *when they have introduced an innovation*, that is, after having applied a new combination of the production factors for the first time. Entrepreneurs may then eventually continue as 'just' leaders and owners of small businesses, that is, managers of what was once an innovation.
- As entrepreneurs are only entrepreneurs during certain periods, they do not constitute any social class in any fundamental sense.
- Entrepreneurs tend to appear in swarms, and these swarms lead to a rise of the economy for a period. Entrepreneurs are therefore important to economic cycles.

A simple time axis of the movement of entrepreneurship as part of the subject of economics is seen in Figure 1.1.

It is still common to discuss entrepreneurs in terms of risk takers, builders of production units, clever individuals and innovators. But Richard Cantillon, Jean Baptiste Say, Carl Menger and Joseph Schumpeter were not the only economists that had ideas about the function that entrepreneurs fill in the economy. They take their place among some other economists in Table 1.1.

1700s	1800s	First half of 1900s
Richard Cantillon coins the concept 'entrepreneur' as a 'middle-man'. The entrepreneur takes a risk, accepts an undertaking and leads the work to accomplish this undertaking.	*Jean Baptiste Say suggests that the profit that the entrepreneur makes is different than that return, which the owner of the financial capital gets. Carl Menger makes a distinction between those who provide the financial capital and those who lead that unit which is set up by using this capital.*	*Joseph Schumpeter describes the entrepreneur as someone who is an innovator and someone who is a leader of a process which he calls 'creative destruction'. The innovation consists of coming up with new combinations of the production factors in the economic value chain.*

Figure 1.1 The first 250 years of the subject of entrepreneurship

Table 1.1 Some suggestions by economists about the function that entrepreneurship fulfils in an economy

- Many economists referred to the entrepreneurial function as just a specific task, like that of a manager in a business. Consequently some economists (for instance, Jean Baptiste Say and John Stuart Mill) saw entrepreneurial profit as a kind of salary.
- To many other economists, the most important function for the entrepreneur is that he or she takes that risk which is associated with starting a business (Richard Cantillon).
- To some economists (for instance, Adam Smith and David Ricardo), the entrepreneur is the person that provides financial capital.
- To still some other economists, above all Joseph Schumpeter, the most important function for entrepreneurship is innovation.
- The entrepreneur is sometimes seen as the coordinator of the production factors and the decision-maker in this context. So is the case made by Carl Menger, Alfred Marshall and John Maynard Keynes.
- The entrepreneur has also been seen among economists as
  - an industrial leader
  - a pure speculator
  - a negotiator
  - a source of information

Source: Bjerke (2007, p. 72).

Later development of the subject of entrepreneurship

Since around 1960 the subject of entrepreneurship has been of interest to business scholars and related social scientists. Some important contributions are:

- Theories of technological development (Donald Schon, 1930–97)
- Behavioural science (David McClelland, 1917–98)
- The entrepreneur as an opportunist (Israel Kirzner, b. 1930)
- Intrapreneurship (Gifford Pinchot III, b. 1944)
- Sociology (William Gartner, b. 1953)
- Small business research (David Birch. b. 1937; David Storey, b. 1947)

Donald Schon (1983) pointed out the importance of what he referred to as *champions* in all technological development. He came up with the following four conclusions:

1. At the outset, new ideas face strong resistance. Schon claimed that a social system's resistance to change can sometimes be extremely forceful. He called this the *dynamic conservatism* of the social system.
2. To overcome this resistance, *selling the idea* becomes vital.
3. People representing the new idea work mainly through the *informal* rather than the formal organization, at least to begin with.
4. Typically, *one person* acts as a champion for the idea.

David McClelland tried to come up with a picture of individual motivation in the context of management and entrepreneurship. According to him, people in those areas are motivated by three principal needs: (1) the need to achieve, (2) the need for power and (3) the need for belonging. The relative importance of these three needs varies between different people according to McClelland. He claimed that entrepreneurs are primarily driven by a *need for achievement*. McClelland also stated that societies where the need for achievement is a norm are developing more dynamically than other societies. He wrote a classic book on this theme, *The Achieving Society*, which was published in 1961 and it points out the importance of entrepreneurship for economic growth in societies like the United States.

Israel Kirzner was not the first to say it, but he was the one who most clearly expressed the idea that entrepreneurs are, above all, *alert to business opportunities* that might appear, that is, they look for unbalances in the economic system that can be exploited to start entrepreneurial operations (Kirzner, 1973).

Gifford Pinchot III coined the term 'intrapreneur' (1985) for an entrepreneur who acts within already existing business firms, that is, who comes up with and realizes new business ideas within the company where he or she is employed (the person could, of course, be the founder of the company or one of them). He defines an intrapreneur as a person who takes a hands-on responsibility to create an innovation of some kind within an organization. The intrapreneur 'may be the creator or inventor but is always the dreamer who figures out how to turn an idea into a profitable reality' (Pinchot III, 1985, p.ix). Some commentators claim that the concept, no matter how attractive it may sound, is a play on words. They assert that entrepreneurs are normally seen as taking personal risks, which employed people do not necessarily have to do.

William Gartner, who is a sociologist, claimed in a seminal and much quoted article (1988) that it is not fruitful to ask who the entrepreneur is. According to him, the important question is: how are organizations created? He even defines entrepreneurship as the creation and establishment of new organizations.

David Birch presented pioneering work about the importance of small businesses in *The Job Creation Process* (1979). He claimed that in a country like the United States, most new jobs are created by small firms. He showed more specifically that small business firms, having not more than 100 employees, had created 80 per cent of new jobs in the United States at the beginning of the 1970s. This conclusion was contrary to the established, taken-for-granted understanding at that time that big companies are the machines of the economy.

David Storey, a British scholar, is contemporary with David Birch. He refers to himself as a small business researcher, not as an entrepreneurship researcher. He points out, for instance in Storey (1980), that:

- Whether a small firm is growing or not is very much up to the entrepreneur/founder.
- The government is important for the development of the small business sector in a society.
- There are major differences between the frequencies in establishment of new firms in different regions of a country.

Entrepreneurship is now a multidisciplinary subject. The phenomenon can be and is studied from many different points of view, from that of the economist, of the sociologist, of the financial theorist, of the historian, of the psychologist, of the anthropologist or of the geographer, to name just a few. Furthermore, much research on the topic probably still takes place in business-related areas and is market based, but, increasingly, the interest in the topic is broadened to other parts of the society, for instance, the public sector and the citizen sector. I will have more to say about this as I move on in this book.

The history of the subject of entrepreneurship has been presented in Figure 1.2.

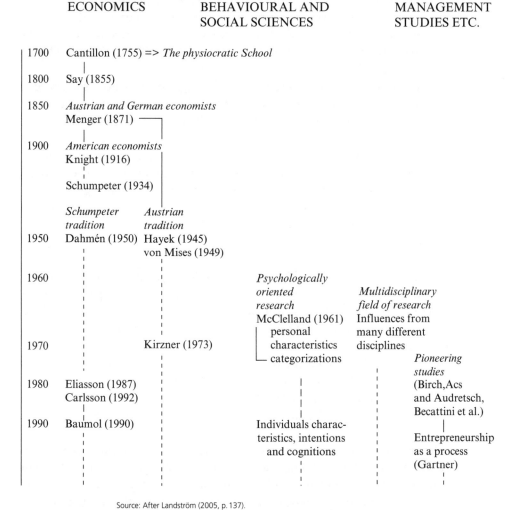

Source: After Landström (2005, p. 137).

Figure 1.2 The history of the entrepreneurship subject

Two views on entrepreneurship today

Interest in and research on entrepreneurship has simply increased exponentially during the past 10 years or so. It is also now possible to see different theoretical orientations and their differences. These two orientations, containing distinctly different 'views' on the subject of entrepreneurship in the society at large, are (Bridge et al., 2009):

1. *The narrow view*: Entrepreneurship is basically an economic phenomenon and is a matter of tracing and exploiting opportunities and of creating something *new*, thereby satisfying *demand in different markets*, new or not. Entrepreneurs in all parts of the society should try to emulate those entrepreneurs, which have been successful in business. Some representatives of this view are, for instance, Dees et al. (2001), Amin et al. (2002) and Dart (2004).

2. *The broad view*: Entrepreneurship belongs to the whole society, not only to its economy and is a question of creating something *new* (not necessarily in business) and thereby satisfying *meaningful needs*, new or not. To be a social entrepreneur (as extension of a business activity to also let it satisfy broader social needs, as an entrepreneur in the public sector or as a citizen who has neither a business firm nor is employed in the public sector) is based on a somewhat different logic than the one ruling in business. This view is represented by, for instance, Hardt (2002), Hjorth and Steyaert (2003), Johannisson (2005) and Bjerke (2007).

Some authors refer to this as the American (United States) and the Scandinavian views (for instance, Bill et al., 2010). This separation, even if there is some truth to it, is a simplification, geographically seen. There are many examples of what could be called the American view in Scandinavia and, above all, in other parts of Europe. There are also a few examples of what could be called the Scandinavian view in the United States. It is also possible to find both views in other parts of the world, for instance, in Australia and New Zealand. What is clear, however, is that *the American view* (what I prefer to call the narrow view) *is dominating everywhere*.

The differences between the narrow and the broad view of entrepreneurship and that there is often a difference between how entrepreneurship is seen in the United States and in Scandinavia becomes clear if you look at how the subject is defined in American and in Scandinavian textbooks. Let me first look at some American examples:

> Entrepreneurship is a way of thinking, reasoning, and acting that is opportunity obsessed, holistic in approach, and leadership balanced. (Timmons, 1999, p. 27)

> An entrepreneur is one who creates a new business in the face of risk and uncertainty for the purpose of achieving profit and growth by identifying opportunities and assembling the necessary resources to capitalize on them. Although many people come up with great business ideas, most of them never act on their ideas. Entrepreneurs do. (Zimmerer and Scarborough, 2005, p. 4)

> Entrepreneurship is a dynamic process of vision, change, and creation. It requires an application of energy and passion towards the creation and implementation of new ideas and creative solutions. Essential ingredients include the willingness to take calculated risks – in terms of time, equity, or career; the ability to formulate an effective venture team; the creative skill to marshal needed resources; the fundamental skill of building a solid business plan; and finally, the vision to recognize opportunity where others see chaos, contradiction, and confusion. (Kuratko and Hodgetts, 2004, p. 30)

Compare this with some Scandinavian definitions:

> Entrepreneurial processes are about identifying, challenging and breaking institutional patterns, to depart temporarily from norms and values in the society. (Lindgren and Packendorff, 2007, p. 29; my translation)

> Entrepreneurship is tangible action as creative organizing in order to realize something different. (Johannisson, 2005, p. 371; my translation)

> Entrepreneurship = to satisfy user values and/or needs – new or old – in new ways. (Bjerke, 2007, p. 17)

Many different themes have appeared when defining entrepreneurship (see Figure 1.3).

Most entrepreneurship theories are of the narrow type and *market based.* Historically seen, the entrepreneurship discourse is based on the economic discourse (Steyaert and Katz, 2004). Most entrepreneurship theories are not positioning themselves *in place or in time,* that is, they are very ahistorical and not specified in terms of in what culture they are valid (Bjerke, 2010). Some examples:

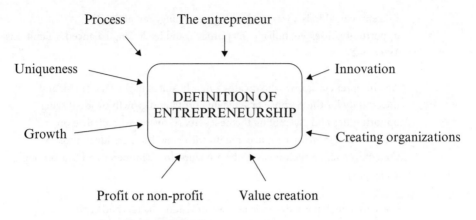

Source: After Coulter (2001, p. 4).

Figure 1.3 Common themes when defining entrepreneurship

- Entrepreneurs are achievement motivated, have a risk-taking propensity, have an internal locus of control, have a need for autonomy, are determined, creative and self-confident and take initiative (Bridge et al., 2009).
- Many entrepreneurs seem to think counter-factually, live more in the present and in the future than in the past, become more involved when making decisions and evaluating things, underestimating costs as well as time required to succeed (Baron, 1998).
- Positive consequences for entrepreneurs of starting a business include creating one's own future, having a high degree of independence, being responsible only to oneself and following in the family's footsteps (Coulter, 2001).

Three things become natural with this type of theories:

- To look at *growth* as something primary (Coulter, 2001; Wickham, 2006; Allen, 2010).
- To see *opportunity recognition* as a distinct and fundamental entrepreneurial behaviour (Gaglio, 1997; Kirzner, 1979; Stevenson and Jarillo, 1990; Venkataraman, 1997).
- To view entrepreneurship as *a (special) type of management* (Drucker, 1985; Stevenson and Jarillo, 1990; Wickham, 2006).

Entrepreneurship and management – again

One consequence of the narrow view on entrepreneurship is, as mentioned, like Wickham (2006, p. 16), to claim that an entrepreneur is a *manager*, that is, a person who handles a situation in an entrepreneurial way. Entrepreneurial management is, according to him, characterized by three things: a focus on change, a focus on an opportunity and a solid stress on management in all situations. Drucker (1985, p. 131) asserts that no matter where in society entrepreneurship takes place, those rules that govern it are, by and large, the same, that what functions or what does not is, by and large, the same and this is also the case for innovation and where to look for it. He claims that in each and every one of these cases, there is a set of conceptions that could be called *entrepreneurial management*. In a book on entrepreneurship (Sexton and Bowman, 1991), there is a heading that reads 'The entrepreneur – a special kind of manager'. Furthermore:

> Unless a new venture develops into a new business and makes sure of being 'managed', it will not survive no matter how brilliant the entrepreneurial idea, how much money it attracts, how good its products, nor even how great the demand for them. (Drucker, 1985, p. 172)

Drucker (1985, p. 23) claims, furthermore, that anybody can make a decision to learn how to become an entrepreneur and behave entrepreneurially. Entrepreneurship is to him behaviour and not any personal characteristics and entrepreneurship is to him based on concepts and theories rather than on intuition.

In line with this is the view that successful entrepreneurship starts with coming up with a *good business plan*.

I claim, however, which I have mentioned before, that I see important differences between an entrepreneur and a manager.

According to the narrow view of entrepreneurship, the entrepreneurs are the key people in the economy. It is they who (Allen, 2010, pp. 5–7):

- generate economic growth,
- build new industries and
- create new jobs.

Entrepreneurship as behaviour or what?

It is obvious that the broad view defines entrepreneurship less specifically than does the narrow view (compare some definitions of entrepreneurship from the United States and from Sweden, provided at the end of the last chapter). In other words:

1. The broad view, unlike the narrow one, does not find it necessary to specify what personally and which behaviour that is *generally* associated with (successful) entrepreneurs.

Furthermore:

2. The result of entrepreneurship, according to the broad view, is normally not very radical. The narrow view commonly asks for more. Most entrepreneurship results, according to the first view, are better seen as more or less constructive imitations of what exists already and they do not have any major effect on our lives as customers or citizens. For this reason it would, with the broad view, possibly be better to talk about the entrepreneur as a 'maker' instead of as a 'creator' (compare Chapter 5).
3. The narrow view claims that entrepreneurs are some kind of extraordinary people; the broad view does not do that.

Lindgren and Packendorff (2007, p. 18) point out that there are some weaknesses in existing entrepreneurship research (that is, what I refer to as the narrow view of entrepreneurship):

- It suggests that entrepreneurship can be measured, predicted and stimulated in an objective and neutral way, which leads to a number of problems because the phenomenon of entrepreneurship is characteristically complex.
- It almost always lets individuals embody entrepreneurship, in spite of the fact that most entrepreneurial acts are performed by people in cooperation.
- Entrepreneurship is operationalized – lacking better data – as freshly registered new firms, which excludes a number of entrepreneurial acts that take place within existing firms and/or do not lead to the start of traditional companies.
- The focus is too narrow most of the time, which excludes, for instance, female entrepreneurs, ethnic minorities and what is referred to as the cultural sector.

The broad view of entrepreneurship

The progressive imitating and the necessarily mundane aspects of entrepreneurship are what Steyaert (2004) calls the prosaic in entrepreneurship. With a prosaic study of entrepreneurship, we leave a dominating focus on building models and general concepts, which is usually supported in the area (Steyaert, 2000), and enter a road to a study of the conversation process which supports the everydayness of entrepreneurial processes.

> The point of departure of prosaic writing is the belief that everyday is the scene where social change and individual creativity take place as a slow result of constant activity. The daily effort of thousands of small steps makes after all a difference . . . As prosaic has a sensitivity for the eventness of an event, for its creative moving ahead, it is highly suspicious of systems and all attempts that try to create all-encompassing patterns. In creating systems, there is a chronic double danger. One is the act of exclusion, things become driven out and end in a state of 'non-existence', and the unnoticed becomes even more unnoticeable. Another is that things which happen accidentally are meaningless (at least to the system being created) and not related but become somehow related, meaningful and are no longer accidental. (Steyaert, 2004, p. 10)

The most basic or at least a natural consequence of the broad view of entrepreneurship is to make a distinct difference between traditional ways of doing business and new business venturing – between 'managerialism' and 'entrepreneurialism' in Hjorth and Johannisson's terminology (1998). Management and organization theory preserve according to Hjorth and Steyaert (2003, pp. 298–9) a special place for entrepreneurship, but this is because of its usefulness as a solution in management theory, that it generates an ever-lasting need for new 'success generators'. The entrepreneurship book became part of the view on management in the 1980s (Peters and Waterman, 1982; Kanter, 1983). The business venture discourse progressed on a broad front and included what was called Thatcherism and Reaganism in the 1980s as well as making the employee an enterprising individual in the 1990s (Peters, 1994a, b; du Gay, 1997). Enterprising (Burchell et al., 1991) represents the entrepreneurial according to managerialism (du Gay, 1997) and is therefore spread quickly to all places where managerialism has become the ruling basis for rationality (Hjorth and Steyaert, 2003, p. 299). It is important for the business discourse during the 1990s that it is almost impossible to define the limit to managerialism: 'attempts to construct a culture of enterprise have proceeded through the progressive enlargement of the territory of the market – the realm of private enterprise and economic rationality – by a series of redefinitions of its objects' (du Gay, 1997, p. 56).

The result became a new target for management knowledge – the employees themselves. They were seen in entrepreneurial terms or at least as parts of an entrepreneurial company. All that could be governed – to become effective – should then function as entrepreneurial management. In order to become successful and to contribute to the success of the company or the healthcare centre or the primary school or the public authority, the employees should develop a knowledge of themselves (Townley, 1995), which centres around the management version of the entrepreneur as the person who takes initiatives, who is looking for opportunities, who takes responsibility, who is reliable, the individual who is enterprising. When Drucker (1985) wrote that he wanted to do for entrepreneurship what he did for management in the 1950s – turn it into a successful discipline – he was prophetic both in terms of how entrepreneurship in terms of enterprising became the ruling power of the new technologies of the self (Martin et al., 1988; Townley, 1995; Deetz, 1998) and how entrepreneurship as an academic discipline emerged during the 1990s (Katz, 1998). How to behave and how to do something about your life was increasingly answered in enterprising terms: manage your life as an entrepreneurial venture and become an enterprising individual. But one question would then be according to Hjorth and Steyaert (2003, p. 299): 'if you managerialize entrepreneurship, can one still speak of entrepreneurship as if it hasn't changed?'

The broad view of entrepreneurship sees no point in creating conceptual systems in order to explain entrepreneurship. If entrepreneurship, powered by its present popularity, is again treated as a primarily economic phenomenon, Hjorth and Steyaert (2003, p. 299) 'fear' that it will disappear again, unable to break through its curse of history. When entrepreneurship got a central position in the 1990s, several high-flying, IT-fuelled ventures were launched, most of them with young bright IT men in the driving seats. Such examples lead us astray, according to the broad view (ibid.). What is needed instead, according to this view, is to invent a new way to talk about what is entrepreneurial such that it will include more of the society than its economic parts.

One aspect of the broad view of entrepreneurship is not to have a focus on the discovery of opportunities but on the creative process in itself, which is made clear by using the verb to enterprise as something ongoing, that is, *entrepreneuring* (Steyaert, 2007). Lindgren and Packendorff (2007) also assert that entrepreneurship research more and more orients itself towards entrepreneurial action processes. Entrepreneurial studies must then be based on a process philosophy (Steyaert, 1997). Entrepreneurship can then even be called *the science of the art of the power of imagination* (Gartner, 2007). Two proponents of the broad view of entrepreneurship, that is Hjorth and

Steyaert, have had such a starting point in their so-called movement books (Steyaert and Hjorth, 2003, 2006; Hjorth and Steyaert, 2004, 2009).

One important difference between the two views of entrepreneurship is that the broad view inevitably looks at entrepreneurship as an activity embedded in a special social (historical, cultural, economic) context. Entrepreneurship is, however, not determined by this context. It is rather a specific response to those limitations that are part of the specific context; it is a special way to *problematize* and to *transform* these limitations.

> Entrepreneurship can [then] be translated as an activity that takes advantage of the *Zwischenraum*, that is of the in-between space (*entre* = between, *prendre* = to take in French). This means that entrepreneurship is an activity that searches and actively creates the distance to what is seen as normal and habitual; it enters and actively creates the between-space as an intensive space and can thus reveal the becomingness of the world. It is further a creative activity in the sense that it connects and reconnects – assembles, dis-assembles and re-assembles – materials, ideas, and so on in a new way. Given rules, plans, norms, models and so on are *transformed* in the process of 'application'. Application, however, has to be understood in a new way. It is not a technical process or the execution of a programme that is fully determined. Rather, 'it would be a concept of application which generates something unpredictable in a totally different context, in contexts which no one can master in advance' (Derrida, 2000, p. 28). *Application* can be rethought as the *space between* rules, regulations, and so on and the concreteness of the situation. (Weiskopf and Steyaert, 2009, p. 196)

The innovative power of entrepreneurship can then no longer be conceptualized as 'creative destruction' in Schumpeter's meaning but rather as a folding which is infused with an attitude in which 'the high value of the present is indissociable from a desperate eagerness to imagine it, to imagine it otherwise than it is, and to transform it not by destroying it but by grasping in it what it is' (Foucault, 1997, p. 311).

> The focus is no longer on the entrepreneur as someone who is surveying the world from above, sees people (workforce), material, so that they become information, values or commodities. He or she is no longer the one who rationally combines these factors in order to produce an output and to achieve something (Spinosa et al., 1997, pp. 57–8). In contrast, we see the entrepreneur as 'someone' (or somebody) who is in-between, or more precisely: we can focus on *entrepreneurship* as the in- betweenness itself (Steyaert, 2005). In this way we realize that it is not the individual (entrepreneur's) intentions that account for the process of entrepreneurship. To put it another way: it is not the intentions in the

individuals' mind but rather it is the tensional traction of the field of incompatible and heterogeneous events (Cooper and Law, 1995, p. 246) that constitutes entrepreneurship as an intensive space and entrepreneuring as the entering of an intensive space of creation and transformation. (Weiskopf and Steyaert, 2009, pp. 196–7)

The broad view of entrepreneurship then also means that an understanding of business entrepreneurs and maybe, above all, of entrepreneurs in other sectors of the society, that is, social entrepreneurs, cannot neglect those contexts in which they exist and that entrepreneurs in different sectors of the society are guided by, at least partly, different logic. Nilsson (2003), for instance, makes a clear distinction between entrepreneurship research in the economy and other entrepreneurship research. This means, for instance, that *business entrepreneurs are satisfying market values through new business ventures,* while *citizen entrepreneurs or entrepreneurs in the public sector are satisfying social values through new activities.*

A criticism of the broad view of entrepreneurship has been directed from the narrow view, which asserts that entrepreneurship research should limit itself and come up with results from what can be seen as what is distinctly entrepreneurial, find its domain or so-called *core,* that is, claims that that the subject should be consolidated (Venkataraman 1997; Low, 2001; Davidsson, 2003; Baron and Shane, 2008). The proponents of the broad view, on the other hand, would be happy to support Johannisson (2005, p. 28, my translation) in the following statement:

> To be enterprising in everyday life is to take initiatives, to take responsibility together with other people that something is done. Entrepreneurship is the antipode to apathy and indifference. Some people picture entrepreneurship as extreme cheerfulness, intellectual malnutrition and a hysterical run for empty places to fill with its own content. It may be so. Nevertheless, an enterprising individual recognizes his or her own humanness, believes that he or she can do something about his or her own situation and is driven by being able to involve others in that project he or she is initiating. Entrepreneurship as persistent and creative business design, sometimes successful, becomes in this perspective just a special case of general enterprising.

Is it possible to combine the narrow and the broad view of entrepreneurship?

Some scholars recommend a broad view on entrepreneurship without completely neglecting the narrow view. What should be kept in mind in a broad view of entrepreneurship is, according to some entrepreneurship research-ers, the following:

- Entrepreneurship is as much a matter of improving imitation as genuine creation of what is new (Johansson, 2010).
- It is too simple to claim that entrepreneurship needs freedom to prosper. It needs in the highest degree resistance to be triggered to achieve great things (Berglund and Gaddefors, 2010).
- There is a risk in claiming that entrepreneurship needs spectacular behaviour and that it excludes more mundane activities close to reality (Bill et al., 2010).

Summary and conclusion

In this chapter, I have provided an overview of the history of the subject of entrepreneurship stressing more recent times. I claim that it is very clear and possible to separate two views of entrepreneurship from each other. I refer to them as the narrow and the broad view of entrepreneurship, respectively.

Think 1.1 Which theorists in the history of the subject of entrepreneur-ship would you use to provide a picture of Bill Gates, Steve Jobs and Richard Branson?

Think 1.2 If you should start a business, which (living or dead) person would you want to talk to?

Think 1.3 In your opinion, which are the three most important character-istics that you should have as an entrepreneur?

Think 1.4 Which is most important – the personal characteristics or the environment – for a successful entrepreneur?

CH 1 – CASE STUDY

Palm Pilot

(Adapted from Barringer and Ireland, 2006, p. 23)

Every day, millions of people use *Palm Pilots* to organize their schedules. The story behind the founding of *Palm*, the leader in the handheld devices industry, is an intriguing tale of the tenacity it takes to pioneer a new technology and successfully bring it to the market.

As a youngster, Jeff Hawkins, *Palm*'s founder, helped his dad and brothers build boats. Hawkins remembers his father as a 'consummate inventor' and believes the skills he acquired as a child helped him to become an entrepreneur. 'Learning to use shop tools, learning to use fiberglass and screws and stuff, is actually very useful in building little computers', Hawkins says. 'Not many people in my business can get involved in as many aspects of product design as I do'.

Hawkins graduated from Cornell in the United States in 1979 with a degree in electrical engineering and went to work for Intel. He stayed only 3 years and then took a job at *GRiD Systems*, a small Silicon Valley start-up whose goal was to design a computer that a person could carry – a crazy concept in the early 1980s. After a short stint at *GRiD*, where he became fascinated with how the brain functions, Hawkins went back to school – to Berkeley – to study how the human brain recognizes patterns. While there he developed 'Palm-Print', a handwriting-recognition software.

After leaving graduate school short of a PhD, Hawkins returned to *GRiD* to see if he could develop pen-based hardware and software to complement his earlier invention. He developed a rudimentary handheld device, called the GRiDPaD, and launched it in 1990. Although it was slow, clunky and ugly, it was a pen-based computer and was innovative for the time. The GRiDPaD had a number of serious limitations, however, and eventually fizzled out. But Hawkins was determined to create a high-quality pen-based computer that people could carry with them and that would give them the power of a PC at their fingertips.

To realize his dream, Hawkins left GRiD and founded his own company, *Palm*, in 1992. His first product was a handheld device for the consumer market called 'Zoomer' – short for 'consumer'. Based on the strength of his reputation, Hawkins got venture-capital financing. He hired Donna Dubinsky, a former *Apple Computer, Inc.* employee who was excited about what Hawkins was trying to accomplish. Dubinsky was a particularly good fit because she lent sales and management skills to *Palm* that Hawkins lacked. The first thing the two decided was that *Palm* would design only software and outsource Zoomer's hardware and operating system to others. While this sounded like a recipe for success, the plan didn't quite pan out. The Zoomer was eventually produced as a collaborative effort between *Palm* and a collection of its suppliers and was essentially 'designed by committee'. It had many interesting features but was slow, had bad text recognition, and was priced at $700, which was much too high for the consumer market. It quickly flopped.

CH 1 – CASE STUDY *(continued)*

Now, Hawkins had tried twice regarding handheld devices. *Palm* survived only because it was frugal and still had money in the bank.

Hawkins and Dubinsky went back to the drawing board and conducted in-depth surveys with people who had purchased the Zoomer, leading to two important realizations. First, consumers did not want their handheld devices to be little PCs; they wanted them to complement their PCs. This would make the devices easier to design and produce. Second, because of the biggest difficulty in building pen-based computers was getting the computers to recognize individual handwriting, Hawkins realized that instead of the handheld device learning everyone's handwriting, everyone would have to learn the handheld device's handwriting. From the insight, 'Graffiti' was developed – the handwriting-recognition software that differentiated the *Palm Pilot* from other handheld devices. With Graffiti, each letter is made by writing in a standardized fashion; no individuality is allowed.

With this new understanding, Hawkins, Dubinsky, and a new partner, Ed Collins, rolled up their sleeves and pressed on. This time *Palm* would build the entire device. Strapped for cash, they sold the company to *U.S. Robotics*, with a strict understanding regarding the relative autonomy of *Palm*. Backed by the company's cash, manufacturing strength and global presence, *Palm* introduced the original *Palm Pilot* in April 1996, and it became the fastest-selling consumer product in history – faster than the PC, the cell phone, the colour television and the VCR. When *Palm Pilot* was a clear winner, Jeff Hawkins was asked how the success of the product made him feel. He replied:

> It feels good. What really feels good is that people like the product. Since we're all product people here, there's nothing else that makes me happier that people saying: 'Hey this is great, it's changed my life'. That feels good.

 DISCUSSION QUESTION

How would you like to characterize Jeff Hawkins as an entrepreneur?

To access the teacher's manual that accompanies this book, please use the following link:

http://goo.gl/DXQas.

2

Our society during the twenty-first century

Introduction

All societies are changing. No society remains the same. In this chapter I bring up some aspects of our modern society of importance to the orientation and content of entrepreneurship.

Our modern society

We could call our modern society an *entrepreneurial* or *post-modern society*. This society is a society changing at a magnitude that may never have been experienced before. There are not many fixed points left. This can be seen in all areas. Politicians must live with big variations in their opinion polls, we are constantly reminded of a turbulent world around us through our TV screens and the big corporations often disappoint us by their lack of ability to keep up employment and repeatedly by their unethical behaviour. But to say that change is part of our everyday life is not enough, however. *Changes* are also *of a different kind. They contain genuine uncertainties.* This kind of uncertainty cannot be eliminated, or even be decreased by more careful planning. Our *changes have changed* (Ferguson, 1980). It is also so that more and more parts of our modern society are influenced by change. *The number of exceptions is increasing.*

Only the fact that we, to an increasing extent, have to deal with more changes which cannot be forecasted or be totally eliminated by more planning, could justify the label *an entrepreneurial society* for the world of today. It is now constantly necessary to be prepared to renew ourselves if we do not want to be left behind. As new courageous acts are the result of circumstances where it is impossible to forecast precisely profit or loss makes the entrepreneur 'the sovereign inventor and explorer' (Hébert and Link, 1982, pp. 45–7). This is another aspect of 'as if', a concept mentioned in the Introduction, that is, in this case to act 'as if' it is possible to forecast the consequences of one's act.

But new kinds of changes are not the only thing characterizing our modern society. Among other things, *IT technology and other technologies play a larger new role*. Castells has even provided a date for and localized the start of what he calls '*the new economy*':

> The new economy emerged in a certain point in time, the 1990s, at a given space, the United States, and around/from specific industries, mainly information technology and finance with biotechnology looming on in the horizon. It was in the late 1990s that the seeds of the information technology revolution, planted in the 1970s, seemed to come to fruition in a wave of new processes and products spurring productivity and stimulating economic competition. Every technical revolution has its own tempo for diffusion in social and economic structures. For reasons, that historians will determine, this particular technical revolution appeared to require about a quarter of a century to retool the world – a much shorter span than the predecessors. (Castells,1998, pp. 147–8)

Technology is more than information technology (IT), but it is this technology that is most widely associated with our modern society. IT can be defined as the infrastructure and knowledge necessary to make information quickly and easily accessible (increasingly it applies to the software and the communication services that link the hardware).

However, IT is not essentially about new firms in a new sector but about new conditions for the whole economy, mainly noted for the industry ('Det nya näringslivet', 2001, p. 20).:

> The popular distinction between the old and the new economy completely misses the point. The most important aspect of the new economy is not the shift to high-tech industries, but the way that IT will improve the efficiency of all parts of the economy, especially old-economy firms. (*The Economist*, 2000, p. 13)

No matter how we look at IT, it is there – *everywhere*. It moves faster and faster. It invades all sectors, all that can be digitalized will be.

It is also now so, that *knowledge is a central success factor*. Our society has become a *knowledge society*. Knowledge and competence is its key resource, its only meaningful resource, as Peter Drucker said a long time ago (Drucker, 1969, p. ix) and 'knowledge workers' are the dominant group in the workforce. It is a society where there are more chances to climb the career ladder than before but also where there is a larger risk of failing trying to do so (*The Economist*, 2001, p. 4). But according to Castells (1998), the relevant borderline is not between the industrial and post-industrial society but between two types of production. The analytical emphasis should, according to him, be moved from post-industrialism to informationalism.

> Economies are increasingly based on knowledge. Finding better ways of doing things has always been the main source of long-term growth. What is new is that a growing chunk of production in the modern economy is in the form of intangibles, based on the exploitation of ideas rather than material things: the so-called 'weightless economy'. In 1900 only one-third of American workers were employed in the service sector, now more than three-quarters are. (*The Economist*, 2000, p. 29)

One interesting aspect of knowledge is that it does not obey the traditional economic laws of scarcity. It does not matter how much knowledge is used, *it is still not used up*! One may even claim that *the more you share it, the larger it becomes*.

However, the most important aspect is not knowledge and competence in itself but who is carrying it and has the ability to use it. Many of the change agents which are of interest in this book, that is entrepreneurs, are of this kind.

Furthermore, we should not forget in our modern society that getting rid of old habits may be equally important, *maybe even more important*, than learning new ones.

Another aspect of our modern society is that *relationships and networks are becoming more important*. Contemporary society is underpinned by all-encompassing networks; network is the primary symbol of our modern society (Holmberg et al., 2002, p. 13). One characteristic of the new info-technological paradigm

> is *the logic of networks* in every system and arrangement of relationships using the new information technology. The network morphology seems to be well suited to the increasingly more complex interaction and the unpredictable patterns of development emerging through the creative power of this interaction (Castells, 1998, pp. 92–3).

Our new entrepreneurial society is based on networking 'because under the new historical conditions, productivity is generated through and competition takes place in a global network of interacting business networks' (ibid., p. 99).

> By transforming the processes for managing information, the new information technology is influencing the activity field of all human beings and makes it

possible to create an infinite number of connections between separate areas as well as between different elements and agents of various operations. A network-based economy emerges with far-reaching internal interdependencies which is increasingly more able to apply its advances within technology, know-how and business organizations on technology, know-how and organizing businesses themselves. Such a virtuous circle should lead to improved productivity and efficiency, given the right conditions in terms of equally dramatic organizational and institutional changes. (Castells, 1998, pp. 99–100)

I mentioned earlier in this section that there is a kind of change in our modern society, a kind of change that contains genuine uncertainties. It is possible to see the network logic as an answer to such a situation, because the network economy has moved 'from change to a situation where everything is in a state of flux' (Kelly, 1998, p. 144). Understanding how these networks are working is the key to understanding how our new entrepreneurial society is working, and the greatest profits in this society are to a large extent to be found in researching and exploiting the power of decentralized and autonomous networks and building new ones.

It is even possible to say that the network economy is changing our identities. What matters today is whether a person belongs to 'the network' or not (Kelly, 1998). At the same time, the more high-tech we become the more 'high-touch' we need (Naisbitt et al., 2001).

I will have more to say about networking in Chapter 8.

Globalization is a concept that is often mentioned when we talk about our modern society. We do not only need each other more as humans. We also need each other more *as nations*. Our new modern society is global because its central activities and its components are organized globally (Castells, 1998). Jonung (2000) associates this new globalized economy with a free and extremely fast flow of ideas, information and capital, a flow, which to a large extent is a result of the IT revolution. Others, such as Eriksson and Ådahl (2000), discuss the new economy in somewhat more political terms, using the market economy (with the United States as a forerunner) as a model. The supporters of this thesis claim that the globalization process facilitates high economic growth for all participants. Its opponents claim, on the other hand, that it is increasing the rifts between rich and poor countries.

At any rate, global markets add to our inability to make meaningful forecasts, which again speaks for that we need entrepreneurship more than ever in all parts of our modern society.

Finally, *the view on capital* has changed in our modern world. We speak less and less of financial capital and more and more of human capital, social capital, cultural capital, structural capital and visual capital, for instance.

Bell (1974) identifies five primary characteristics with our post-industrial society:

- Changes in the economy, which lead to a focus on service rather than production.
- Changes in the social structure placing higher value on professional and technical skills.
- Changes from the practical to the theoretical as a source of ideas and a greater stress on research and development compared to principles for its implementation.
- Changes in controlling the technology and a greater interest in technological changes.
- A kind of intellectual technology related to advanced information systems.

I would like to summarize the situation in our modern society in the following way:

- Most societies are a product of history. This does not mean that they are best suited to solve present and future problems.
- The analytical units in the society of today are not traditional production factors but reflecting human actors (Storper, 1997).
- Innovation cannot be planned in advance to any essential degree. It is a result of what may look like random meetings of different 'pictures'.
- Interpretations and constructed pictures are steering people, not 'reality' as such (if it even exists) (Öhrström, 2005, p. 64).
- Successful societies of today keep away from imitating and copying forces faster than they are able to copy new development (Öhrström, 2005, p. 64).
- Society cannot successfully be renewed from the top or from the centre. For this to be done continuous learning by all key actors at all levels is necessary.

Freedom as autonomy–freedom as potential

Maravelias (2009, pp. 15–18) has an interesting discussion about how freedom in our society has gone *from being autonomous to having potential*. Through Descartes, Hegel and Kant, the European philosophical tradition has above all conceived *freedom as autonomy*; to able to decide without being influenced by external forces and limitation and being independent of passions and natural drives (Foucault, 1991; Liedman, 2004). One central premise of such freedom has been a human being's capacity to develop a profound self-understanding on the basis of which self-consciousness and ability to reflect become possible. Only pure and rational subjects are free (in the meaning autonomous) in this view. Based on this type of thought, freedom is discussed mainly in 'negative' terms, that is, as the absence of coercion and domination and more generally, as the absence of power (Preston, 1987).

Even if the conception of freedom as the necessity to be able to distance oneself from the world – and from oneself – still dominates Western thought, it does not exhaust the current meaning of the expression 'being free' (Preston, 1987; de Carolis, 1996). In our everyday language being free tends this way to have at one's disposal concrete possibilities, in other words, having the ability to initiate and complete certain actions (de Carolis, 1996; Liedman, 2004). Understanding freedom this way is not the same as keeping an autonomous distance to one's environment. On the contrary, the conception is based on the idea that the individual maintains an intimate relationship to one's position to act. Someone who wishes to become a member cannot keep a physical and psychological distance to other members in this group. He or she must take an active part in the group's practices. Similarly, a person who runs into a transitory possibility has no time to act on his or her reflective awareness of the role to be played and the ideal to live up to. Acting freely in such situations is more a matter of making agile and instinctive choices on the basis of an unconstrained confidence in one's own possibility, in other words, to act more entrepreneurially.

From this perspective a person is consequently free if he or she is ready to exploit the innumerable chances offered by the world. Such an understanding of freedom, which Maravelias (2009) refer to as *freedom as potential*, implies that the subject becomes involved in the environment and that such intimate interaction with the environment is encouraged – because without it, the potential of doing and accomplishing things does not exist (de Carolis, 1996). This idea of freedom is substantially different from the former, especially in two regards. First, it does not lead to any distance between self and others, that is, that individuals are independent in the sense of the term above. To act freely then implies instead to act frictionlessly because the act is intimately integrated with its environment in the society. That is to say, freedom of an individual is not based on any self-conscious distance but on the individuals' willingness and ability to mould him- or herself in the social structure even if it means that it is not certain how much of oneself is given up. The person who is free in this regard does not wish to stand beside the world, looking at it and analysing it from a distance but he or she wants to belong to it in a way that lets him or her move around like a fish in water. Second, when the power to seize a possibility is accentuated before autonomy, power is no longer any antithesis to freedom but it becomes an integrated part of freedom. What is then emphasized is that freedom does not mean freedom from power, but that it requires power to act and to seize the possibilities. In other words, if freedom as autonomy means freedom from power, freedom as potential means to have freedom to seize possibilities through some kind of distributed power.

In our age of a politics built up as a kind of post-welfare, we have reasons to assume that the meaning of freedom as potential will become more dominating and pushing the notion of freedom as autonomy to the margins of social practices. In our present society, it is so, according to Rose (1999) that we are always in continuous training (we never completely leave school behind us), we are always at work (even at home) and we can never keep our private life outside work. This is because, he says, existing institutions of work and education are not distributed around any central but on a dispersed principle of power and control. Hence, rather than in the form of centrally distributed roles, rights and obligations, power and control are distributed in the networked flow of possibilities.

Hence, the common denominator of these financial, technological and political transformations is that they create and distribute possibilities, that access to these possibilities is not evenly distributed and that they can decreasingly be guaranteed (Castells, 1998; Hardt and Negri, 2004). It is more pragmatic under such circumstances to try to develop one's power to seize possibilities by remaining alert and open and by constantly being connected, to learn and to change (Maravelias, 2009, pp. 15–18).

The post-bureaucratic world does not does take, even primarily, something away from employees – their protected zones of autonomy – it provides them with possibilities. In other words, post-bureaucracy provides individuals with access to possibilities on the basis of judgements of their willingness and ability to use their potential to transform themselves in ways that make them use their possibilities.

> Such principles of organization do not differentiate individuals in terms of what types and levels of autonomy they should be given and what regulated rights they have, but in terms of who has and who does not have (entrepreneurial) potential, and accordingly, who should and who should not be granted access to

[possibilities]. What this implies is that freedom is transformed from a derivative of individual rights and regulated demands and duties, to a derivative of individuals' potential. Those who lack potential are not given [possibilities], and even if they were, their lack of potential would make them unable to use them. In post-bureaucracy, *freedom would thus become the mark of an elite and the privilege of those who already have.* (Maravelias, 2009, p. 26)

The post-bureaucratic person is not primarily subordinated roles that are worked out by an authority, because from this perspective, directives in the post-bureaucratic world are not distributed according to roles, but possibilities are worked out as temporary roles, which make it possible for individuals to exploit possibilities of the tasks and projects that are at hand. Rather than a slave or a silent rebel, the post-bureaucratic person therefore emerges as an *opportunist*, who is constantly fighting against all kinds of subordination, even against subordination to him- or herself (Virno, 1996; Sennett, 1998).

To summarize, Maravelias (2009) claims that society has developed from discussing freedom in terms of *not being oppressed*, that is, a more advanced democracy from the centre and outwards, to discussing freedom as *equal possibilities in the society*, which to a large extent must take place locally. This has, as I see it, several consequences. It will be harder to see how power is exerted. Furthermore, as the possibilities to exploit possibilities are so different in societies today, we may have *increased inequality* in our modern society.

The growing citizen involvement

By social entrepreneurship, I mean all entrepreneurial activities in the society that are not limited only to private profits. These exist to a large extent in the business sector but above all in the public sector and to an increasing extent in the third sector, which I refer to as the citizen sector. This citizen sector was strong during the nineteenth century, but expansion during the twentieth century placed it in the backseat. During the last 30 years the trend has changed, however, and this has led to a revival of the citizen sector (sometimes denoted as *the social economy*) for three reasons (the discussion here follows Murray, 2009):

1. The user has also become his or her own producer to a large extent.
2. Increased social imperatives exist.
3. The green revolution has been harder to avoid.

The user has also become his or her own producer to a large extent

The user (the everyday consumer) has to a large extent become his or her own producer; he or she is today more active in being part of coming up with and adding value to what he or she thinks he or she needs. The consumer has become what Toffler calls a *prosumer* (Toffler, 1980). What has become critical to him or her is now how different kinds of support and possibilities are designed to have a manageable normal day rather than being a passive receiver of service and support by society. *The support economy has taken over from the commodity economy* as an organizing principle (Maxmin and Zuboff, 2002). The production in the society (in the wide sense of it) is no longer clearly going on in a separate sector that produces goods and services for other parts of society to choose from, but the whole arrangement is *to an increasing extent built up around the user.* A transformation of the relationships between consumers and markets and between the citizens themselves has taken place. The production process is to a decreasing extent a linear process where the consumer is the end of the chain. The decisive middle hands are these days those who have the knowledge and the confidence to put together the relevant support packages. Those are the ones who put the knowledge economy together.

The institutional consequences of this are far-reaching. The systems are now organized around the households. These households have not been isolated from each other, however, but have become connected in a variety of shapes – physically, virtually, discursively and emotionally – rather than built up around centralized institutions. The spread of mutual interest and support groups has become a pattern during the last 30 years – connected through the Internet or by various kinds of events and in study groups. This is a long way from the passive consumer and the mechanical worker of the early twentieth century. The modern society positions every household by itself *and* in cooperation as a kind of '*living centres*' in distributed systems – the vitality of the whole becomes dependent on the vitality of the individual innumerable components. This justifies asking new questions about what permits and what prevents households being participants (feeling a kind of inclusiveness), questions of what the relationships and possibilities (access) look like, questions about how dwellings are to be built and where they are to be placed, questions about necessary skills and working times (and working places) for individual citizens today, questions about tax design and tax relief, just to mention a few. The society of today is simply incompatible with long working hours in one place with minimum wages, with compensation only in money and with an educational system that is not suited to the specific and very varied skills of modern life.

Increased social imperatives exist

Social issues are harder to manage

Second, the pressure has increased on the state-driven infrastructure that is supposed to provide social service. One type of pressure comes from the sheer size and growth of demand for such services. In many industrialized countries there are dramatic rising trends in, for instance, obesity, chronic disease and demographic ageing, all of which have been described as time bombs.

These trends constitute a double challenge for existing structures. First of all, there is a growing mismatch between social service as it has traditionally been given and new needs – in most countries hospital care was, for instance, originally built up to handle acute rather than chronic diseases. At the same time, the chronic diseases are those that are expanding at the moment. Furthermore, it has proven difficult to combine increased service needs with necessary cost efficiency. Schools, hospitals, nursing homes and prisons have cost structures, which, to a large extent, are of a fixed kind and difficult to reduce in a more work-intensive service.

As a result of this, these sections of society require an increasingly large part of its national resources. With ruling trends, the major parts (both in terms of value added and employment) in the economies of the Western world in 2020 and beyond will not be cars, ships, steel, computers or personal finances, but instead health, education and care. The public and the citizen sectors, as well as the environment, will no longer be tributaries to the business sector but instead the main streams of society, central for the employment and the economy of the country as a whole. And this will be a major financial issue.

There are two responses to these challenges. The generally most common policy-based approach has been to try to design technical solutions in order to upgrade those institutions where service is given. In the case of hospital care, for instance, those industrial models, which once were associated with Henry Ford and later Toyota, have been adapted in order to try to speed up the patient flow through hospitals. Costs have been cut through outsourcing and repeated efficiency drives. Hospitals have become bigger and more specialized. Prices have been set on what once was free and quasi-market arrangements have been established in order to bring in economic discipline among personnel and others concerned. But the pressure has continued to increase relentlessly. In terms of health and some other social issues in general and environmental issues in particular the most effective answers have been of a preventive nature, but these have, as we know, proven to be very difficult to establish in the public sector and in markets the way they look today.

Another approach has also turned up to try to cope with the problems. This approach is still more or less at an explorative stage, but has nevertheless turned out to become more and more important. During the past 10 years or so a number of attempts have appeared to involve citizens and the civic society as partners in public service. Ministers have occasionally acted as champions to bring in the citizen sector into areas related to health and similar general social issues. They have welcomed the assistance of parents in schools and of patients in the governance of hospitals.

Both those who work in public service as well as some politicians have become very aware of the apparent disconnections between social institutions and many issues and needs that exist among those who use this service. They admit that active citizens are central to many of the big social issues. To those with chronic diseases, households and their supportive networks are central components of what have been the primary producers of service.

In these cases, citizens are active agents, not passive consumers. They need resources and abilities, and support and relationships that existing social services cannot provide. This, together with that pressure on costs that exists, are factors behind what could be called a *co-designed public service* and the acknowledgement of the role that *the third-sector organizations play in providing service to citizens.*

Persistent voices

At the same time as public authorities have tried to involve citizens, it is obvious that the latter have, to a large extent, radically changed attitudes as members of the society. It was a highly recognized report from Stanford Research Institute that in 1978 gave the wider public a hint about a fundamental shift among consumers (Murray, 2009, p. 13). The research in question was led by Arnold Mitchell, the consumer futurist, who made a distinction between *outer-directed consumers* who are primarily directed by external acceptance and social position, and *inner-directed consumers*, that included narcissistic, experiential and socially conscious consumers. When the former were two-thirds of the population, the latter had grown to 20 per cent and were seen as a development away from the outer-directed consumers. This report calmed the fear that existed among some major companies that the generation after 1968 to a large extent would stop consuming commodities available in a market. This generation became instead the start of what became known as the *post-modern citizen* – as a producer and/or as a consumer – who is interested in matters of identity, the meaning in life and self-employment rather than consumption of standardized products. The French social analyst André Gorz called it *a new subjectivity*, which is no longer moulded round the supply and demand of the economy the way it looked at the time (Gorz, 1999). To the post-modern, individualized citizen life becomes a formation process, where career has to step back to different projects and where the picaresque becomes as important as formal plans.

Post-Fordist manufacturing was partly an answer to these changes. It was an industrial revolution by itself, which made it possible for companies to manage complex links of supply and which allowed them to respond to a very different and varied demand. At the end of twentieth century the post-modern consumer became used to a varied economy, which was oriented towards consumers, with fast food and quick fashion changes. This shift indicates a change from an economy dominated by concrete goods and services to an economy centred on service, information and communication – what is sometimes referred to as a *cognitive capitalism*. The means of production become subordinated to the communication codes. This is a world where images, symbols, culture, ideology and values take the driving seat. Production and circulation of these codes, which are mainly situated in cities, also means rather different types of production culture and labour demand. The development towards an individualized public service is also an aspect of these trends as well as the shift in cultural policy from delivering finished cultural products to enabling an expressive life (Murray, 2009, p. 14).

This is the personal cultural economy. But there is another significant development of cooperation. The disjunction between the existing sensitivity of the active citizen and the insensitive organizations that came up in an earlier period – companies, public bureaucracies, mass-political parties and the state church – has led to a multiplication of different social movements and of citizens that take the issue into their own hands. In several areas these have been leading social enterprises and innovators during the past 30 years or so.

These changes are not only influencing the 'rules of the game' within which different authorities and the public market operate. They have opened the very game itself to new social initiatives, to a more active role for the citizens to play on the field and to new value-based necessities.

As movements they gain support from different parts of the society, both from those inside authorities and those outside. All activities in these movements start voluntarily and they remain that way. Many of them involve personnel who are paid by donations or grants or start their own initiatives within the market economy.

There is a new awareness, a commitment to what is being produced and how this is done, in using one's possibilities as a citizen, consumer and worker in order to decide on one's own what is meaningful. It is a movement that goes *from passivity to action*. And out of this comes a way of value-based initiatives, some within the citizen sector, but there are also those that are seen in the market or start from the public sector. As movements this wave has developed its own form of network organization, its own mixture of paid work and voluntarism and its own culture. It is a source of a great variation of social innovations as well, which in many cases are focusing themselves on those issues that authorities and the market have not been able to handle successfully.

Distributive production and the social economy

These developments are in many ways running in parallel with those distributive systems that emanate as an aspect of new technological possibilities. They are not completely determined by the new technology – there are examples that predate that – but the new technologies are doing much to reinforce and facilitate them. Technology also plays a role in supporting and multiplying these trends. This is partly because one characteristic of these systems is that they contain a strong element of mutuality.

The arguments here are of two kinds (Murray, 2009, p. 17). *First of all* there are a number of difficult-to-manage social issues which demand an increasingly larger slice of the economy of a country, of which many neither the public sector nor the market have had the ability to solve in a satisfactory manner. *Second*, there are a great number of new initiatives both from within the public sector and from the households, cooperative and voluntary organizations as well as from the citizens themselves more directly that are characterized by a kind of distributive systems, which to a large extent are possible due to the new technology. These distributive systems are part of what is often called the social economy, which is consequently very important for these innovations and for the service and those relationships that come out of them.

The green revolution has been harder to avoid

The environmental movement of today is an example of the praxis and the type of organizations which exist with the new social movements and which also may be seen as one example of the renewed social economy. Those who are involved have set an agenda for the twenty-first century (Murray, 2009, p. 17) – concerning energy, food, waste, transport and the whole subject of well-being and life style. In each and every one of these, the citizen networks have developed their own political economy with protests, production and consumption. They have created a strong wave of alternative technologies, of new forms of consumption and distribution, which now constitutes its own international micro economy.

Many of these innovations have been taken up and been reinforced by the markets and the public economy. Large companies and public institutions have often found it difficult to graft those distributive microsystems in their structures, even if some have succeeded in doing so.

The deployment period

There are consequently reasons as to why those entrepreneurs, who, with a social interest in mind, act outside or inside business to get a larger role in the society. But what does the employment period look like, that period which to a larger and larger extent is to bring us into the new society?

Social entrepreneurs are in a way not a new solution by themselves but a necessary part of it due to the remorseless growth of social and environmental issues which neither governments nor the markets, the way they look today, are able to stem (Murray, 2009, p. 19). These issues can no longer be confined within the economy of the state, but have consequences for the way production is organized in the market and the way in which production and consumption take place at home.

The shift to a network paradigm has the potential to transform the relationships between the organizational and institutional centres and their peripheries. The new distributive systems are not managing the complexity from the centre; this is done in a complex, but distributive, way more and more from outside this centre – to household and service users and in the work places to local managers and workers. Those who are at the margin have something that those in the centre can never have – knowledge of the details – what are the specific time, place, special events and, in the case of consumers and citizens, needs and wishes. This is the potential. But to realize this, a new kind of commitment is required with and for users. New relationships at work and new terms of employment and compensations are necessary.

This concerns those who operate on the private market. But it is, in a way, of greater importance to the so-called authorities. For the moment the economy is divided between a hierarchical and centralized state, a number of companies that exist in different markets and a number of small organizations, informal associations and groups (which are citizen based). But the important thing is that the new techno-economic paradigm connected to the new social movements makes it possible to think of this distribution in a new way – a distribution that makes it possible to combine the energy and the complexity of a distributive responsibility with the integrating capacity of modern systems societies, which contain a strong citizen sector and intimate connections between this sector, the public sector and the market sector.

Substantial structural reforms and institutional changes are necessary in order for a society of this kind to function effectively. New infrastructures, tools, platforms and means to distribute resources, new kinds of organizations and maybe above all new ways to link the formal and the informal economies to each other are needed. This means a far-reaching programme and realized informal initiatives to social innovations on a scale that has not been seen since the second half of the 1800s. The existing crisis provides possibilities for *a social innovative activity* – which so far has been marginalized – *to take place next to private innovation activities on society's stage.*

This book is a contribution to the discussion about how to design the innovative activities of this new society.

Summary and conclusion

What has been said in this chapter points at a necessity for humankind to act in an entrepreneurial way today as never before, but also at the orientation that we can expect the entrepreneurship will have in the future, that is, to be gradually more of a social entrepreneurial kind.

Think 2.1   What new aspects are really needed today in order to start a business/entrepreneurial activity? Is there anything that you had to think of when you started a business/entrepreneurial activity, say, 50 years ago that you do not have to think of today?

Think 2.2   What will probably be more important when you start a business/entrepreneurial activity, say, 20 years from now?

Think 2.3   Think of six different products:
P1: Food
P2: Telephones
P3: Bicycles
P4: Tools
P5: Magazines
P6: Clothes

Also think of six different target groups:
T1: Teachers
T2: Hospitals
T3: Senior citizens
T4: Mothers
T5: Children
T6: Students

Finally think of six different needs:
N1: Communication
N2: Experiences
N3: Freedom
N4: Environment
N5: Culture
N6: Security

Let chance, for instance a dice, choose any of the products, one target group and one need. Find out a possible business based on this combination.

Think 2.4   How can you be entrepreneurial in your own home? Give an example.

CH 2 – CASE STUDY

Microsoft

(Adapted from Burns, 2011, p. 6)

Microsoft is one the world's most outstanding business success stories. Born in 1955 in Seattle, United States, Bill Gates and his friend Paul Allen, begged, borrowed and boot-legged time on his school's computer to undertake software commissions. The two went to Harvard University together and used the school's computer to start their own business. Bill's big break came when he approached *Altair*, a computer company in Albuquerque, New Mexico, and tried to sell a customized version of a programming language, BASIC, to them to be used on their computers. The only problem was that that, at the time, he and Paul Allen had not finished writing it. He had a vision of what it would look like and how it would function, but no software. It was not finished until a couple of weeks later and with that *Microsoft* came about. The programme was later sold to *Apple*, *Commodore* and *IBM*. *IBM* then commissioned *Microsoft* to develop its own operative system and that was how *Microsoft* Disk Operating System (MS DOS) came about. By 1980, *Microsoft*, which was founded in the late 1970s, was seen as a successful start-up with a turnover of $8 million from just 38 employees. The company floated its shares on the US stock market in 1986 and the company's stock price has made four billionaires and an estimated 12 000 millionaires from *Microsoft* employees.

The growth of *Microsoft* has been amazing. With a turnover of more than $58 billion and with 93 000 employees, *Microsoft* is today the world's largest software company and it has produced a number of products and services, including the *Microsoft* operating system and *Microsoft* Office package. And its ambitions are still far from over. The company has expanded to markets like video game consoles (Xbox), interactive television, Internet access (MSN) and search engines (Bing). As its major market matures, it has been looking to transform its software applications to Web-based services.

In 2008 Bill Gates retired from day-to-day activities of the company as one of the world's richest men. He remains chairman of its board and will continue as advisor to its key projects.

 DISCUSSION QUESTION

> This is a very hypothetical question, but would a company like *Microsoft* be able to start in today's world? (You are welcome to look for more information around the start of *Microsoft* on the Internet to answer the question.)

To access the teacher's manual that accompanies this book, please use the following link:

http://goo.gl/DXQas.

3

All these preneurs

Introduction

It is not difficult to understand that entrepreneurs can be found everywhere – they are needed everywhere. This chapter starts by looking at entrepreneurs in society, where this society is divided into three sectors: the business sector, the public sector and the citizen sector. This chapter ends by looking at one type of entrepreneurship which constitutes a connection between two of these three sectors of society, one type which is of special interest to me in my profession and which I also believe is of interest to many of the readers of this book, what we commonly call academic entrepreneurship.

Entrepreneurship in different sectors of society

Most entrepreneurship scholars today, like myself, do not want to limit entrepreneurship to specific personal traits or specific (for instance, economic) behaviour. The broad view of entrepreneurship (to which I belong) claims, furthermore, more distinctively that entrepreneurs can be found in the whole society, not only in its economy. Johannisson, for instance (2005, p. 27; my translation), puts it such that 'venturing is something that belongs to all kinds of life' or 'the market is too small an arena for entrepreneurship, only the whole human existence is big enough' (p. 39; my translation).

I see three sectors in society, which are (Figure 3.1):

- The public sector
- The business sector
- The citizen sector (or 'the third sector')

It is also so, that only part of these sectors consists of entrepreneurship, that is, people who 'not just are' and 'act as if', people who are a bit more proactive than most others in satisfying other people's demand and/or need through new businesses or new activities over and above 'just' being employed in the

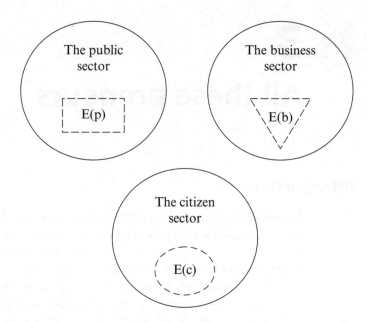

Figure 3.1 The three sectors of a society

public sector, running a business or 'just' being a citizen. These are within the broken lines in Figure 3.1:

E(p): Entrepreneurs in the public sector
E(b): Entrepreneurs in the business sector
E(c): Entrepreneurs in the citizen sector

It is possible to associate the above types of entrepreneurs with three different types of places where they operate (compare Bjerke, 2010):

- In institutions in the public sector
- In markets in the business sector
- In private or public places in the citizen sector

By this it is possible to see three kinds of entrepreneurs in a society:

- *Entrepreneurs in the public sector* = People employed in different institutions in the public sector, who 'are not just' and 'act as if' for the common good at the same time as they are 'just' employed there.
- *Business entrepreneurs* = Enterprising and innovative people, who are financially driven and who focus on demand in different markets and try to satisfy these through new products and services.

- *Citizen entrepreneurs* = Enterprising and innovative people, who are idea-driven and direct their interest towards social needs though new activities. This can take place in private places (for instance, in sheltered workshops at elderly's homes) or in public places outside the public sector or in markets (for instance, in public squares, in public lecture events or on the Internet).

This broad classification is in line with what the statement made by Steyaert and Katz (2004), when they (1) say that entrepreneurship takes place in many different places and in different situations; (2) claim that these places and situations are political in the wide sense of the term; and (3) state that entrepreneurship is a question of everyday activities rather than a result of an elite group. It is also possible to put as Berglund and Johansson do (2008, p. 2; my translation):

> To see that entrepreneurship in fact expresses itself in a variety of places, and not only locate it to so-called incubators or science parks. To see that people through their entrepreneurship create a variety of values for society and not just the economic ones that so easily come in focus.

Compare these statements with what I earlier referred to as the broad and narrow views of entrepreneurship.

It is important to realize that Figure 3.1. is meant to illustrate that not all (probably most) that takes place in the society is entrepreneurial. There are so many activities (probably most of them) in the traditional sectors of society *that are not entrepreneurial*. To put it differently, it is, of course, possible to be a citizen, be employed in the public sector and/or run a business *without acting 'as if'*. Furthermore, entrepreneurial activities take place where many non-entrepreneurial activities also take place. *Institutions* are associated with the public sector, *markets* are associated with the business sector and *private and public places* are associated with what is sometimes called *the third sector*, the way I look at it (my name for the third sector is *the citizen sector*).

If we 'stress' the entrepreneurs in Figure 3.1 we get Figure 3.2.

I see all *entrepreneurs* in the public sector and all *entrepreneurs* in the citizen sector, but only some business entrepreneurs, as *social entrepreneurs*, which are the shaded fields in Figure 3.2. I see all entrepreneurs as social entrepreneurs who are not run by a profit motive but by a social idea or entrepreneurs

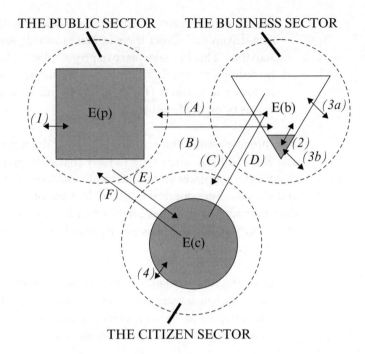

Figure 3.2 Entrepreneurs in different sectors of a society

who next to their profit motives have a clear objective to satisfy non-commercial citizen needs in a society.

There are all kinds of connections between the different entrepreneurial parts of Figure 3.2 and between these parts and the rest of the society for instance:

- From or to *entrepreneurs* in the public sector and *other parts of* the same sector. This can be people who go from 'just being' employed in this sector to coming up with *new* ways to perform their tasks or people, who after having done so 'go back' to 'just' administer them as part of their employment (these connections are marked 1 in Figure 3.2).
- From or to *entrepreneurs* in the business sector to *social entrepreneurs* in the same sector. This can be business entrepreneurs who change their entrepreneurial ventures in a more socially oriented direction or social entrepreneurs within the business sector who after having developed new socially oriented activities within the business sector move into running them in a more commercial, but still entrepreneurial, way (these connections are marked 2 in Figure 3.2).
- From or to *entrepreneurs* in the business sector and other, non-

entrepreneurial parts of, the same sector. This can be traditional business people who move between being entrepreneurial business people and being non-entrepreneurial business people (*3a*) and socially oriented business entrepreneurs who move between being socially oriented business entrepreneurs and being non-social non-entrepreneurial oriented business people (*3b*).

- From or to *citizen entrepreneurs* (that is social entrepreneurs in the citizen sector) to other parts of the citizen sector. This can be people who have run citizen entrepreneurial ventures as a project and who move to 'just be' citizens or citizens who move from what it means to be a citizen and start citizen entrepreneurial ventures (as citizens) (These connections are marked with *4* in Figure 3.2).
- There are several possible connections *between* the different sectors. Some examples (which are also marked in Figure 3.2) are:
  - **A.** *From market to institution*: A consulting company, who helps a local community with its place marketing.
  - **B.** *From institution to market*: A local community, who privatizes its waste disposal management.
  - **C.** *From market to private or public place*: A company, which applies corporate social responsibility (CSR) in a more tangible way.
  - **D.** *From private or public place to market*: An organization, which is mainly operated by volunteers, assists women to start their own businesses.
  - **E.** *From institution to private or public place*: Three employees in a local community who start a soccer club among teenagers.
  - **F.** *From private or public place to institution*: Two citizen entrepreneurs, who run a seminar in a local community, where the participants are members of a locally dominant political group.
- Finally, there are several different possibilities to a *cooperation* between the three sectors (entrepreneurial or not) (there are no such connections marked in Figure 3.2).

A model similar to the one in Figure 3.2 has been suggested by Nicholls (2006). It is given in Figure 3.3.

A clear difference between Figures 3.1 and 3.2 compared to Figure 3.3 is that in Figures 3.1 and 3.2 different entrepreneurs are seen as clearly separated from each other while social entrepreneurs in Figure 3.3 bridge over the traditional sectors of the society. I prefer Figures 3.1 and 3.2 for at least two reasons:

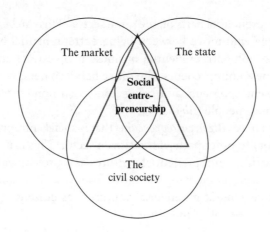

Source: Nicholls (2006, p. 229).

Figure 3.3 The three estates of society

1. Even if social entrepreneurs in general may appear in any sector of the society and even if it is common that social entrepreneurs are bridging the different sectors of the society (the reader will find many such social entrepreneurs in this book), I assert that those social entrepreneurs that operate in the citizen sector are somewhat different. Furthermore, there are lots of citizen entrepreneurs that are not running a business of any kind or not employed in the public sector. It is easy to think that those scholars who stress that social entrepreneurs *always* bridge the different sectors of society only look at those social entrepreneurs, who in fact do so. This kind of bridging is also common in many countries, where the public sector is not as large as it is in countries like Sweden. But many citizen entrepreneurs do not enter other sectors, but 'are not just' and 'act as if' *just being citizens*, that is, not being business entrepreneurs or publicly employed. To stress planning and organizational skills for all entrepreneurs, good knowledge of management and marketing plus efficiency, effectiveness and economic effects easily neglects the political and ideological functions of social entrepreneurs (Parkinson and Howorth, 2008). It is not enough to bring over so many of the views of business entrepreneurs to the views of social entrepreneurs, the way I look at it. This is 'disarming' the social entrepreneurs from the possibilities to come up, in their 'own' way, with more or less innovative solutions and suggestions and to keep the distance from business entrepreneurs and from other parts of the society (Cho, 2006).

2. I also claim that business entrepreneurs and social entrepreneurs build on *at least partly different logic*, which cannot be combined in any straightforward or simple way. I will shortly return to this.

As stated on several occasions, in all entrepreneurial situations it is necessary:

- 'Not just to be', that is, to, for instance, not just be employed by the public sector, business person or citizen but also come up with new solutions to satisfy demand and needs (this independent of doing it in the same sector or doing it in another sector). Another aspect of this is that entrepreneurs never can be positioned or appointed. They must act on their own free will.
- 'To act as if' (Gartner et al., 1992), that is, not being constrained by existing or predicted resources (which will probably lead to functioning the same way as before) but think and act in a new (entrepreneurial) way instead of as before (full of duties and administratively), to act in such an interesting way to other people that they will provide new resources. Another way to phrase this is to say that entrepreneurship is never about what is already done or finished but always about something which is 'on its way to becoming something' (Gartner et al., 1992).

It is relevant in this context to realize that 'increasing the connections between entrepreneurship and society, we get the chance to see the new multiverse of entrepreneurship with its variety of social, cultural, ecological, civic and artistic possibilities' (Steyaert and Katz, 2004, p. 193). There *are*, however, as aforementioned, limits on applying the results of research on business entrepreneurs onto social entrepreneurs, for instance, to citizen entrepreneurs:

- Even if social entrepreneurs as well as business entrepreneurs are good at networking, social entrepreneurs exploit network relations *in a much broader field* (Dennis, 2000; Blundel and Smith, 2001; BarNir and Smith, 2002).
- Social entrepreneurs use their networks not only to leverage resources and strengthen their own ventures, which is primary to business entrepreneurs, but also *to deliver impact and to create new social value* (Nicholls, 2006, p. 225).
- Social entrepreneurs operate in *a more diversified and dynamically strategic landscape* than traditional business entrepreneurs (O'Gorman, 2006). Even if they never compromise in their social mission, social entrepreneurs are looking for alliances and cooperative possibilities where they can most easily find them. Many social entrepreneurs work *at the same time* with local governments, welfare institutions, volunteering groups and banks (Nicholls, 2006, p. 225).
- Social entrepreneurs often show *a much larger variation* in the form of

organization under which they operate than do business entrepreneurs (ibid., pp. 225–6).

- Economies of scale are *not as obvious* for social entrepreneurs as for business entrepreneurs. The former may often get maximum impact by remaining small and local and through deepening their activities rather than broadening them (ibid., p. 226).
- Social entrepreneurs are often looking for a social space where traditional business activities and the public sector *have not* shown any major interest and they improve on and create new social capital through institutional or gradual improvement and innovations (ibid.).
- Social entrepreneurs are often very *politically involved* (which is not the same as working for a specific political party) and they are often *effective activists* and/or *campaigners and catalysts of a wider social change* than what is the case for business entrepreneurs (ibid.).
- The urge to change the terms of engagement within their own sector, not for their own benefit but *for the benefits of their stakeholders,* often marks social entrepreneurs out as quite distinct from business entrepreneurs (ibid.).
- The primary interest behind an increased participation in their own interest areas as social entrepreneurs is not to gain themselves, but in order *for those in which they are interested to benefit from it.*
- The ultimate aim (even if it may not be attainable) for social entrepreneurs is to do so well that *they are no longer needed.* This is not the case for business entrepreneurs (ibid.).
- Paton (2003) asserts that social entrepreneurs and business entrepreneurs live *in different meaning-worlds.* To bring the business-venturing mind to social entrepreneurship could undermine what is the strength of social entrepreneurs (Krashinsky, 1998), neglecting the dialogical and political praxis which is central to social entrepreneurship (Cho, 2006).
- The important interest among social entrepreneurs is to stress the satisfaction of different *needs* while for the business entrepreneurs it is to stress the satisfaction of different *demands.* I do not, by this, claim that there are clear differences between demands and needs.

Most entrepreneurship theories are *market based.* The differences between the narrow and the broad view of entrepreneurship are much clearer among business entrepreneurs than among other kinds of entrepreneurs. Some concepts associated with the narrow view of entrepreneurship are:

- Need for achievement
- An economic phenomenon
- Growth

- Using opportunities
- A special type of management
- Business planning
- Extraordinary behaviour among extraordinary people

The narrow view of entrepreneurship is discussed in more detail in Chapter 4.

Some concepts associated with the broad view of entrepreneurship are:

- A phenomenon dependent on culture and place
- Not only an economic phenomenon
- Not just to be and act as if in everyday life
- Imaginative power
- Entrepreneurs are not a type of managers
- Too much planning may stifle creativity
- Extraordinary acts among ordinary people

The broad view of entrepreneurship is discussed in more detail in Chapter 5.

Entrepreneurship theories based on the narrow view largely have the ambition to try to *explain*. There are also attempts to *understand* entrepreneurship, which are above all used by the broad view of entrepreneurship (more about understanding entrepreneurship as different from explaining entrepreneurship comes in Chapter 11). *Market* is above all (at least traditionally) a *space-based* concept but entrepreneurship research has increasingly started to stress the importance of *place* (more about entrepreneurship theories related to space and place comes in Chapter 11).

The public sector can be seen in terms of 'space' as well as in terms of 'place'. It has created a space for itself in the economy by requiring people in a society to pay taxes, tariffs and charges to an amount that, in a country like Sweden, is more than half its gross national product. At the same time, activities in the public sector (entrepreneurial or not) take place in institutions like schools, hospitals, courts and public political and quasi-political offices at national, regional and local levels. Movements like labour unions and producers' and consumers' cooperatives have today become rather institutionalized and may very well be seen as belonging to the public sector (or to the business sector in the latter case), even though they once started in the citizen sector.

Entrepreneurship at central political level can be seen as *a more collective form of entrepreneurship* that focuses on broader actions and outcomes as a response to changes characterizing the global age (de Bruin, 2003). This means to stress entrepreneurship at a national government and political level. It is, however, rather clear that there is a need for a new terminology to be developed to convey better the nature of the state and to conceptualize the reconfiguration of the role of the state in our modern society. The 'welfare state' concept is now outmoded. Jessop (1994, p. 251) argues that 'a Schumpeterian workfare state is more suited in form and function to an emerging post-Fordism state'. Similarly, Audretsch and Thurik (1999) observe that industrialized countries have changed from the *'managerial economy'* of the previous industrial era to a knowledge-based *'entrepreneurial economy'*. De Bruin (2003) suggests the term *'the strategic state'*: 'The strategic state could be the principal actor in laying the foundations for building a strong, socially inclusive economy within the globally connected world' (p. 156).

Some small city-states are doing just that. According to Pereira (2004), the Singaporean government has chosen to evolve from a developing country to an entrepreneurial state.

According to Osborne and Gaebler (1992) there are nine characteristics that characterize *the new form of entrepreneurial government* in general. These are to support competition, empower citizens, judge activities through their results, be driven by objectives, redefine clients as customers, prevent problems from arising rather than providing service afterwards, concentrate on generating resources rather than using them, participative leadership, preferring markets to bureaucratic mechanisms and to focus on catalysing all sectors to solve citizen problems.

According to so-called conventional wisdom, organizations in the public sector cannot be innovative. Bureaucracies are normally regarded as lacking the competitive spur that drives businesses to create new products and services. Their rules are regarded as squeezing out anything creative or original. From the point of view of outsiders their employees are thought to be penalized for mistakes made but never rewarded for taking successful risks. So, while business develops new computer chips, ePads, ever more modern airplanes and wonder drugs, the slow and stagnant public sector acts as a drag on everybody else, so people say.

This opinion can be found everywhere. But it is at odds with the history of innovation (Mulgan, 2007, p. 4). Two of the most profound innovations that have been made during the last 50 years are the Internet and World Wide Web. Both came out of public institutions, however, DARPA in the first case and CERN in the second. If we look even further back in history, business has not been very innovative during most of human history, at least not until

the end of 1800s. The most important innovations came instead in communication, material and energy through support from wealthy patrons, from
governments and from the military. The idea that business and markets are
central to innovation in the society, or 'innovation machines' to use Baumol's
phrase (Baumol, 2002), is, in a historical perspective, rather new.

Even today the caricature of public institutions as stagnated enemies of creativity and innovation is disproven by thousands of public employees around
the world who have discovered new ways to combat AIDS and innovations
that promote health in other respects, for instance, vaccinating large portions
of the population or within the education or application of new methods
such as political intelligence or auctions of radio spectrums.

There are, however, good reasons to doubt the public sector's ability to be
innovators. Innovators normally succeed in spite of, not because of, dominant structures and systems. Too many good ideas lead to frustration, are
filed in registers or are simply forgotten. Public services remain bad at learning new models – even if they exist in their neighbourhood – and only a small
number of governments have any role, budget or structure that is devoted
to innovative issues as their *main task* within welfare, security, health and
environment. So that, even if they say they support innovation, there is no
government that has anything remotely near an army of public employees to
inspect and to monitor, or for that matter, to support technological research
and development (Mulgan, 2007, p. 4).

Pressure on the public to renew itself is mounting however. We have already
mentioned that, in the twenty-first century economies, the largest sectors
will not be cars, steel or even IT. In the advanced economies the largest
sectors will instead be health and care. Education accounts for 5–10 per cent
of GNP (gross national product). Health and care, both for children and
elderly, is growing fast and already constitutes 5 per cent in some economies. These are all sectors where government is the major player, either as
provider, funder or regulator, and they are all sectors where innovation takes
place in a very different way from how it was done in dominating economies
during the last century.

Public institutions, like other innovations, cannot be institutionalized or
planned to any major degree. But there are many things that governments
can do to improve the chances of new ideas coming up to improve value to
the public. They can do more to cultivate and scan the background from
which new ideas come, they can recruit innovators who have proven to be
successful, they can deliberately design and test promising new ideas; they

can provide markets for solutions and outcomes and they can create space where radical new ideas can evolve (Mulgan, 2007, p. 5).

Citizen entrepreneurship takes place in different *places*, some of them private and some of them public. Social entrepreneurs in general and citizen entrepreneurs in particular will be discussed in Chapter 6.

Academic entrepreneurship

Some entrepreneurship does not take place in separate sectors in the society but between two sectors, so to say. One example of this is cooperation between universities and industry, that is, between the public sector and the business sector. It is called *academic entrepreneurship*. There are, according to Bengtsson (2006, pp. 22–4), a number of trends in the society which create possibilities for entrepreneurship and business enterprising that this can lead to in academic environments, even if the picture is complex:

- The knowledge-based economy of today makes creation of knowledge in general, including research, important to economic development. More and more work requires education and special knowledge of different kinds. High technology plays an important role in this economy and leads to large investments in research and development. That academic entrepreneurship and business enterprising that may become its consequence is an important part of the process of spreading new knowledge to industry. Through academic entrepreneurship and that business enterprising that might follow, new steps of research may be spread and tested commercially. In that way new commercial experiences may be gained.
- There are great expectations from the political system and from different authorities that the role of universities is to be more salient in innovation. There is now relatively large concentration on making the academic environment produce more entrepreneurs, businesses and innovations. This concentration is given, among other reasons, in order to strengthen different scientific research environments but also to stimulate entrepreneurship and academic business enterprising in different organizations in incubators close to universities.
- A number of technological breakthroughs in, for instance nano-technology, biomedicine and bioinformatics could play a large future economic role in new businesses and equivalents. Within these areas, the connections between universities and industry are close.
- Most major companies in countries like Sweden are increasingly investing in more development work close to application. The need for new

research-based knowledge and development work, which they do not do themselves, is satisfied by organizing networks together with external partners. Universities with relevant research are usually part of these networks.

The picture of entrepreneurship and that business enterprising which may come out of academic environments becomes more complex, however. Let us take the example of Sweden.

- Sweden is a very research-intensive country, usually among the top countries in this respect, but this consists mainly of investments in research and development in a few large companies like Ericsson and AstraZeneca. This is the major explanation for Sweden's research intensity. At the same time, studies show that this lead to relatively few innovations and low economic growth compared to other OECD countries. This situation, that is, the high level of research and development with low-gear economic effects, has been called 'the Swedish paradox' (Edquist and McKelvey, 1998). However, independently of how one should interpret this paradox, it is clear that a huge number of ideas and much knowledge and many businesses in this country's research-intensive sectors come from activities at universities. It is therefore important that academic entrepreneurship and other enterprising are developing as in other industrialized countries. 'One of the most striking aspects of the development since World War II has been the growing importance of academic research's contribution to the continuing development of industrialized countries' (Henrekson and Rosenberg, 2000, p. 9; my translation).
- Growth in business start-ups coming from the academic world is slow and clearly lower than in other business start-ups. Even if the academically based start-ups are generally at a high level of innovation, they seem to remain small most of the time.
- Researchers and teachers have generally limited experience from contacts with commercial environments. The academic environments have even sometimes been hostile to commercial initiatives in Sweden. It has turned out, furthermore, that researchers founding businesses are less willing to take risks than other entrepreneurs. This is sometimes because they want to keep up their academic positions and therefore will not invest too much time or effort in their business enterprises.

In order to stimulate the start and earlier development of new business start-ups coming from the academic world, it has become increasingly common for universities and the equivalent to develop special organizations, so-called incubators (sometimes called science parks), which concentrate on the early development stage of academic business start-ups. The role of incubators is to make the transfer of technology and commercialization between university and industry more effective.

> Science parks are organizations that stimulate technology and knowledge transfer between university and industry. This is, above all, meant to take place by the research park providing suitable premises geographically close to a university or equivalent educational institution and by creating and exploiting formal as well as informal cooperation and networks between the university environments and the business firms in the park. The first business park was started in 1951 by Stanford University and was called Stanford Research Park. It then took some time before the idea about science parks was spread to Europe. The first European parks were Cambridge Science Park in England, ZIRST in Grenoble and Sophia Antopolis in France. They were established in the beginning of 1970s. In Scandinavia Ideon's science park was established in Lund in 1983. In science parks there are normally four types of businesses. There are technology- and research-based business start-ups based on some idea from academic or other entrepreneurs. Another group is established small and medium-sized technology-based firms. A third group consists of units, often research and development units, belonging to big firms which want to come closer to the university's research and to an educated staff. Finally, there is a group of service firms which sell everything from cleaning and restaurant services to management consultancy to the firms in the science park and other firms in the neighbourhood. (Bengtsson, 2006, p. 97; my translation)

Summary and conclusion

In this chapter I have provided an overview of different entrepreneurs that may exist in a society, divided into the three sectors: public sector, business sector and citizen sector (sometimes called 'the third sector'). I have also looked at common cooperative efforts between university and industry today, which is called academic entrepreneurship.

Think 3.1 How could your educational institution/university become more entrepreneurial?

Think 3.2 What kind of entrepreneur would you like to be and why?

Think 3.3 Do you see any differences between a senior academic entrepreneur and a junior student entrepreneur?

Think 3.4 What should a fruitful business incubator or science park look like from an entrepreneurial point of view in your opinion?

CH 3 – CASE STUDY

Freeplay Energy

(Adapted from Barringer and Ireland, 2006, pp. 351–2)

Have you ever had your cell phone battery go dead when you needed it the most? What if you could reach behind the back of your phone when it happens, turn a crank for 30 seconds and generate enough power for 5 minutes more talking time? If your answer is yes, put a little money aside. *Freeplay Energy*, a British electronics company, has already developed a half-pound, hand-cranked generator for *Motorola* cell phones and is working on devices for other manufacturers' phones.

Freeplay Energy has an interesting start-up history. In 1991, the British inventor Trevor Baylis saw a television programme about AIDS in Africa. A comment was made during the programme that advice on how to prevent the spread of AIDS could be disseminated to people by radio, if only radios and in particular batteries weren't so expensive. Trevor asked himself why radios could not be powered the same way as clocks by winding them up to produce power. Trevor built a prototype of his idea that he called a 'clockwork radio'. The idea was promising and enough backing could be generated to carry out the necessary scientific and market research study to make the clockwork radio a reality.

While Trevor was completing his work, the clockwork radio concept was featured in a British television documentary that was seen by Chris Staines, another British inventor. Staines and his business partner, Rory Stear, immediately realized the potential for self-sufficient electronics could go much further than radio. The partners decided to take Trevor's idea to the next level. Their next step was to obtain a grant from the British government to commercialize the idea and the self-sufficient energy industry and *Freeplay Energy* (the company that started to commercialize the idea) was born.

After finishing the clockwork radio, *Freeplay Energy* started to produce hand-cranked radios that were distributed by AIDS relief agencies in Africa. The benefits of the radios were immediately recognized and *Freeplay Energy* generates interest and support from a number of humanitarian agencies, including the Red Cross, CARE, the European Union and the United Nations. More than 150 000 *Freeplay Energy* radios were produced and distributed to at least 40 developing countries. It is estimated that these self-sufficient windup radios have benefitted over 3 million people directly and more than 30 million people indirectly by providing them with a vehicle for information and education despite the lack of electricity and batteries in their communities.

To further investigate the possible applications of its clockwork radio technology, *Freeplay Energy* quickly evolved into a commercial company focusing on designing and producing useful self-sufficient energy products. The members of the company knew that they could apply their technology to almost any small electrical device, including flashlights, cell phones, laptop computers and various types of radios. They also knew that users often get caught trying to use these types of devices when their batteries are low and no source of electricity is readily available. The company has branched out further and now

CH 3 – CASE STUDY *(continued)*

produces self-sufficient energy via solar panels, rechargeable batteries and similar developmental possibilities.

The most compelling aspect of *Freeplay Energy*'s offerings is that they appeal to almost all socioeconomic groups. The products are accessible and valuable in areas where the consumers cannot afford batteries or electricity. As mentioned, several of the products from *Freeplay Energy* are distributed by relief agencies. The company's products are also accessible and valuable to middle-class and affluent consumers who are constantly on the go. Trevor Baylis says that he wants to 'make energy available to anybody any time'. He also says that 'what makes me the happiest is if I can improve life among the poorest in developing countries. I feel like a citizen of the world and I want to act like one.'

 DISCUSSION QUESTION

What kind of entrepreneur is Trevor Baylis in your opinion?

To access the teacher's manual that accompanies this book, please use the following link:

http://goo.gl/DXQas.

4

Business entrepreneurship: the narrow view

Introduction

This chapter is about business entrepreneurs according to the narrow view, that is, it is more or less about rationally thinking business starters, who come up with new business solutions mainly by being good business planners, by being clever managers and by being open to business opportunities that appear and/or are created in different markets.

Entrepreneurial myths

The narrow view of entrepreneurship is relatively homogeneous. There are, however, still a number of myths about entrepreneurs around, even if we stick to business entrepreneurs and have a narrow view of the subject (Bjerke, 1989, pp. 526–7; Timmons, 1999, pp. 47–8; Coulter, 2001, pp. 8–9; Kuratko and Hodgetts, 2004, pp. 30–3). For instance, whether *you are born an entrepreneur or not* is a much-discussed subject. Some commentators claim that entrepreneurship is primarily a matter of inborn qualities. Others claim that entrepreneurship comes forward under favourable external circumstances, that is, when cultural, family and social conditions are propitious. My opinion is, even if there is no general agreement on the issue, that entrepreneurial qualities cannot be compared with such congenital talents as an ear for music or a strong skeletal structure. I have seen entrepreneurship appear under such differing circumstances and implemented by such completely different people that I am inclined to say that, in principle, practically anybody could be an entrepreneur.

One common opinion is *that entrepreneurship often leads to failure.* Considering that entrepreneurship means to do something differently (to 'act as if' and to 'make a difference' as I call it) and to do something which is, at least partly, new and that many activities associated with entrepreneurship cannot be planned to any major degree, entrepreneurship is often a question of taking risks. However, even if the entrepreneur is not unwilling to take a risk, entrepreneurship is more of calculated risk-taking than a shot in the dark. Furthermore, there are situations where, if the entrepreneur is to succeed, risks have to be minimized and sometimes even avoided. It is even possible to say that entrepreneurship never fails even if mistakes can be made, if the entrepreneur uses his or her false steps as moments of learning.

I often hear that *all you need as an entrepreneur is a good idea*. As I see it, a good idea is only one part of the equation to become a successful entrepreneur. To get an understanding of existing requirements wherever you are in the entrepreneurial process, to attack possibilities systematically when you start and to take on challenges as you go on can also be key ingredients in succeeding as an entrepreneur. But it shows again and again that the entrepreneur's own qualities (even if, as mentioned, these 'qualities' are not generalizable) are more decisive than anything else in an entrepreneurial success. It is a common statement that it is better to combine a top-quality entrepreneur with a low quality idea than the opposite. A good idea can always be frittered away, but a good entrepreneur can achieve miracles with an inferior idea.

It seems to be a common conception that *the most important thing for an entrepreneur is to have access to money*. It is true that much financial capital may be needed when undertaking a major entrepreneurial project. It is also true that many entrepreneurial attempts may fail due to shortage of such capital. It is, however, not correct to claim that money is the decisive factor to succeed when undertaking something new in the first place. There are many entrepreneurial start-ups that take place *as if* the necessary resources were there (another aspect of the concept 'as if'). Furthermore, money is for the entrepreneur what paint and brushes are for the artist – dead matter in itself, which in the right hands may create inimitable results. Furthermore, it may be so in a problematic stage of an entrepreneurial project that lack of financial resources may be a sign that other circumstances like leadership qualities, degree of motivation or imagination and willpower are not what they should be.

It is common to hear the statement that *entrepreneurship only takes place in small contexts and in small organizations*. Entrepreneurship is not something that takes place only when an activity is started (which is normally small, at least in the beginning). It has become increasingly obvious in our modern society that every activity, in order to survive, no matter what age and size must renew itself from time to time, at least to some to some extent, and this even if it has grown big (I have talked about what is required in our society today in this respect in Chapter 2).

Some business entrepreneurial schools in the narrow view of entrepreneurship

In spite of the fact that the narrow view of entrepreneurship is relatively homogeneous, it is rather rich. One way to illustrate this is to look at some entrepreneurial schools, which could be seen as belonging to this view. I bring up the following schools:

- Macro and micro schools.
- Schools with the ambition to map the entrepreneurial process.
- Schools building either on the supply or the demand in the economy.
- Schools discussing the phenomenon psychologically or behaviourally.

Macro and micro schools

Kuratko and Hodgetts (2004) suggest a classification of entrepreneurial schools in two groups: macro schools (based on factors beyond the control of entrepreneurs) and micro schools (based on factors which the entrepreneur can control).

Macro schools can be broken down into the *environmental school*, which focuses on factors in the sociopolitical environment which positively or negatively affect the development of the entrepreneur; and the *financial/capital school*, which focuses on opportunities for the entrepreneur to look for and to find venture capital during different phases of the development of a business venture. Furthermore, the *displacement school* is counted as a member of this group; this considers the consequences for the entrepreneur of being outside certain political, cultural or economic situations.

Micro schools consist of the *entrepreneurial trait school*, which aims to identify the personality traits, which characterize successful entrepreneurs; the *venture opportunity school*, which focuses on the process of searching for opportunities to exploit a business opportunity; and the *strategic formulation school*, which stresses the planning process for effective business development.

Entrepreneurial description models

Different entrepreneurial description models are summarized in Table 4.1.

Table 4.1 Entrepreneurial description models

The entrepreneurial model	Central focus or purpose	Assumption	Behaviour and skills	Situation
'Great person' school	The entrepreneur has an intuitive ability – a sixth sense – and traits and instincts with which he or she is born	Without this 'in-born' intuition, the individual would be like the rest of us mortals, who 'lack what it takes'	Intuition, vigour, energy, persistence, and self-esteem	Start-up
Psychological characteristics school	Entrepreneurs have unique values, attitudes, and needs that drive them	People behave in accordance with their values; behaviour results from attempts to satisfy needs	Personal values, risk-taking, need for achievement and others	Start-up
Classical school	The central characteristic of entrepreneurial behaviour is innovation	The critical aspect of entrepreneurship is in the process of doing rather than owning	Innovation, creativity and discovery	Start-up and early growth
Management school	Entrepreneurs are organizers of an economic venture; they are people who organize, own and assume the risk	Entrepreneurs can be developed or trained in the technical function of management	Production planning, people organizing, capitalization and budgeting	Early growth and maturity
Leadership school	Entrepreneurs are leaders of people; they have the ability to adapt their style to the needs of people	An entrepreneur cannot accomplish his or her goals alone, but depends on others	Motivating, directing and leading	Early growth and maturity
Intrapreneurship school	Entrepreneurial skills can be useful in complex organizations; intrapreneurship is the development of independent units to create, market and expand service	Organizations need to adapt to survive; entrepreneurial activity leads to organizational building and entrepreneurs becoming managers	Alertness to opportunities, maximizing decisions	Maturity and change

Source: Cunningham and Lischeron (1991, p. 47).

Supply and demand schools

A relatively common ground for classification is to divide studies of entrepreneurship into *supply schools* focusing on the availability of suitable individuals to occupy entrepreneurial roles, and *demand schools*, where focus is on the number and nature of entrepreneurial roles which need to be filled (Thornton, 1999, p. 20ff.).

Factors influencing the supply of entrepreneurship can in turn be divided (Bridge et al., 2009) into:

- *Population growth and density.* Expanding population and growing population density in some regions can mean that more people are considering self-employment as a means of securing an income.
- *Age structure.* Entrepreneurial attitudes, skills and resources are acquired over time and consequently age can have an impact on entrepreneurship.
- *Immigration.* Immigrants need work like everybody else, but may have problems in accessing existing jobs. Starting their own businesses could be an alternative.
- *Participation.* Increased participation in the labour market, especially among women, increases the number of people who are prepared to consider self-employment.
- *Income levels and unemployment.* High-income levels can mean that a person has too much to lose by leaving a permanent job. Unemployment, on the other hand, increases interest in starting on one's own.

Similarly, factors that influence the demand for entrepreneurship can be divided into (ibid.):

- *Economic development.* Economic development can affect the interest in starting new companies. In developed countries, high salaries may discourage people from trying self-employment. However, in developing countries, even low per capita income may have a positive impact on the self-employment rate.
- *Technological development.* In recent years the speed of technological development, which reduces the advantages of scale, has created new opportunities for small business start-ups.
- *Globalization.* Globalization makes people more aware of the diverse range of opportunities which do in fact exist; this may stimulate phenomena such as ethnic restaurants.
- *Industrial structure and clustering.* The break-up of monopolies and the

reduction of protectionism have offered more opportunities for small business start-ups and have trends such as localization in clusters.

Psychological and behavioural schools

These could be subdivided into the personality school, the social demographic school, the cognitive school and the behavioural school.

The personality school

The explaining task of research, which governs the narrow view of entrepreneurship, looks at finding patterns and regularities – not strict deterministic, sufficient and necessary relationships, which would be unrealistic in social sciences, but at least those that could be seen as average or typical (most common). The ultimate ambition for such a researcher would be to get a clear picture of the true entrepreneur, for instance, in terms of personality. Personality can, in turn, be defined in terms of patterns and regularities in action, feelings and thoughts that are characteristics of the individual (Snyder and Cantor, 1998). Some personality traits which by tradition have been identified with entrepreneurs (Bridge et al., 2009) are:

- *Achievement motivation*: When individuals accomplish something that they consider as worthwhile, their self-esteem is enhanced and they are encouraged to take on other demanding assignments. Enterprising people are constantly on the lookout for challenges.
- *Risk-taking propensity*: Proactive achievers break new ground, but their behaviour is risky. The outcomes of enterprising undertakings are less certain than conservative ones and enterprising individuals must have the capacity to tolerate risks and the psychological make-up and mental resources to cope with failure.
- *Locus of control*: Enterprising people believe that they themselves make things happen in a given situation and they underplay the importance of luck and fate. They make things happen; things do not just happen to them. In essence they feel that they exercise considerable control over events in their everyday world.
- *Need for autonomy*: This may follow from a feeling of being in control, but it is not the same thing. Enterprising people have a strong desire to go it alone. In interviews with enterprising people they repeatedly refer to the need to control their own lives.
- *Determination*: Enterprising people also possess determination. They normally complete their projects and a certain degree of persistence is necessary for success.

- *Initiative*: A person may have a strong need for achievement, may possess determination, may welcome the chance to do his or her own things and to exercise control over his or her environment when pursuing an assigned project and may, when presented with an opening, exercise many enterprising qualities. If, however, he or she does not actively take the initiative and seek openings and opportunities, the enterprise will be limited in its results.
- *Creativity*: The ability to come up with something new is not evenly distributed in a population. Some people tend to have more originality than others and to have the ability to come up with solutions that fly in the face of established knowledge. They are also inclined to be more adaptable and prepared to consider a larger range of alternative approaches.
- *Self-confidence and trust*: It is most unlikely that enterprising people lack self-confidence. Proactivity, creativity and achievement are not accomplished without changes, sometimes major ones. Along with self-confidence goes trust. In reality, successful enterprise requires the coordination of disparate inputs, and a degree of trust in those who contribute.

Other personality traits which are often associated with entrepreneurs (Timmons, 1999; Zimmerer and Scarborough, 2005; Delmar, 2006; Allen, 2010) are:

- *Responsibility*: Entrepreneurs feel a deep sense of personal responsibility for the outcome of the venture they start. They prefer to be in control of their resources and use those resources to achieve self-determined goals.
- *Opportunity obsession*: Successful entrepreneurs are obsessed with opportunity. Their obsession with opportunity is what guides the entrepreneurs when dealing with important issues.
- *Desire for immediate feedback*: Entrepreneurs enjoy running their businesses, but they like to know how they are doing and are constantly looking for feedback.
- *Future orientation*: Entrepreneurs have a sense of constantly searching for opportunities. They look ahead and are less worried about what was done yesterday than with what should be done tomorrow. Entrepreneurs see an opportunity where other people only see problems if anything at all, a characteristic that often makes them the object of ridicule (at least until they succeed).
- *Tolerance of ambiguity*: The start-up process is by its very nature dynamic, uncertain, complex and ambiguous. Entrepreneurs, however, seem to work well in this type of environment, possibly because it is challenging, exciting and offers more opportunity than a structured environment.

- *Over-optimism*: Over-optimism is closely related to the feeling of being in control, because both are related to the expectation of success. When entrepreneurs are asked about their chances for succeeding, they tend to be extremely optimistic.
- *High commitment*: An extraordinary level of commitment is commonly required from entrepreneurial ventures. Entrepreneurs often live under high and constant pressures – first for their firms to survive start-up, then for them to stay alive and finally for them to grow. They have to be the top priority for the entrepreneur's time, emotions and loyalty.
- *Leadership*: Entrepreneurs are patient leaders, partly to be first with a tangible vision and managing for the longer haul, partly to be a model for their team and to motivate its members.

Much has been said over the years about entrepreneurs as risk takers beyond the ordinary. This is worth a few comments in the context of our new entrepreneurial society. Traditionally it is assumed that entrepreneurs run four kinds of risks in their endeavour (Kuratko and Hodgetts, 2004): (1) financial risk – putting one's financial savings, maybe even house and property, at stake in an entrepreneurial effort; (2) career risk – not being able to go back to one's old job if the venture should fail; (3) family and social risk – neglecting family and friends because a new entrepreneurial effort uses much of the entrepreneur's time and energy; and (4) psychological risk – risking one's own well-being.

However, how does the risk of undertaking something compare with the risk of not doing so? Is it not so in our new entrepreneurial society that the quickest way to go under is *not* to do something? I can see great risks – financially, in terms of career, family and social life and, perhaps above all, psychologically – in sitting down still in the belief that the future will simply be a repetition of today. The concept of 'risk' gets a new meaning in our new entrepreneurial society!

The personality school has endured much criticism. It has been unable to differentiate clearly between entrepreneurial small business owners and equally successful professional executives in more established organizations (Carson et al., 1995). Most of those factors believed to be entrepreneurial have not been found to be unique to entrepreneurs but common to many successful individuals (Boyd and Vozikis, 1994). Most entrepreneurs do not possess all the enterprise traits identified, and many of the traits are also possessed by those who could hardly be described as entrepreneurs (Bridge et al., 2009). To use only the personality school approach may even lead to problems identifying those aspects of a person that are *not* specifically entrepreneurial. One example is a large and very careful study of 11 400 people in the UK (the cohort contained 1300 entrepreneurs) who were born in the first week of March 1958. When compared with the rest of the cohort the entrepreneurs did not turn out to be either more persistent, self-motivated or risk-taking Almost the only factor that distinguished the entrepreneurs from the others was that those who became entrepreneurs were more likely to have received an economic gift or an inheritance which could be turned into money (*The Economist*, 1998).

There are theoretical as well as methodological problems associated with an approach based on the personality school (Delmar, 2006). The school does not recognize that entrepreneurship is a dynamic, constantly changing process. A person is not always an entrepreneur. Different entrepreneurial qualities may also be needed in different phases of an entrepreneurial venture (Carson et al., 1995). The personality trait approach can easily lead to the conclusion that the entrepreneur springs from the cradle with all faculties, drives and qualities preformed, needing only the opportunity to exploit them.

> Part of the problem with trait approaches arises from how the entrepreneur and entrepreneurship are defined. In the first instance a focus only on the individual who establishes a new venture is arguably too narrow. It fails to recognise sufficiently the entrepreneurial potential of people who work to develop and grow established enterprises. In addition, there is the difficulty raised by the fact that entrepreneurs are not an easily identifiable, homogeneous group. Entrepreneurs, it appears, come in all shapes and sizes, from different backgrounds, with varying motivations and aspirations. They are variously represented and addressed in the literature as opportunists or craftworkers, technical entrepreneurs or so-called intrapreneurs. (Carson et al., 1995, pp. 51–52)

The social-demographical school

Sociodemographic circumstances can explain entrepreneurs to some extent:

- Some regions or communities encourage entrepreneurship more than others because they have institutions ready to help small firms (Curran and Blackburn, 1991). Such localities could be said to be more favourably disposed to the notion of entrepreneurship (Bridge et al., 2009, p. 75).
- People who have self-employed parents are overrepresented among those who are self-employed themselves (Shapero and Sokol, 1982; Delmar and Davidsson, 2000).

- Education and work experience influence entrepreneurship. Two groups are overrepresented among those who start a business (Delmar and Davidsson, 2000, p. 4): (1) individuals previously self-employed trying to start a new business and (2) unemployed individuals trying to start a business as a way of earning a living. As regards education most studies indicate a positive effect on self-employment, at least for low versus intermediate levels of education.
- Ethnicity: self-employment is often suggested as a way for new immigrants to establish themselves in a new society. However, the interest in self-employment differs widely between different categories of immigrants.
- Those people who find themselves in an in-between situation in life seem to be more inclined to seek entrepreneurial outlets than those who are in 'the middle of things' (Dollinger, 2003, p. 43). Examples of such situations, apart from immigration, are between military and civilian life, between student life and career, and between prison and freedom.
- Gender and age. To run a business seems to be associated with gender to some extent – men start more businesses than do women (I will look at women as entrepreneurs more specifically in Chapter 9). It is also conditioned by age. According to Brockhaus (1982), most businesses are started by people 33–45 years old (Landström and Löwegren, 2009, p. 47).

However, no sociodemographic (or other individual level) variables have turned out to be particularly strong predictors of self-employment (Delmar and Davidsson, 2000, p. 2).

The cognitive school

Theories that try to explain behaviour by how people perceive and comprehend information surrounding them are called *cognitive theories* (Delmar, 2006, p. 159). They may be better at explaining entrepreneurship because they consider that interaction which exists between people and their environment. These models can be divided in two groups (Delmar, 2006, pp. 166–74): attitude-based models, and (2) models for motivation in achievement contexts.

An attitude is a key concept in motivation theories. An attitude is an evaluation of an object or a concept, that is, to what extent an object or a concept is judged as good or bad (Eagly and Chaiken, 1993). When modelling people, psychologists tend to make a distinction between *distal* and *proximal* factors affecting behaviour (Ackerman and Humphreys, 1990). A distal factor explains general behaviours (such as eating, sleeping or having sex). A proximal factor defines the more concrete situation in which the individual finds him or herself. Actual behaviour is better explained by proximal factors (task characteristics) than by distal factors (traits and needs). Attitude is a proximal factor. Attitudes can provide some basis for explanation. They may influence a person's choice but they say very little about the level of effort and persistence employed (Locke, 1991). In order to do this a more *planned behaviour* is needed (Ajzen, 1991).

Two proximal factors discussed in models in achievement contexts, according to Delmar (2006), are *perceived self-efficacy* (Boyd and Vozikis, 1994) and *perceived intrinsic motivation*. Intrinsic motivation can be seen both as an antecedent to and as a consequence of high self-efficacy (Bandura, 1995).

To understanding-oriented researchers of entrepreneurship who are not using these types of models the explaining-oriented results can seem somewhat self-explanatory. Who can deny, for instance, that a person who experiences positive attitudes towards starting a business and who feels that he or she is efficient and motivated enough to make it, has a higher chance of succeeding than others? The models in question should not, however, according to their advocates be seen in this way. They are attempts to come up with constructs such as 'planned behaviour', 'perceived self-efficacy' and 'intrinsic motivation' which should provide the grounds for the establishment of tests, which through quantitative analysis are to be used as better instruments for forecasting who will be an entrepreneur and who will start a business. This is a natural and respected aim *if you are an explaining-oriented researcher*. (I will be back to research aiming for explanations and research aiming for understanding and also to models and interpretations in Chapter 11.)

The behavioural school

The aim is here to look at a larger complex of behaviour and how elements within them are related to supporting entrepreneurship. Examples of variables that may be contained in such complex are:

- ability to make judgements and decisions
- goal-oriented behaviour
- planning behaviour
- taking on responsibility
- creativity
- technical skills

- networking ability
- knowledge of project management

According to Landström and Löwegren (2009, p. 49), the concept of *intentions* is important in entrepreneurial psychological and behavioural models – an intention concerns a person's interest and willingness to execute a specific act – in the case of business entrepreneurs to start a business. One condition is then that the person in question has control over his or her situation, which in the case of the entrepreneur leads to a focus on his or her knowledge to start a business.

Entrepreneurship and handling opportunities

Entrepreneurship using the narrow view is commonly defined as the process by which individuals purposefully and consciously pursue opportunities without regard to resources they currently control (Stevenson and Jarillo, 1990). The essence of entrepreneurship behaviour is in such a view seen as identifying opportunities and putting useful ideas into action (Ireland et al., 2003).

According to Gaglio and Katz (2001, p. 95), 'understanding the opportunity identification process represents one of the core intellectual questions for the domain of entrepreneurship'. Mariotti and Glackin (2010, p. 13) assert that there is a simple definition of 'entrepreneur' that captures the essentials: 'An entrepreneur recognizes opportunities where other people see only problems'. According to Baron and Shane (2008, p. 5), entrepreneurship involves the key actions of identifying an opportunity that is potentially valuable in the sense that it can be exploited in practical business terms and yield sustainable profits. 'The entrepreneur always searches for change, responds to it, and exploits it as an opportunity' (Drucker, 1985, p. 25). Kirzner (1979) asserts that the mentality of entrepreneurs differs because they are driven by *entrepreneurial alertness*, which he suggests is a distinctive set of perceptual and cognitive processing skills that directs the opportunity recognition process.

An opportunity is seen by Barringer and Ireland (2006, p. 28) as 'a favorable set of circumstances that creates a need for a new product, service, or business'. Coulter (2001, p. 53) sees opportunities as 'positive external environment trends or changes that provide unique and distinct possibilities for innovating and creating value'.

> The opportunities themselves often emerge from changes in economic, technological, governmental, and social factors. When entrepreneurs notice links

or connections between these changes, ideas for new ventures may quickly follow. (Baron and Shane, 2008, p. 13)

Timmons (1999) defines a business opportunity as an idea, plus four characteristics:

1. It is attractive to customers.
2. It will work in your business environment.
3. It can be executed in the window of opportunity (which is the amount of time you have to get your business idea to the market) that exists.
4. You have the resources and skills to create the business or you know someone who does and who might want to form a business with you.

Opportunities are often seen as noticeable circumstances. Such circumstances may be (Mariotti and Glackin, 2010, p. 16):

1. *Problems* that your business can solve.
2. *Changes* in laws, situations or trends.
3. *Inventions* of totally new products or services.
4. *Competition.* If you can find a way to beat the competition on price, location, quality, reputation, reliability or speed, you may create a very successful business with an existing product or service.
5. *Technological advances.* Scientists may invent new technology, but entrepreneurs figure out how to use and sell new products based on it.

Opportunities are claimed to generally arise from two major sources – the information people have that helps them to notice new business opportunities, and changes in the external world that generate opportunities (Baron and Shane, 2008, p. 39). According to one economist, Ács (2002, p. 12), opportunities for discovering or creating goods and services in the future exist precisely because of the dispersion of information. This dispersion creates the opportunity in the first place. Second, the very same dispersion presents hurdles for exploiting the opportunity profitably, because of the absence or failure of current markets for future goods and services. It is therefore, according to Ács (ibid.) necessary to understand, (1) how opportunities for the creation of new goods and services arise in a market economy, and (2) how and in what ways individual differences determine whether hurdles in the discovering, creating and exploiting opportunities are overcome.

There has been a debate in the field of entrepreneurship as to whether opportunities exist in the external world or are created by human minds (see, for instance, Forbes, 2005). Baron and Shane (2008, p. 84) believe that there is no basis for controversy over this issue. Opportunities, according to them, as *potentials*, come into existence in the external world as a result of changes in conditions in the society. However, they remain merely potentials until they are recognized by somebody's perceptual and cognitive skills. In a sense, therefore, according to these two authors, opportunities both exist 'out there' and are a creation of human thought. Maybe a solution to whether opportunities are there to be discovered or created could be to talk about *opportunity formation*. Hjorth and Johannisson (2003) refer to this process as '*articulation*'.

Now to one critical question: how useful is it to look at recognizing and exploiting opportunities as necessary for entrepreneurs to succeed? I think that even from the point of view of the narrow view of entrepreneurship, it is possible to make two solid comments in answering this question:

1. The highly recognized Global Entrepreneurship Monitor studies on the variation of entrepreneurship inclination across countries have come to the conclusion (for instance, Bosma and Harding, 2007), that early-stage entrepreneurship is more likely to be *necessity-based* in middle- or low-income countries, where entrepreneurship in many cases may be the only option for making a living, than *opportunity-driven* which is the case in high-income countries.
2. A more serious criticism against the usefulness of looking at opportunity recognition and exploitation as a *necessary* entrepreneurial characteristic is probably that the success of that type of research which most of the narrow view of entrepreneurship is based on and which is trying to promote this skill as a primary and necessary entrepreneurial quality is judged by its ability *to make a forecast*. I think it is *possible* to look at opportunity recognition and exploitation as a variable in a model of factual entrepreneurial behaviour, but that is most of the time *after the fact* and this is often *not a very adequate explanation for what has actually been going on*. To claim that opportunity recognition and exploitation is a *necessary* requirement to succeed as an entrepreneur (logically related to having a good business plan, aiming for growth and having the skills of a good manager) *before* you go for a business start-up, I simply find very doubtful, in practice as well as in theory. One study in the narrow entrepreneurial tradition (Gartner and Carter, 2003) even claims that the desire to start a business more often than not comes before looking for a business opportunity.

Consequences of starting a business

Much has been written about the positive consequences for entrepreneurs of starting a business; some examples follow (Coulter, 2001; Bjerke and Hultman, 2002; Zimmerer and Scarborough, 2005):

- to tackle opportunities
- the opportunity to create one's own future, to achieve and to mean something
- to be able to use one's own abilities and talents fully
- to have a high degree of independence, to make one's own decisions without restrictions
- to be responsible only to oneself
- to gain financial advantages
- to have the chance to have fun
- to follow in the family footsteps

The same authors (Coulter, 2001; Bjerke and Hultman, 2002; Zimmerer and Scarborough, 2005;) have, of course, something to say about the negative consequences of entrepreneurs from starting a business:

- change and uncertainty
- a multitude of sometimes contradictory decisions to make
- being forced to make economic choices
- risk
- uncertain financial flows
- much work
- the possibility of failure

Different kinds of new business ventures and business entrepreneurs

It is common to distinguish between *lifestyle firms* and *growth firms* when talking about business start-ups (Burns, 2011). Lifestyle firms are set up primarily to undertake an activity that the owner-manager enjoys while also providing an adequate income, for example craft-based businesses. Expansion is not an issue, and once a level of activity that provides a reasonable income is reached, management becomes routine. Growth firms are set up with the intention of expansion, which normally requires exceptional entrepreneurial qualities of their starters.

There are, of course, other classifications of business entrepreneurs. Today, we can imagine new ones, for instance, technopreneurs, e-entrepreneurs, academic entrepreneurs and team entrepreneurs. One classification that I suggested in an earlier book (when I only knew the narrow view of entrepreneurship, but which I found useful) was (Bjerke, 1989):

- First a distinction between *independent entrepreneurs*, that is, business entrepreneurs who start businesses on their own and often become their owners, and *intrapreneurs*, that is, business entrepreneurs who start new business ventures for their employers.
- Independent entrepreneurs can then be classified into:
  A. *Extrapreneurs*, that is, people who leave their employment, taking along ideas that have come up in the course of employment and start their own venture;
  B. *Novopreneurs*, that is, people who get an idea which does not compete with the activities of their employer and start a new venture to exploit their creative potential;
  C. *Interpreneurs*, that is, people who connect ideas, resources and possibilities from different sources and start a venture based on this;
  D. *Renovateurs*, that is, people who save businesses in trouble and start a new venture based on the best pieces of the old one.

I came to the following conclusions through studying the above entrepreneurial types over the years at that time:

- extrapreneurs and renovateurs are common in critical situations,
- the majority of new business ventures are started by extrapreneurs,
- most countries have some kind of government institution supporting novopreneurs and their innovations,
- renovateurs seem to have become more common,
- novopreneurs seem to have become more rare.

Summary and conclusion

This chapter has summarized the narrow view of entrepreneurship. A number of entrepreneurial schools have been considered. Furthermore, a central aspect of the narrow view of entrepreneurship has been discussed, that is, the entrepreneur's ability to discover or create opportunities and to exploit these. Also, some aspects of the consequences of starting a business and different types of new businesses and business entrepreneurs were provided.

Think 4.1   Which strong sides and which weak sides do you see in the narrow view of entrepreneurship?

Think 4.2   Statistics claim that the most common type of a business entrepreneur is an extrapreneur, that is, a person who leaves his or her employment and starts something of his or her own in a similar field which he and she has been working with before. Why is it so?

Think 4.3   Statistics claim that about half of those businesses being started in the world are done so for necessity reasons, that is, to be able to support your family, etc. How much of 'the narrow view of entrepreneurship' is there among these?

Think 4.4   What does it mean to be rational as an entrepreneur?

CH 4 – CASE STUDY

3M

(Adapted from Burns, 2011, pp. 496–8)

3M has been known for decades as an entrepreneurial company that pursues growth through innovation. It generates a quarter of its annual revenues from products less than 5 years old. 3M started life as the *Minnesota Mining and Manufacturing Company* back in 1902. Its most successful product – flexible sandpaper – still forms an important part of its product line but this now comprises of over 60 000 products that range from adhesive tapes to office supplies, medical supplies and equipment to traffic and safety signs, magnetic tapes and CDs to electrical equipment. Originally, innovation was encouraged informally by the founders, but over more than a century some of these rules have been formalized more explicitly. But most important of all, a culture that encourages innovation has built up. And because this culture has built up a history of success, it perpetuates itself.

3M started life selling a somewhat inferior quality of sandpaper. The only way they could do this was by getting close to the customer – demonstrating it to the workmen that used it and persuading them to specify the product – an early form of relationship selling. This was the first strategic thrust of the fledgling business – get close to the customer and understand their needs.

However, the company was desperate to move away from selling a commodity product. Competing primarily on price and its closeness to the customer led it to discover market opportunities that it had the expertise to capitalize on. The first such product was Three-M-Ite™ Abrasive – an abrasive cloth using aluminium oxide for durability in place of a natural abrasive. This was followed by waterproof sandpaper – an idea bought from an inventor who subsequently came to work for 3M. This was followed shortly by Wetordry™ – a product designed for use by the car industry in finishing bodywork. And with this the second strategic thrust of the company was developed – to seek out niche markets, no matter how small, which would allow it to charge a premium price for its products. The company began to realize that many small niche markets could prove to be more profitable than a few large ones.

In the 1990s this began to change somewhat to the extent that some technologies became more sophisticated and the investment needed to develop new products increased. Therefore the return required became larger and markets needed to be correspondingly bigger. Luckily the world was increasingly becoming a global marketplace. At the same time, competition was becoming tougher and the rapidity of technological change and shortening of product life cycles made 3M recognize the need to dominate any market niche quickly. Speed of response was vital. By the 1990s, many of the market niches 3M was pioneering were turning out to be not that small at all, particularly in the global market place. So, the approach remained the same, but the speed of response and size of market niche, worldwide, increased.

The company really started to diversify when it entered the tape market in the 1920s,

CH 4 – CASE STUDY *(continued)*

but even this built on its expertise in coatings, backings and adhesives. What is more, the way the first product evolved demonstrates perfectly how an entrepreneurial architecture works. By being close to its customers *3M* saw a problem that it was able to solve for them through its technical expertise. In selling Wetordry™ to car-body finishers, an employee realized how difficult it was for the painters to produce the latest fad in car painting – two tone paintwork. The result was the development of masking tape – imperfect at first, but developed over the years 'out-of-hours' by an employee to what we know it to be today and from the technology developed the Scotch™ range of branded tapes. So, the third strategic thrust was developed – having identified a market opportunity through closeness to the customer, diversify into these related areas. Once *3M* found a niche product to offer in a new market, it soon developed other related products and developed a dominant position in the new market. In the 1990s *3M* came to recognize that it did best when it introduced radically innovative products into a niche market in which it already had a toehold.

This experience also taught *3M* the value of research but in particular to value maverick inventors who were so attached to their ideas that they would push them through despite the bureaucracy of the company. It was in the late 1920s that it developed the policy of allowing researchers to spend up to 15 per cent of their time working on their own projects. To this day, it tries to make innovation part of the corporate culture by encouraging staff to spend 15 per cent of their time working on pet ideas that they hope one day will become new products for the company. They can also get money to buy equipment and hire extra help. To get an idea accepted, they must first get the personal backing of a member of the main board. Then an inter-disciplinary team of engineers, marketing specialists and accountants are set up to take the idea further. Failure is not punished, but success is well rewarded.

Perhaps the best-known contemporary example of the success of this policy is the development of the Post-It® Note by Art Frye in the 1980s. He was working for a way to mark places in a hymn book – a paper marker that would stick, but not permanently. At the same time the company had developed a new glue, which, unfortunately as it seemed at the time, would not dry. Art spotted a use for the product but what was different was the way he went about persuading his bosses to back the project. He produced the product, complete with its distinctive yellow colour, and distributed it to secretaries who started using it throughout *3M*. Art then cut their supplies, insisting that there would be no more unless the company officially backed the product. The rest is history.

So the fourth strategic thrust of the company was developed – to pursue product development and innovation at every level in the organization through research. This was formalized when the Central Research Laboratory was set up in 1937, but maverick research continued to be encouraged. In 1940, a New Product Department was developed to explore the viability of new products or technologies unrelated to existing ones. In 1943, a Product Fabrications Laboratory was set up to develop manufacturing processes. In the 1980s four Sector Labs were created with a view to being more responsive to the market

CH 4 – CASE STUDY *(continued)*

place and undertaking medium-term research (5–10 years): industrial and consumer, life sciences, electronic and information technologies and graphic technologies. The Central Lab, renamed the Corporate Lab, was maintained to undertake more long-term research (over 10 years). In addition most of the divisions had their own labs undertaking short-term, development research (1–5 years).

3M has always been admired for its ability to share knowledge across the organization and link technologies to produce numerous products that could be sold in different markets. One example is Scotchlite™ Reflective Sheeting used for road signs, developed in the 1940s – in fact as a result of failed research to develop reflective road markings. This combined research from three different laboratories to produce signs with a waterproof base onto which a covering of an opaque, light-reflecting pigment was added followed by microscopic beads. This was all sealed with a thin coat of plastic to ensure weather durability. Strategy five had emerged – get different parts of the organization to communicate and work together and, most important of all, share knowledge.

This became formalized in the 1950s with the establishment of the Technical Forum, with the aim of sharing knowledge across the company. It held annual shows. Out of this came the Technical Council, made up of technical directors and technical personnel, which met several times a year to review research and address common problems. Alongside this the Manufacturing Council and then the Marketing Council were established. At the same time technical directors and researchers regularly moved around the different divisions. The fifth strategy was in place – share knowledge.

The culture in *3M* evolved out of its place of origin and has been called 'Minnesota nice'. It has been described as non-political, low ego, egalitarian and non-hierarchical as well as hardworking and self-critical. It has also, at least in its earlier days, been described as paternalistic in its approach to employees. Above all, *3M* is achievement oriented and achievement, particularly in research, was rewarded, often through promotion. For example successful new products teams were spun off to form new divisions. The leader of the team often became general manager of the new division and this was seen as a great motivator. Lesser achievements were also acknowledged. Researchers who consistently achieved 'high standards of originality, dedication and integrity in the technical field' – as judged by their peers, not management – were invited to join the exclusive 'Calton Society'. The 'Golden Step' and 'Pathfinder' awards were also given to those helping develop successful new products. Achievement was lauded at all levels. Strategy six was emerging – encourage achievement through reward.

Today *3M* faces many challenges to maintaining its reputation for innovation. As it becomes larger and more complex, involved in different markets with different products and technologies, at different stages of their life cycle, it recognizes that different managerial approaches may be necessary. The 'maverick', high-risk approach to research and development may not be appropriate in certain sectors. The 25 per cent rule – the proportion of new product sales – may not be achievable by all divisions. *3M* also faces stiffer

CH 4 – CASE STUDY *(continued)*

competition, which means that cost economies have had to be made to maintain profit-ability. As a result the 15 per cent rule – slack time to research new products – is under severe pressure, to the point where it is described as more of an attitude rather than a reality. Nevertheless, *3M* has for over a century successfully practiced entrepreneurship (of the type called intrapreneurship sometimes).

 DISCUSSION QUESTION

Explain, using the narrow view of entrepreneurship, why *3M* is so successful.

To access the teacher's manual that accompanies this book, please use the following link:

http://goo.gl/DXQas.

5

Business entrepreneurship: the broad view

Introduction

This chapter offers an alternative to the narrow view of business entrepreneurship described in the previous chapter, that is, what I call the broad view of entrepreneurship.

Rational and natural way of doing business

To behave rationally can be defined as consciously behaving logically and consistently in relationship to those objectives that exist and/or in relation to those means that exist. To behave rationally is sometimes interpreted such that you know your objectives and your means so well that you can behave optimally. To be entrepreneurial, that is, to be enterprising by suggesting or generating new solutions to existing or new problems does have to mean, however, that you only consider those means that you control at present or those which you with confidence can say will come in the future (Stevenson and Jarillo, 1990), but act 'as if' you are so interesting to your environment that more references will be generated as you move on.

But is it not possible just to combine existing resources in a better way or use them to reach new ambitions? Lévi-Strauss (1966) is here introducing a new dichotomy, which is between the engineer's and the so-called bricoleur's way of thinking. The first could be called a rational way of thinking and the second a natural way of thinking and that dichotomy can be applied to that special way of doing business which is entrepreneurship.

The word bricoleur (as well as entrepreneur) comes from French. In the old sense, the verb 'bricoler' applied to some external, natural movement, for instance, a ball rebounding, a dog straying or a horse swerving from its direct course to avoid an obstacle. In our own time the 'bricoleur' is still someone who works naturally, almost instinctively, compared to those of a crafts person, unlike an engineer who is rationally executing his or her profession, based on that knowledge acquired at school (Lévi-Strauss, 1966, pp. 16–17). The 'bricoleur' has no precise equivalent in English. He or she is a person who undertakes odd jobs and is a Jack-of-all-trades or a kind of professional do-it-yourself man or woman, but as Lévi-Strauss makes clear, he or she is of a different standing from, for instance, the English 'odd job man or woman' or handy person. The bricoleur has a variety of skills, which, even if they are many, still are limited. Furthermore, he or she always tries to make do with what is at hand. The engineer, on the other hand (Lévi-Strauss' terminology) acquires those skills and means that are necessary to fulfil the purposes behind a project that he or she has taken on. In principle, there are, at least in theory, as many skills and means as there are projects for an engineer. The skills and means of a bricoleur, on the other hand, cannot be defined in terms of projects. The bricoleur is collecting skills and means according to the principle that 'they may always come to be of some use' (Lévi-Strauss, 1966, p. 18).

The engineer always tries to get free from and get outside of those limitations that exist in a given context at a given place at a given time. The bricoleur, on the other hand, feels that this is not possible but sometimes he or she even uses a given context, place and time in a clever (or at least natural) way to achieve what he or she wants. The engineer chooses means from all directions rationally according to the needs of a specific project. The bricoleur chooses in a natural way projects considering what skills and means he or she has access to and are at hand at the same time as he or she is considering what he or she wants to achieve. It is a big mistake, however, according to Lévi-Strauss (1966, p. 21) to see the engineer's and the bricoleur's thinking as stages or phases in a knowledge development.

The broad view of entrepreneurship, which is presented in this chapter, has many bricoleurial (that is, natural instead of rational) characteristics. I will go back to bricoleurs in Chapter 8, when I look at rational and natural entrepreneurial start-ups.

Four business-makers

In this chapter I want to present four different suggestions to having a more broad view on entrepreneurship. The four suggestions have, however, several common characteristics. They are:

- entrepreneurs as *sense-makers*
- entrepreneurs as *language-makers*

- entrepreneurs as *culture-makers*
- entrepreneurs as *history-makers*

The reason why I use 'maker' instead of 'creator' (for instance, 'culture-maker' instead of 'culture creator') is that the broad view wants, as mentioned before, to study extraordinary acts among ordinary people (not among extraordinary people like in the narrow view). The point is then, most of the time, to use what is at hand, that is, among sense-makers to focus on what is meaningful or can be made meaningful, among language-makers to use the building blocks of language, so-called memes, among culture-makers to focus on the basic values in the culture and among history-makers to use more or less clear life styles. When they do this, however, they are more of 'makers' than 'creators' (compare professions like shoe-maker and saddle-maker with professions like film creator or fashion creators). There are, as we know, cases of very radical and innovative entrepreneurship, where what we may call super-entrepreneurs are in action, but these are exceptions rather than types. In these cases, it may be justified to speak of entrepreneurs more as 'creators' than as 'makers'. The borderline between creating and making is certainly very vague.

Everybody is a sense-maker, language-maker and culture-maker one way or the other. The point here is to look at entrepreneurs *as* sense-makers, language-makers or culture-makers. To see an entrepreneur as a history-maker is, according to Spinosa et al. (1997), different from the other three views above. These authors see entrepreneurs alone as history-makers. For instance, entrepreneurs have a particular ability to interpret the implicit style of their time, to understand what is in the air so to say, and out of this, they are able to disclose a space that others can use.

These broad views of business entrepreneurs are, as mentioned, intimately related. Which you focus on as a researcher is a matter of taste.

Baumol (1993) asserts that because entrepreneurs change the world we live in, no level of description can catch what they do. But I want to claim, that precisely by studying entrepreneurs when they use contexts as well as when they change them and show how this is done, this leads to an understanding of theoretical pictures of them.

Entrepreneurs as sense-makers

To look at entrepreneurs as sense-makers means to study them by building on social phenomenology, the way I look at it. This means, for instance:

- The interesting world for entrepreneurs is the life-world, the experienced everyday life, that reality which is constructed socially by and between people, not any abstract theoretical world.
- Life-world is socially constructed, but individually based (Sanner, 1997, p. 39).
- Sense-making takes place in a continuous process characterized by dialogues and communicative exchanges between people.
- This approach, which is based on phenomenology as presented originally by Edmund Husserl, has clear dialectic undertones.

I have, in another context, which was theories of methods, described this view as *the actors' view* (Arbnor and Bjerke, 1994, 2009).

The social phenomenology idea is based on four dialectically interrelated, processes for sense-making (Berger and Luckmann, 1966 [1981]; Arbnor and Andersson, 1977):

1. *Subjectification.* Consciousness of self is an important part of the consciousness of an individual. To be conscious means here that an individual has interpreted his or her situation, that he or she knows what has been interpreted and has an opinion of what it means. A subjectification means for an entrepreneur, for instance, that he or she starts to understand the business situation and its organizational form.
2. *Externalization.* In our life-world there are continuous externalizations between people. People meet people. We interpret each other. We act against or with each other. We show ourselves. An entrepreneur describes and tells the environment about the meaning with what he or she is doing, for instance how he or she is starting to look at his or her business situation.
3. *Objectification.* An interpretation or an act is manifested through externalization and positioned as 'objective' (more correctly, 'objectified', that is looked at and treated as objective without being it) through objectification. Externalization and objectification 'can take place simultaneously' and may therefore be difficult to separate. Externalizing new knowledge perceived by other people can be the beginning of objectification. But externalizations can also be influenced by previous objectifications and thereby confirm partly existing knowledge. An objectification by an entrepreneur means, for instance, that his or her venture becomes more accepted and established. This takes place, above all, if the entrepreneur is experienced as successful.
4. *Internalization.* This is the process by which earlier objectifications influence coming subjectifications and externalizations, that is, the historical

influence which the socially constructed reality may have on subjectification and externalization of the individual. Internalization for the entrepreneur can mean, for instance, taking on the generally established understanding of business venturing in his or her own situation.

These four processes need to be *institutionalized* and *legitimized* to function in the long term (Berger and Luckmann, 1966 [1981]; Arbnor and Andersson, 1977):

⇨ *Institutionalization.* Socially constructed reality has more or less fixed forms and is taken more or less for granted. Institutionalizations such rules of law, organizational diagrams and business (including entrepreneurial) educational programmes can have a dominant influence on any situation, where an entrepreneur perceives him or herself to be.
⇨ *Legitimization.* This is often seen as important in establishing oneself as a new business start-up person, the sense that one has something to provide and to get acceptance for trying to do so.

The whole process of sense-making through the above mentioned dialectical processes is illustrated in Figure 5.1.

As mentioned, life-world is socially constructed but individually based. All acts, including entrepreneurial ones, take place in a context. We may call such context, after Hjorth and Johannisson (1998), the *organizing* context. This context is institutionalized as well as constituting a potential and a possibility. It may support entrepreneurship at the same time as embedding an entrepreneur in a social context (Winnicott, 1971; Stacey, 1996).

For an entrepreneur it is possible to see three contexts (Sanner, 1997):

1. *The commercial context.* This context concerns production, distribution and exchange in a market for goods and services. The entrepreneur is rewarded there if his/her offer is satisfactory. Those who, in the end, will judge what is 'good' or not are the users of the outcome of the entrepreneurial efforts.
2. *The institutional context.* This context is characterized by rules and requirements that the entrepreneur must follow in his or her sense-making to gain support and legitimacy. The entrepreneur and other actors of interest to his or her venture are participating in this sense-making effort, taking into account its rules and requirements.
3. *The personal context.* Family and friends are often important to the entrepreneur's attempt to realize his or her ambitions.

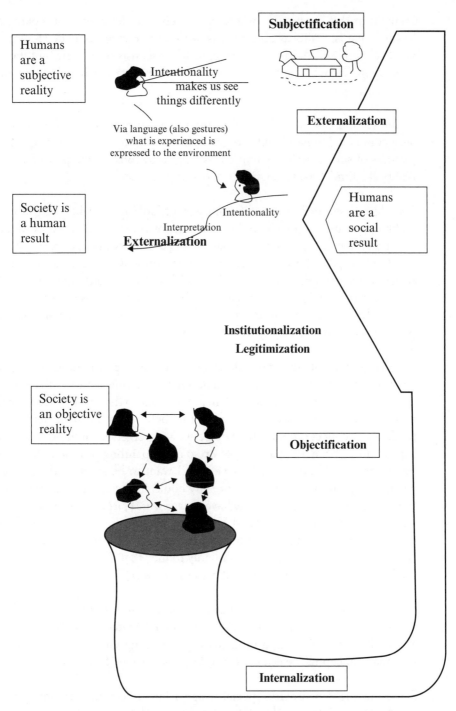

Figure 5.1 Social construction of reality

It might in this context be of interest to separate three ways of looking at 'reality', that is, reality as objective, as perceived or as sense-made (Smircich and Stubbart, 1985). In the first case, reality is seen as something 'out there', a reality to discover and to depict. Reality is then seen as full of contexts and as *objective*.

In the second case, reality, built on the same assumptions, is often seen as very complex. Human ability to generate more holistic and encompassing pictures of such a reality is limited. We can only look at one part of such a reality at a time. Reality can then be seen as *perceived*.

The third case offers a very different way of looking at reality. In this case reality is not believed to be full of contexts, of which we, limited as we are as human beings, can see only a part. Instead it is assumed, consciously or unconsciously, to be controlled by our intentionality, we enact a reality which we have *made sense of*, a reality which means something to us. If this reality exists as such, or if it does not, is of less importance, as it is of no interest whether or our perception is right or wrong. People, for instance, entrepreneurs act here *as if* reality were this way.

In order to illustrate the whole thing, let me use my apartment in Sweden as an example. *Objectively* it consists of about 118 m² and contains five rooms and a kitchen. I *perceive* the apartment as big, but also that the kitchen is small and that the storage space in the cellar that belongs to the apartment has a tendency to collect mould. These objective and perceived circumstances can explain how I have the space to put up so many paintings on the wall and so many carpets on the floor as I have, that I want to be alone in the kitchen when I cook and why I do not store any books in the cellar. But what does the apartment mean to me? How have I *made sense of* it? Among other things I have been married twice (and have become a widower twice) and that during my two marriages, together with my two wives, I have collected many souvenirs that *mean* a lot to me, and only to me (that meaning can certainly not be described in simple terms of cause and effect)!

Sense-making can be conceptualized as *the reciprocal interaction of seeking information and constructing meaning with action*. Created meaning influences action. Reciprocally, action influences the meaning you give to an action. One may conceptualize *action as meaningful behaviour* (Sanner, 1997, p. 38).

Sense-making can provide special insights into uncertain and ambiguous situations, for instance, when taking on a new and innovative activity related to an entrepreneurial venture. It is important for an entrepreneur to enact possibilities, not being restricted by any fixed ideas or definitions of what the business is all about. The environment can be acted upon in order to widen these possibilities for the business enterprise and in order to include other actors. A broad network widens the environment through social constructions and then enlarges the room to act (I will return to the importance of networking in relation to entrepreneurial start-ups in Chapter 8). Developing a problem into a possibility can be achieved through entrepreneurial sense-making of reality (Sanner, 1997).

Sense-making concerns the future but tends to be retrospective. Thinking of future actions involves imagining that they have already occurred and anticipating and making sense of their consequences (Gartner et al., 1992). One could say that we use *the meaning we place in experience of our everyday life* (Schutz, 1967, p. 73) as an *interpretative scheme* for our actions. We could also say that we, often unconsciously, *act according to or enact a narrative*. Somebody might enact the narrative 'I will present myself as an unconcerned person' or the narrative 'incredibly experienced in relating to the opposite sex'. An entrepreneur might enact the narrative 'I have been around before' or 'I know what I am doing'.

Interpretative schemes, which we often take for granted (although without being able to tell somebody else their full content), make it possible for us to 'recognize', 'interpret' and 'negotiate' even strange and unanticipated situations and thus to continue confirming and reconfirming meaning in the course of interaction with others (Ranson et al., 1980). But these schemes may also work as blinkers in a situation which should be seen as new.

Sense-making, however, is more than a process of recalling existing interpretative schemes or playing out old narratives. If that were true, no new learning could take place (Gioia, 1986). Instead, sense-making and construction of meaning involve associating new experience with existing knowledge, sometimes modifying existing schemes and narratives to incorporate new knowledge and also, even if infrequently, dramatically restructuring existing knowledge or creating new knowledge by using intuition and revelation (Bartunek, 1984).

Entrepreneurs as language-makers

Think about language as reality. To work symbolically through language and thereby transcend our biological limits is a hallmark of humanity and can even be counted as the most significant feature of a human being. Our acts are not only controlled by our intentions, but acts as well as intentions are controlled by the language we use. Genuinely new problems require genuinely new solutions. We do not find these genuinely new solutions if we do not have the appropriate language for it (Bjerke, 1989, p. 135). I look at it as an interesting possibility to try to understand entrepreneurs *through* the language they use and how they often must coin new concepts in order to succeed.

There are many examples of the magic and importance of language in our everyday life:

- Many companies try to make the concept 'employee' or 'worker' more humane by talking about, say, 'member of the crew', 'associate' or 'crucial resource'.
- 'Restructuring' or 'downsizing' are euphemisms used in some companies when they cut down. They refuse to say that they 'fire' anybody.
- How many times have we heard empty phrases in top-heavy bureaucracies, where the mode of presentation is what is most important and the medium is the message? When we listen to these people we often ask ourselves: 'What did they say – really?'
- Why, in some countries, are they changing the term 'public sector' to 'common sector'?

Language has certainly entered the theory and practice of business in the past 20–30 years:

- ⇨ A company is defined by its *language*. The symbols, concepts, visions and focus of the senior managers offer a better understanding of the company in question than either its plans or decisions.
- ⇨ Every moment is a *symbolic* moment. Even to ignore this as a business leader is symbolic.
- ⇨ The vocabulary of a company can be an important *asset*, but it can also be a major *liability*.
- ⇨ To renew a company it may be necessary to identify those who hold to the *relics* of its old language (Arbnor et al., 1980). Words rarely shake off their etymology and their origin. The point is to clarify the original ideas underlying the language being used in a company in order to reveal those who are still living in an outdated world.

Many of the most important artefacts are purely symbolic, with no *a priori* physical manifestations. *Concepts* are incredibly important artefacts. They are memes often resulting from a long 'cultural' process, or they may be expressions of deliberate rhetorical innovation. When *Xerox* went from the copying machine company to 'the document company', or when *Mercedes-Benz* talked about selling 'mobility' instead of cars, these notions were highly significant as artefacts. When *Observer* (a very successful Stockholm headquartered company) launched concepts such as 'communication audit' and 'value-creating communications' they created mental analysts for reframing the company's business, which started as press clippings where they were the world's leader. The power of concepts is further proven by how extremely conserving they can be. When *IBM* set up a personal computer division and called it the 'entry products division' this, of course, reflected a whole world view out of touch with emerging reality. (Normann, 2001, p. 244)

The great language philosopher, Ludwig Wittgenstein, coined the brilliant concept *language game*. This concept serves several purposes. *First*, Wittgenstein wanted to stress that language is used and functions in many different ways beyond the trivial sense of, for instance, pointing something out, asking questions or giving commands. Language is used one way when we tell a story, another when we participate in a debate and still another when we do mathematics. Here we can really talk about different language games. *Second*, Wittgenstein wanted to draw attention to the fact that the meaning of a linguistic expression is determined by its use *within* that language game to which it belongs. *Third*, the concept accentuates the fact that speech acts are related to other social acts. *Fourth*, 'game' indicates an activity that can be done for its own sake; there is no specific purpose to which all use of language is subordinated. In this context, Wittgenstein stresses the concept *life form* where a language game takes place in a natural way contrary to a purposeful activity. *Fifth*, one is reminded by the concept of language game that the use of language is an activity governed by rules.

If we follow Wittgenstein we must deny that understanding in the life-world *consists* of something special, a mental process in particular. Instead we should ask ourselves *what is the situation* in which we use the concept 'understanding' in a language game. Furthermore, there are no generally valid or exact conditions for somebody to say that he or she thinks or understands. If that were the case it would be meaningful to ask for the *moment* when somebody thought or understood for the first time. This would naturally lead to the idea of mental processes. Such questions, however, are not asked in the games using this concept *in everyday life*. There, understanding is something which takes place *between people*.

This provides us with a basis for discussing how to use language in order better to understand entrepreneurship, language which enables entrepreneurs to become the free and creative human beings they deserve to be (see, for instance, Hjorth and Johannisson, 1998 and 2000). Concepts from everyday life, such as interplay, passion, vision, initiative and responsibility could be utilized to stimulate entrepreneurial acts. Ambiguous concepts could be used to compare different understandings of entrepreneurship, action and behaviour, problems with possibilities or circumstances with meaning. Vocabulary could be re-established by, for instance, talking about becoming rather than being, or using terms from arts and theatre such as inspiration, creativity and spontaneity. Ingrained concepts such as coordinating or understanding could be re-interpreted. The use of verbs could be increased and the use of nouns decreased; organizing instead of organization, or why not 'entrepreneuring' instead of entrepreneurship? Finally, new words could be constructed in order to enliven old ideas, such 'cre-activity' for what entrepreneurs are doing and 'observ-actor' to denote the person who studies a phenomenon (from an understanding point of view).

I have mentioned before that I see clear differences between management and entrepreneurship. Let me put up two vocabularies, which could be contained in these two activities:

Management	Entrepreneurship
– Planning	– Learning
– Totalization	– Simplification
– Unity	– Variety
– Systems	– Social units
– Structure	– Process
– We are	– We become
– Efficiency	– Commitment
– Fit	– Excitement
– Marketing	– Networking
– Economies of scale	– Small is beautiful
– Education	– Culture
– Models	– Creative language

I see two different language patterns in these vocabularies – and by this two different thinking patterns and two different action patterns!

The relationships between language and entrepreneurship could be considered from very different angles. In order not to lead the discussion too far, let me just plant some 'seeds for thought' concerning entrepreneurs as language-makers with the reader:

- We *can*, as researchers, talk about creating new business ventures without having experienced it. Entrepreneurs cannot do this, however – as entrepreneurs.

- We *cannot create* new business ventures without talking about it.
- We do not understand entrepreneurship *before* we speak its language.
- To be an entrepreneur *always means*, at least partly, modifying one's language.
- A problem is not completely formulated until *it is solved*.
- To renew businesses (and so also language) in a firm it may be necessary that somebody comes in *from outside*.
- A word can only get its *full* meaning in a concrete context and in concrete action.
- If we do not talk about entrepreneurship, it will not take place. *The word can give space to it.*
- Entrepreneurs do not succeed very well *if they do not practice what they preach.*

Entrepreneurs as culture-makers

Let me illustrate entrepreneurs as culture-makers by presenting a larger study, which I conducted during the 1990s when I lived and worked in South East Asia. The study is discussed more in detail in (Arbnor and Bjerke, 2009, pp. 286–96). It was started by two friends and professors of business, one from Europe and one from the United States, who had received research grants to conduct comparative studies of the business culture among SMEs in Europe and the United States and who contacted me. They asked if I was interested in using some of this research grant to conduct a similar study of the culture among SMEs in South East Asia. I took on the challenge.

I started by thinking about how I could do what I promised. I realized very soon that it was an impossible task to study SMEs all over South East Asia. That task was simply too challenging. I then decided to limit the study to the business culture of such businesses among overseas Chinese in that part of the region, that is, Chinese that once lived in mainland China and for different reasons left that country and established themselves in countries around its coast. They were about 50 million people at that time in those countries in South East Asia, where they, in fact, dominated the business activities: Indonesia, Singapore, Malaysia, Thailand, Taiwan, Hong Kong and the Philippines (Lasserre and Schütte, 1995, p. 100).

Malaysia	*6 million*	*Thailand*	*6*
Indonesia	*8*	*Singapore*	*2*
Philippines	*1*	*Hong Kong*	*6*
Taiwan	*21*	*Total*	*50 million*

I soon realized that the public definition of an SME differed among the seven countries, for instance:

- Hong Kong limited the number of employees in SMEs to 100 in manufacturing and to 50 in non-manufacturing firms.
- Malaysia limited its public interest in SMEs to manufacturing only and preferred to talk about 'small- and medium-sized industries' (SMIs) to stress this fact.
- The Philippines divided enterprises below 200 employees into 'medium' (those with 100–199) employees), 'small' (with 10–99 employees) and 'cottage enterprises' (1–9 employees). If the value of a cottage enterprise's assets fell below a specified amount, it was called a 'micro enterprise'.

I therefore adopted the following pragmatic definition of an SME to use in the study:

SME = A small or medium-sized enterprise is one which is independently owned and operated, which is in business for profit and which is not dominating its field of operation.

I also adopted a pragmatic definition of culture as follows:

CULTURE = Basic values, assumptions and beliefs (which are mainly unconscious) and which influence everyday behaviour (which is mainly taken for granted).

The study continued with a search for information from five different sources (according to Figure 5.2) and I assumed that I could find the content of overseas Chinese business culture by finding the common denominator between those sources (**X** in Figure 5.2).

Overseas Chinese culture, so I thought, should manifest itself in all the five perspectives in Figure 5.2. It should manifest itself in action and thinking among power holders in the seven countries in question; in the economy and small business in the region; among what other researchers had found out about the Chinese way to do business; and in stories and material from real overseas Chinese business practice.

There is reason to describe to some extent what I found through my five perspectives, once some central points are brought up. The study took 3 years to complete (part-time).

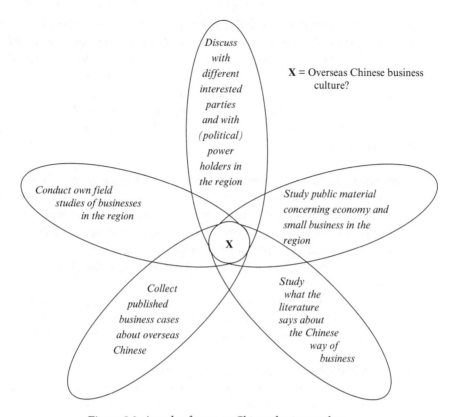

Figure 5.2 A study of overseas Chinese business culture

Discuss with different interested parties and with (political) power holders in the region

I visited the seven countries several times to discuss my research interests. I concentrated on three types of institutions:

1. governmental institutions involved in SMEs as a part of their area of interest
2. universities
3. SME interest groups, employers' confederations, industrial associations and the like.

All the seven countries had (1) governmental institutions with names like the Ministry of Industry and Trade (Malaysia), the Industrial Development Authority and the Agency for Development of Small Industry (Indonesia) or the Bureau of Industrial Promotion Policy and Planning (Thailand).

All of them had public material that was given to the researcher. However, most of this material concerned what *they wanted to do, not what they had actually done* and *very little concerned the SME sector* in the country. Also, very few university departments (2) showed any interest in small- and medium-sized business at the time. SME interest groups and industrial associations (3) existed in all seven countries, but in none of these cases were they specifically (or at least not openly) concerned with Chinese business alone.

Some results from discussions and readings from this perspective were:

- All seven countries, with the exception of Hong Kong, had very interventionist governments. Two of them, that is, Singapore and Taiwan, had been 'designed' by public policies more than the others.
- Due to this, SMEs had been crowded out in many industries in the seven countries.
- As a result of the former two points, it was no surprise that the proportion of SMEs was highest in Hong Kong among the seven countries.
- There was no support until very recently for SMEs in any of the seven countries.
- Most of the seven countries had developed a dualistic national structure with a relatively rich and prosperous (or at least active in terms of various kinds of businesses) capital and a very poor countryside. Exceptions were Singapore and Hong Kong, which had no agricultural business worth mentioning.

Study public material concerning economy and small business in the region

There turned out to be a rich body of material concerning the economy of the seven countries in general, but very little material concerning their SME sectors. Most material was attained by the researcher from APEC (Asia Pacific Economic Cooperation – a supranational institution with an office in Singapore). They provided me with several comparative studies of countries in the Asia-Pacific region, which I studied critically and methodically and chose information from. Some examples of results from this perspective were:

- The countries varied from very rich (Singapore) to rather poor (Indonesia and the Philippines).
- All the countries had moved from being commodity-based to becom-

ing manufacturing-based – and some even further to becoming service-based.

- There was no way to understand the South East Asian boom without understanding the overseas Chinese.
- If the overseas Chinese were an economy of their own, they would probably been the third largest economy in the world.
- The overseas Chinese started as traders and, to some extent, as contract workers. Many of them left their homeland because their lives were impoverished there and they were often treated harshly and as outsiders in the communities where they settled.
- Overseas Chinese, when entering business, concentrated on family businesses in order to keep themselves together by ties of blood, geography and business procedures.
- The overseas Chinese ran an extremely efficient opportunity-seeking machine and were moving funds around in networks.

Study what the literature says about the Chinese way of business

I studied the Chinese way of business through about 20 major works and about 100 articles, most of the latter in so-called recognized scientific journals. Some results from this perspective were:

- Overseas Chinese were very secretive about what they are doing.
- Overseas Chinese (as Chinese in general) were very superstitious, fatalistic and intuitive.
- The businesses of overseas Chinese were often a second-generation business as part of the inheritance from the first-generation patriarch.
- The businesses of overseas Chinese could survive in an industry with a very small margin as long as the turnover of sales is reasonably high.
- Long-range planning rarely existed in an overseas Chinese business.
- The manager/owner of the overseas Chinese business was a natural networker.
- If an overseas Chinese business was growing, it was often split into several units, the sizes of which were not larger than could be controlled by a family.

Collect published business cases about overseas Chinese and Conduct own field studies of businesses in the region

(These two sources are combined here, because they came up with very similar results.) I found 43 published case studies that told the stories of overseas Chinese businessmen (no women) – a surprisingly low number.

In order to come up with more stories I paid consulting companies to go to small business people for them to tell their stories in their local language and to translate those stories into English for me. Six such field studies were made in Malaysia and eight in Indonesia. These were two countries not represented among the 43 published cases mentioned earlier. The consulting companies had a directive to find 'what in their opinion were typical companies in their country'. They were also given an interview guide to follow as far as possible. They had 3 months to do the job. They were provided with a large list of generally formulated questions and issues that I wanted answers to, but otherwise, for practical reasons (only me and one assistant were involved in this large project), the consulting companies were left by and large to themselves until a one-day discussion was held individually with each of them at the same time as they handed over their material.

Some results from these two perspectives were:

- Overseas Chinese SMEs were commonly subcontracted.
- Management was based on person-to-person transactions to minimize bureaucracy and paperwork.
- Very few standard procedures existed in overseas Chinese businesses.
- Overseas Chinese SMEs could be personally influenced by the founder/owner to the extent that it may lead to confusion among employees.
- Promotions among employees were made from inside in overseas Chinese businesses.
- Overseas Chinese SMEs gave priority to manufacturing.
- The meaning of marketing in overseas Chinese SMEs did not include advertising, sales promotions or public relation activities.

I constructed a systems model of the overseas Chinese business culture shown in Figure 5.3.

Figure 5.3 should be read such that every *component*, that is, every 'basic value, belief and assumption' influences every other component in a complex pattern of mutual relationships.

I mentioned in the introductory chapter that not all small (or middle-sized) business firms are entrepreneurial. This is the same for overseas Chinese, of course. I believe, however, that it is possible to interpret aspects of overseas Chinese entrepreneurs as culture-makers as follows:

o Material success is personal success
o Always be ready for a negotiation

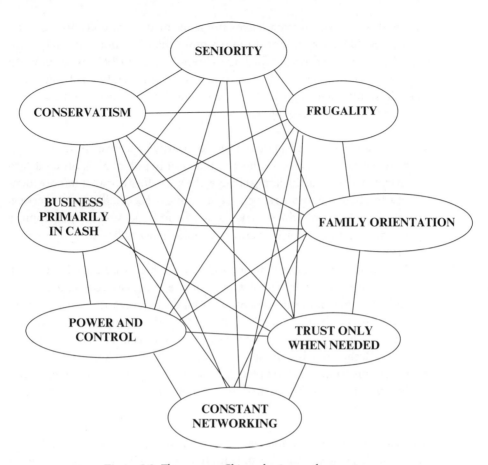

Figure 5.3 The overseas Chinese business culture system

- ○ Commit yourself quickly, if it looks promising; backing from the environment comes (eventually) later
- ○ Play the role that seems suitable – do not care who is really 'you'
- ○ To be secretive is a power; keep it within the family
- ○ Control everything
- ○ Never lose your face
- ○ Contacts, contacts, contacts
- ○ Take risks (if the signs are right)

Entrepreneurs as history-makers

Spinosa et al. (1997) has presented a theory that looks at only some people as *history-makers*. Entrepreneurs belong to this group. This theory is based on the idea that we all experience anomalies or disharmonies in our lives. Most of us, however, do not do much more than just noticing such situations. But there are those, according to Spinosa et al. (1997), who act when they face such situations and who present ways in which to challenge them. They do so by disclosing what the authors call 'the life styles' in the society. This can be done in three different ways:

- *Articulation* is the most familiar type of 'clarifying a style'. It occurs when a style, which so far 'is in the air', but is only potential, is brought into sharper focus. In articulating change, the style does not alter its core identity, but becomes more recognizable among users of a product or service, the acquisition of which makes this life style possible. Articulation is the most common form of entrepreneurship according to Spinosa et al. (1997).
- *Reconfiguration* is a more substantial way in which a style can be focused. In this case some marginal aspect of the practices coordinated by a style becomes more dominant. This kind of change is less frequent in everyday life than articulation. In the case of reconfiguration, a greater sense of integrity is generally *not* experienced (as in the case of articulation). Rather, one has the sense of gaining wider horizons.
- *Cross-appropriation* takes place when some part of society takes over a lifestyle from another part of the society, a style that it could not have generated on its own but that it finds useful.

Articulation, reconfiguration and cross-appropriation are three different ways in which disclosed skills can work to bring about meaningful historical change of a disclosed reality. All of these three changes are called *historical* by Spinosa et al. (1997) because people sense them as a continuation of the past: the practices that become newly important are not unfamiliar. Spinosa et al. (1997) are, therefore, contrasting their notion of continuous, marginal historical change with discontinuous change and look only at the first ones.

One may ask, of course, why it is that our potentialities as history-makers are discovered by so few? Spinosa et al. (1997) assert that there are three ways to understand this. All of them can be seen as aspects of social phenomenology:

- Our common sense works to cover up our role as possible disclosers of new reality. Common-sense practices cover the situation that everyday common sense is neither fixed nor rationally justified. The ultimate 'ground' of understanding is simply shared, but not yet disclosed, practice – there is no *right* way of doing things.
- Once we have become habituated to a style, it becomes invisible for us.

It becomes part of what we take for granted in our everyday reality. If someone behaves in a way that does not fit in with our dominant style, we can fashion his or her behaviour to fit with ours.

- Because we do not cope with the style of, for instance, our culture or our company or our generation directly – we simply *express this style* when we cope with things and with each other – we have no *direct* way to handle it or come alive to it and transform it. Our practices are designed for dealing with things but not for dealing with practices for dealing with things and especially not for dealing with the coordination of practices for dealing with things. We do not normally sense our potential as disclosers, because we are more interested in the things we disclose than in the disclosing as such.

> Through these three ordinary tendencies to overlook our role as disclosers, we lose sensitivity to occluded, marginal, or neighboring ways of doing things. By definition an occluded, marginal, or neighboring practice is one that we generally pass over, either by not noticing its unusualness when we engage in it or by not engaging at all. Special sensitivity to marginal, neighboring, or occluded practice, however, is precisely at the core of entrepreneurship. This sensitivity generates the art, not science, of invention in business. (Spinosa et al., 1997, p. 30)

Spinosa et al. (1997) claim that three widespread ways of thinking about entrepreneurship right now (entrepreneurship as theory, entrepreneurship as pragmatism and entrepreneurship as driven by cultural values) are not enough for several reasons (this criticism is more relevant in the narrow view of entrepreneurship than in the broad view):

- They are not genuinely innovative; to reduce entrepreneurship to a number of fairly stable and regular procedures places us virtually outside of change.
- They only try to satisfy those needs that exist already or which can be discovered or created without talking about how a person as an entrepreneur is changing the *general* way in which we handle things and people in some domain.
- They are deeply antihistorical.

The authors instead suggest a composite case of entrepreneurship which:

- has the ability to act on *the links* between innovation and implementation;
- exists to develop a feeling for *the roots* of our way of being;
- creates domains for history-makers by attaching itself to perceived anomalies. The essential issue, according to the authors, is what they

call historical, unlike the dominant ways of thinking by developing specific skills, by being pragmatic or by living according to one's culture;

- plays a leading role in determining which needs are important and in making change occur *as it does*;
- brings up and makes central what is only implicitly understood but still moves with its time (articulation), takes up an innovation and, above all through speech acts, turns it into a practice (reconfiguration) or finds other domains for entrepreneurship (cross-appropriation).

Spinosa et al. (1997) claim that entrepreneurship is human activity at its best (p. 66).

Summary and conclusion

After first having discussed rational and natural entrepreneurship, this chapter has presented four proposals for how to look at entrepreneurs according to the broad view of the subject, that is, entrepreneurs as sense-makers, language-makers, culture-makers and history-makers. It is obvious that these are very closely related and may gain from being combined.

Think 5.1 Which of the broad views of entrepreneurship above, if any, could inspire you, if you wanted to start an entrepreneurial activity?

Think 5.2 What are the weaknesses of the above broad views of entrepreneurship in your opinion?

Think 5.3 Which of the broad views above would you like to combine? Why?

Think 5.4 Why are most business start-ups very innovative?

CH 5 – CASE STUDY

The Artisan's Haven

(Adapted from Hisrich and Peters, 1992, pp. 611–13)

John and Katie Owen were confronted with a serious problem eight years ago. John was fired from his job with a large chemical company, where he had worked for 33 years. After having worked for one company for so long and giving the firm his best years, John was emotionally upset over his dismissal. It was not as though he had made a big mistake or that he had done anything wrong. He was simply one of the older employees whom the company wanted to replace with younger, more energetic people. A recession gave the firm the opportunity it needed to make wholesale changes in personnel.

Finding a job during a recession is not easy, and for a 55-year-old man whose experience is limited to one industry, it is almost impossible. John felt helpless. He did not know what to do, and his frustration turned into anger as he realized for the first time in his working life that he was just a pawn in a great game of corporation chess. After several weeks of fear, anxiety and doubt, John reached a major turning point in his life. He knew that he never wanted to work for anyone or any firm again.

The decision not to work for others was a major one, but John still did not know what to do. Should he retire? If he did, it would not be a comfortable retirement. Should he start his own business? If so, what kind of business should it be? He knew that he did not want to be involved with chemicals. Even before he was fired, John had begun to have reservations about producing dangerous chemicals and dumping waste into rivers. But his pay was good, and he did not have the time to think about these deep questions too seriously. It was more important to John to pay his bills, to take nice vacations and, in general, to have fun.

Although John liked to take credit for the idea, Katie was the one who suggested that he should consider opening a store to sell arts and crafts. John's hobby for many years had been making gold jewellery, and he had become a very good goldsmith. Katie was an amateur interior designer, and she also enjoyed doing cross-stich and making dried floral arrangements. Starting a business to sell something they enjoyed making and knew something about seemed like a very good idea. In addition, John and Katie could work together in this kind of business, and Katie had always wanted to spend more time with John.

One year after John had been dismissed, they started their first store in the city where they lived, and it was very successful. Their location was excellent, and their merchandise was high quality. Everything they did just seemed to work, and 6 years later they owned six stores in the area.

At this point, John and Katie were both 62 years old, and they were more secure financially than they had ever been. One thing they dreamed of doing was retiring to a nice southern country and enjoying life there. To prepare for this, they decided to sell their stores and moved to a larger university town in a more southerly region of their own country. A couple whom they were very close to had moved to this town several years

CH 5 – CASE STUDY *(continued)*

before, and John and Katie had visited them several times. They liked the town, they liked its university and they liked the climate. The move seemed like the right thing to do.

John and Katie settled very quickly into their new life in their new place. They joined a local church, which consumed a fair amount of their time. Katie became actively involved with the women's club of that church and John joined the Lion's Club and was able to contribute a great deal of time to many of their projects.

However, one thing was missing. While they were in business, John and Katie enjoyed making decisions and watching the bottom line of their income statement change to reflect the quality of their judgement. None of their activities in their university town provided the same sense of excitement and satisfaction that owning and operating a business had provided. After 1 year, John asked Katie about opening a new store where they lived now, and Katie agreed.

One year after they had moved to their new town, the Owens opened *The Artisan's Haven* downtown, directly across from the administrative building of the university and the community responded enthusiastically. The store sold handmade gold and silver jewellery, pottery, dried floral arrangements, woodcrafts and various other handmade objects. Upon entering the store, customers were overwhelmed by the quality of the merchandise. It looked like it could have come out of a fancy top-quality magazine. All the merchandise was made with great care and attention to detail.

Part of the immediate success of the new store was due to the popularity of arts and crafts at the time. But the Owens themselves were the main attraction. John and Katie seemed to be very satisfied with life, and the rapport they developed with their customers was nothing but short of amazing. They offered evening classes to teach their customers how to make many of the items sold in the store. Katie became an interior decorator whose advice was sought by many prominent and influential people in the community. John organized the artists and crafts people in the wider area of where they lived into a guild. As a result of their work, the Owens developed a large, wealthy customer base and an excellent supply of high-quality goods to sell.

 DISCUSSION QUESTION

What aspects of entrepreneurs as a sense-maker, as a language-maker, as a culture-maker and as a history-maker can you see in the above case?

To access the teacher's manual that accompanies this book, please use the following link:

http://goo.gl/DXQas.

6

Social entrepreneurship

Introduction

This chapter presents one type of entrepreneurs, which have been considered in academic settings for no more than about 10 years, but which seem to be increasingly important to the future of our communities, that is, social entrepreneurs.

Why is there a third sector?

Westerdahl (2001) provides three proposals as to why there is a *citizen sector* (a *third sector*, a *social economy*):

- *The vacuum hypothesis*: The stagnating and even shrinkage of the public sector and (in some cases) decline in large areas of the business sector has created a space for other actors. This hypothesis is, according to Westerdahl, the most important one of the three.
- *The global hypothesis (the identity hypothesis)*: At the same time as we are experiencing more globalization we also note a greater wish for local and regional identity.
- *The influence hypothesis*: We are experiencing an increased questioning of the public sector's handling of tax revenues connected to a wish for a greater influence over the way in which this is done.

Thus the three hypotheses – if they are correct – show that the transformation of society currently under way in the Western world exhibits certain development features suggesting a probability that, whether by necessity or by voluntary commitment, certain social elements of the economy will assume increased importance for certain actors. This makes it possible for activities conducted under social-economic forms to expand. The extent to which these activities can make use of this potential for expansion is determined primarily by their strength, their competitiveness and the attitude towards them of other actors in society. (Westlund, 2001, p. 435)

Estimated *employment* in the third sector is 8–10 per cent in Western Europe (somewhat less in Sweden due to its large common sector and considerably more, for instance, in Greece). Studies show that the *increase* of employment in the third sector is increasing in the whole Western world. Between 1980–90, the increase was 40 per cent in France, 36 per cent in Germany and 41 per cent in the United States (Salomon and Anheier, 1994) and in 20 Western European regions the increase was 44 per cent (Westlund and Westerdahl, 1997). All numbers are very uncertain here, however (and in a sense misleading), among other things due to *the large proportion of part-time work in the citizen sector* (Vasi, 2009, p. 169) and its many *volunteers*. The so-called not-for-profit sector in the United States (which refers to all social entrepreneurs, not only those in the citizen sector) is much higher than in Europe and is estimated to 7 per cent of GNP, which is probably twice as high as in Great Britain (Burns, 2011, p. 454).

> In almost all industrialised countries, we are witnessing today a remarkable growth in the 'third sector', i.e. in socio-economic initiatives which belong neither to the traditional private for-profit sector nor to the public sector. These initiatives generally derive their impetus from voluntary organizations, and operate under a wide variety of legal structures. In many ways they represent the new or renewed expression of civil society against a background of economic crisis, the weakening of social bonds and difficulties of the welfare state. (Defourney, 2001, p. 1)

Social entrepreneurs and citizen entrepreneurs

As mentioned already there is a *difference between social entrepreneurs and citizen entrepreneurs*. By *social entrepreneurship* I mean all entrepreneurial activities in society, no matter where they are going, which are not run for private profit reasons but an activity which aims at satisfying different social needs (possibly in combination with an interest in profit).

As the reader will have noted in Chapter 3, I have found a reason to make a separation of three sectors in the society and associated types of situations, where entrepreneurship takes place. This is the public sector with its institutions, the business sector with its markets and the citizen sector, which contains different private and public places. Those social entrepreneurial activities that take place in the citizen sector I refer to as *citizen entrepreneurship*.

So, there is social entrepreneurship, taking place in the public sector. One example is a business school, which is presented as entrepreneurial (Lundqvist, 2009), even if most universities can hardly be called entrepreneurial. There *is also* one type of social entrepreneurship that takes place in the business sector, for instance, a natural social responsibility with small business firms according to Sundin (2009). There are, however, studies in Great Britain, for instance, which state that the social contributions made by small business firms often stop with the economic contributions (ODPM, 2003, Ch. 2). In the same way it is possible to say that most citizen activities are not entrepreneurial, even if some of them are. This can be summarized by saying that all *entrepreneurial* activities that take place in the public sector and the citizen sector can be called social entrepreneurship, but that *only some* entrepreneurial activities that take place in the business sector should be seen as social entrepreneurship.

Nicholls (2006, p. 229) provides a list of contexts for social entrepreneurship (Table 6.1). Referring to this table, I want to speak of social *entrepreneurs* only in the first case (grassroots) and to some extent the next three (institutional, political and spiritual), however, only before they have become too institutionalized. The fifth (philanthropic), I do not count as *entrepreneurial* at all, because it does not contain any *new* solutions (even if such attempts may be financed through this channel).

Social entrepreneurs (or citizen entrepreneurs) are not new in society. We just have to think about names like Florence Nightingale and Mahatma Gandhi. What is new now, however, is that the amount of social entrepreneurial activities is much greater than ever before in history (Bornstein, 2004, pp. 3–6). There are, according to Nicholls (2006), studies in, for example, Great Britain that show that the number of newly started social entrepreneurial projects there *is larger than* the number of newly started pure business entrepreneurial projects. During 2003 it is estimated that 6.6 per cent of the adult population of Great Britain was involved in some kind of activity which basically had a purpose of use to the society as a new or ongoing operation. This was higher than what the GEM estimated the business entrepreneurial start-up activities to be in Great Britain, which was 6.4 per cent. Among other things a new social entrepreneurial minister was appointed in Great Britain in 2001.

It has been claimed that the concept '*social entrepreneur*' appeared for the first time in the literature with Banks (1972) There are many, who assert that the Englishman Michael Young (1915–2002) is the world's most successful social entrepreneur (for instance, Mawson, 2008). He started more than 60 social enterprises during his lifetime, started a number of 'Schools of Social Entrepreneurs' in Great Britain and its first university for distance learning (Open University). The Open University is an example of what I referred to as a distributive system in Chapter 1. Its first student applications

Table 6.1 Contexts for social entrepreneurship

Origins	Social market failure	Means	Ends	Example
Grassroots	Lack of institutional support	Critical social innovation	Coordinated creation of social capital through local/community action	Housing associations
Institutional	Changing social landscape	Normative social innovation	Social entrepreneurship champions new social institutions	Open University
Political	Retreat of centralized government control from society	Market socialism	Introduction of enterprise/private sector market philosophy into public sphere	Public–private finance initiatives (e.g. London Underground)
Spiritual	Decline of church influence in society	Commercialization of congregation- and church-based activities	Revitalize role of faith in public affairs	CAFOOD/ Fair Trade Foundation
Philanthropic	Lack of finance for development of social capital	Foundations coordinating charity giving as social entrepreneurial start-up funding	Link business and social innovation	Skoll Foundation and community education

were in 1970, the year Intel was born, so they were pioneers for a new type of education using old communication technology. The Web has greatly extended the range of its interactions – through forums, chat-rooms, peer-to-peer-contacts, accessible material as well as videos. Around 180 000 students are now interacting with this university from home. There are 16 000 conferences, of which 2000 are run by students with 110 000 participants. Its websites for student guidance have 70 000 hits per week. With a turnover of £420 million a year, the Open University is an example of a new form of social multinational operating in 40 countries with 4000 full-time and 7000 part-time staff. It is worth pointing out that the Vice-Chancellor has been one of the top managers in Microsoft's education product group (Murray, 2009, p. 15).

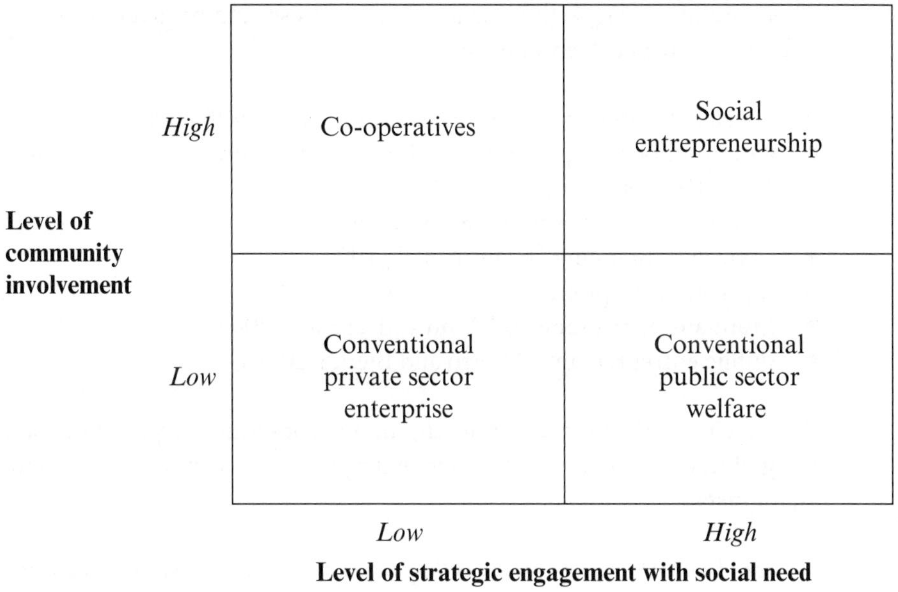

	Low (strategic engagement)	High (strategic engagement)
High	Co-operatives	Social entrepreneurship
Low	Conventional private sector enterprise	Conventional public sector welfare

Level of community involvement (vertical axis, High / Low)

Low   *High*

Level of strategic engagement with social need

Source: Nicholls, 2006, p. 230.

Figure 6.1 One positioning of social entrepreneurship

Whatever way we look at it, social entrepreneurship is always about engagement (Figure 6.1).

Historically areas in which social entrepreneurs have been operating have been (Nicholls, 2006, p. 228):

- poverty alleviation through empowerment (e.g. the micro-finance movement);
- healthcare, ranging from small-scale support for the mentally ill 'in the community' to larger-scale ventures tackling the HIV/AIDS pandemic;
- education and training, such as widening participation and the democratization of knowledge transfer;
- environmental preservation and sustainable development, such as 'green' energy projects;
- community regeneration, such as housing associations;
- welfare projects, such as employment for the unemployed or homeless and drug and alcohol abuse projects;
- advocacy and campaigning, such as Fair Trade and human rights promotion.

There are many suggestions as to what names should be given to those we refer to as citizen entrepreneurs:

- Social entrepreneurs (Boschee, 1998; Brinckerhoff, 2000)
- Community entrepreneurs (De Leeuw, 1999; Johannisson and Nilsson, 1989; Dupuis and de Bruin, 2003)
- Non-profit entrepreneurs (Skloot, 1995)
- Civic entrepreneurs (Henton et al., 1997)
- Idealistic entrepreneurs (Piore and Sabel, 1984)
- Mundane entrepreneurs (Rehn and Taalas, 2004)
- Public entrepreneurs (Hjorth and Bjerke, 2006)

If it were possible, there are more *definitions of a social entrepreneur* or something of that kind than of a business entrepreneur. It can be loosely defined as, for instance:

> *Social entrepreneurship combines the passion of a social mission with an image of business-like discipline, innovation, and determination commonly associated with, for instance, the high-tech pioneers of Silicon Valley. (Dees, 1998, p.1)*

or

> *Social entrepreneurship is the use of entrepreneurial behaviour for social rather than profit objectives. (Burns, 2011, p. 454)*

One example of a Scandinavian definition is:

> *A social entrepreneur is a person who takes an innovative initiative in order to develop functions which are useful for society. (Gawell et al., 2009, p. 8; my translation)*

So, citizen entrepreneurship or social entrepreneurship are far from any *unambiguous* concepts. Furthermore, there is no (and there probably will never be) any *neutral* view of what a citizen entrepreneur is doing and what he or she should do. Among other things *political* aspects always come in here by necessity (Steyaert and Katz, 2004, p. 180; Boddice, 2009, p. 137). Citizen entrepreneurship is always *by its very nature* a political phenomenon (Cho, 2006, p. 36).

Citizen enterprisers and citizen innovators

According to Grenier (2009, pp. 174–5) it is possible to see *two kinds of citizen entrepreneurs*: 'citizen enterprisers' (for instance, Borzaga and Defourney, 2001; Martin and Thompson, 2010) and 'citizen innovators' (for instance, Steyaert, 1997, 2004; Bornstein, 2004). It is often so, however, that the concept 'citizen entrepreneur' (or equivalent) either is used without specifying which of the two is referred to or as an umbrella term, that deliberately encompasses both possibilities (Grenier, 2009, p. 175). But it is not easy to separate the two. Citizen enterprisers are often meant to be innovative as well, even if it is not part of the name itself. Furthermore, there are studies showing that not only citizen innovators but also citizen enterprisers are interested in local issues, collective and private actions, local communities and local political fights (Dey and Steyaert, 2010, p. 98). In Sweden, the citizen entrepreneurial issue is different from most other countries. Citizen enterprising issues are to a large extent managed there by the public sector through its different institutions. The author of this book is a Swedish scholar and therefore more interested in citizen innovators than citizen enterprisers, that is, citizen entrepreneurs that act in the citizen sector with the logic which exists in different *public places* (compare the definition of social entrepreneurs by Gawell et al., 2009 above). By public places I refer to *physical, virtual, discursive and/or emotional* arenas which, in principle, every citizen has access to and which, still in principle, every citizen should feel responsibility for. I refer to them as *public entrepreneurs*. (Please notice that public entrepreneurs do not refer to entrepreneurs operating in the public sector, but entrepreneurs operating in public *places*, places which, by the way, are often publicly owned. I refer to the former entrepreneurs as *public sector entrepreneurs*). Citizen enterprisers, who have sheltered workshops and the like or people's homes as their operative location, usually do not operate in *public* places. Protest movements like Attac or Reclaim the City are operating in public places as well (for a discussion of Attac as an entrepreneurial movement, see Gawell, 2009, in Swedish), but it is possible to make a distinction between *value-creating citizen entrepreneurs* and *critical citizen entrepreneurs* (Nicholls, 2006, p. 235). I am more interested in the former (even if it is hard to draw a strict line between the two, of course).

Nicholls (2010) argues that he can see *three* types of social entrepreneurs in the scientific discussion: (1) the hero that solves difficult social problems; (2) the one who successfully uses business entrepreneurs' methods to solve social problems, and (3) social entrepreneurs with their own logic based on the values of the local community and social justice.

There are many suggestions to what could be meant by social entrepreneurs as *citizen entrepreneurs*:

- social enterprisers
- entrepreneurs in the social economy
- participants in associations
- participants in protest movements
- business entrepreneurs devoted to CSR
- cultural activists
- proponents of fair trade
- environmental activists
- managers of public events
- public entrepreneurs

All of these are generally not what we call public entrepreneurs or, to put it differently, only in some cases. We will, as mentioned, return to them in the next chapter.

Another type of entrepreneurs of interest here is what could be called the *local community entrepreneurial magnets* (citizens, who are able to attract entrepreneurs to start or move their entrepreneurial ventures to the community of the citizens in question without necessarily being entrepreneurs themselves). Some differences between them and business entrepreneurs can be seen in Table 6.2 (Johannisson and Nilsson, 1989, p. 5; the authors refer to what I name local community entrepreneurial magnets as just *community entrepreneurs*).

Table 6.2 Differences between business entrepreneurs and community entrepreneurs

Business entrepreneurs	Community entrepreneurs
Look at society as a means to reach personal goals	Look at the development of society as an essential goal
Strengthen their own self-esteem and competence	Make conscious moves and assist in building self-esteem and competence with other citizens
Put themselves at the top of their organization	Participate as coordinator at grass-roots level
Look at authorities and other stakeholders in society as obstacles and threats if they do not serve the entrepreneurs' own purpose	Approach authorities and external actors as potential supporters and suppliers of resources
Exploit opportunities to build their own network	Use and build arenas where different networks can be connected

It has been suggested that social entrepreneurs as citizen entrepreneurs can express themselves *in at least three different ways* (Vasi, 2009, pp. 160–1):

1. Some initiatives focus on *disseminating a package of innovations* needed to solve common problems. This form of entrepreneurial activity attempts to serve widespread needs because it assumes that 'information and technical resources can be reconfigured into user-friendly forms that will make them available to marginalized groups' (Alvord et al., 2002, p. 10). Once such packages are constructed by various experts – a difficult task, because it requires substantial creativity to adapt materials and resources for low-cost usage – they can be disseminated by individuals and agencies with relatively few resources.
2. Some forms involve *building capacities* or working with marginalized populations to identify capacities needed for self-help. This approach is based on two main assumptions: local groups possess the best knowledge on which issues are most important, and local actors may solve their problems if they have access to more resources and better capacity to act. Therefore, entrepreneurship directed at capacity building requires paying special attention to local constituents and resource providers.
3. Some initiatives focus on *mobilizing grassroots groups* to form alliances against abusive elites or institutions. As noted by Alvord et al. (2002), the assumption underlying this approach is that marginalized groups can solve their own problems if they have increased access to political institutions. This form of entrepreneurship is highly politicized and may involve activities that challenge powerful antagonists.

There are many that assert that social entrepreneurs have their roots in that history which is about *local service and development* (Grenier, 2009, p. 199). Citizen entrepreneurship can even be seen as a universal attempt in a society to answer to specific local needs (ibid., p. 199). It is this local history that feeds their passion for creating activities of importance to society (Emerson and Twersky, 1996, pp. 2–3).

One question that a social entrepreneur should constantly ask is 'Why am I doing this?' placing emphasis on 'I' and 'this'. To do something *for* somebody else neither explains why it is *you* who does it, nor how something came to be characterized as a 'problem' (Boddice, 2009, p. 148).

One unsolved issue in social entrepreneurship (unlike in business entrepreneurship) is how to measure its *effect*. A number of qualitative and quantitative measures have been suggested recently. The most recognized one is a model for 'social return on investment' (SROI) which was suggested by the Roberts Enterprise Development Foundation (REDF) in the United States (Emerson, 1999) and then refined in England by New Economics Foundation (2004). These measures have, however, not in any way been generally accepted (REDF has even, according to Nicholls, 2006, stopped using SROI). There are consequently few agreed upon or even available benchmarks or 'best practice' for the effect of social entrepreneurial operations. The establishment of the effect of social entrepreneurial operations will, therefore, continue to be open for criticism and discussions. One major problem in this context is that a limited and quantitative objective of many social entrepreneurial operations may lead to operational short-sightedness and an inability to focus on more basic social structural issues in their planning and implementation strategies. This may reduce their long-term results as well as their sustainability.

Finally, there are many negative trends in our society, for instance, lower participation in elections, higher contempt of politicians and decreased involvement in the civic society. Whether social entrepreneurs will be able to *counterbalance* these negative trends is a very open question.

Examples of how different groups in the society may need citizen entrepreneurial achievements are shown in Table 6.3 (Dees et al., 2002, p. 143).

Let us look at public entrepreneurs more closely.

Public entrepreneurs

As I have mentioned on several occasions, public entrepreneurs are one kind of citizen entrepreneurs, that is, social innovators. Citizen innovators normally operate in public places. By public places I mean *physical, virtual, discursive and/or emotional arenas* which, in principle, all citizens have the right to participate in and which all citizens should feel responsibility for. Public entrepreneurs are often not on the institutional decision-maker's agenda (Hjorth and Bjerke, 2006, p. 120).

Talking about public entrepreneurs in different citizen situations opens the door for a new discussion of entrepreneurs as a social force (Hjorth and Bjerke, 2006, p. 99). Public entrepreneurs are social entrepreneurs but this statement requires some elucidation (compare Hjorth, 2009; Hjorth and Bjerke, 2006). Public entrepreneurs are seen in the innovative group of citizen entrepreneurs (citizen entrepreneurs are, as we know, social entrepreneurs operating in the citizen sector of the society), not in the enterprising group. Social entrepreneurs are in general, and citizen entrepreneurs

Table 6.3 Communities likely to work with and need citizen entrepreneurs

Types of communities	Defining features
Geographical	Historically isolated and underresourced or abused areas
Marginalized	Stigmatized groups often viewed as nonconformist particularly with regard to work, personal and residential maintenance and sexual practices
Age groupings dependent on working population	Populations segmented by virtue of their need for services, support and control they seem unable to provide for themselves
Special interest groups	Affiliations that advocate for recognition, preservation or expansion of issues or entities that cannot speak for themselves
Groups that self-identify through religious, ethnic, racial or national membership	Alliances built through a sense of common history, often shared hardships and hopes for a better future
Affiliate groups aligned through pursuit of similar activities	Devotion to what are often leisure activities or specialized ways of carrying out particular types of work

in particular, commonly seen as people who are correcting such unsatisfactory states of the society through social entrepreneurship. Public entrepreneurs do not, first of all, devote themselves to such corrections, but make more people in a society feel that they are part of that society instead of feeling alienated. That is, they devote themselves to building *citizenry*. It is no simple matter to determine what is meant by 'citizenry', of course, but it can, in principle, be seen as 'a collective engagement (affective relation) that generates an assemblage (a project, a group of people)' (Hjorth, 2009, p. 216). Social entrepreneurship is today used primarily when discussing how to 'fix' problems with a withering 'welfare state' (Dreyfus and Rabinow, 1982), including 'reinventing government' (Osborne and Gaebler, 1992). Public entrepreneurs do not try (at least not first of all) to make the institutions' job better or to replace the market. There are even those who claim (for instance, Spinosa et al., 1997) that the concept 'market' does not adequately catch those negotiation processes and those democratic structures that exist in a well-functioning citizen arrangement. Furthermore, theoretical views like *convention theory* (Wilkinson, 1997; Renard, 2002) and *analysis of networks* (Callon, 1986, 1999; Latour, 1993) have further challenged and provided new pictures of how economic mechanisms function in our world. (Convention theories are about how the world trade of many fruits and vegetables are more controlled by governments and agreements than by market forces. I will return to the actors network in Chapter 11). It is therefore not surprising that established entrepreneurial models to some extent can only be used to understand citizen entrepreneurs (Nicholls, 2006).

So, public entrepreneurs are not the same as holders of official positions or producers offering products and/or services where rules of supply and demand are valid, but they are *citizens who involve other citizens in making some marginal phenomena more central (more public) in a society*. Public entrepreneurs are consequently not interested in correcting unsatisfactory states of things in our society but in getting other citizens to focus on and develop the social capital in a society in order to passionately increase the inclusiveness and decrease the amount of alienation there! (The limit between 'fixing problems', 'developing the social capital' and 'increase the inclusiveness and decrease the amount of alienation' is not very clear, of course.)

One might think that *social exclusion* (the opposite of 'inclusiveness') is a clear and distinct concept, but that is far from the case (Blackburn and Ram, 2006). First of all, we should make a distinction between a 'strong' and a 'weak' version of the concept:

> In the 'weak' version of the concept, the solution consists of supporting excluded people's unprivileged conditions and support their integration in the mainstream of the society. 'Stronger' versions of this concept are also stressing the role of those who lead to exclusion and consequently attempt to find solutions to find solutions that decrease their power. (Blackburn and Ram, 2006, p. 74)

Second, on the government's part and from more or less the side of public institutions it has been claimed that the 'solution' would be to start more citizen enterprises, where the concept of 'enterprise' is seen as an essential, not to say a decisive, factor in our new society. Unfortunately, nor is the concept of 'citizen enterprises' very clear.

At any rate, I do not believe that it is enough to increase the number of so-called citizen enterprises. Citizen innovators, that is, public entrepreneurs, should be given more attention, the way I look at it.

The *public sphere* in a society is the arena for interventions in the society that link the institutional structured public sector with the mundane everyday practical maintenance of citizenry in the civic society (Hjorth and Bjerke, 2006, p. 109). This is where the public entrepreneurs are operating. In complex societies 'the civic society consists of the intermediary structure between the political system on one hand and the private sectors of the lifeworld and the functional systems on the other' (Habermas, 1996, p. 373).

> I believe that 'the public sphere' is at stake. We urgently need new ideas and tactics for imagining what the public should be today, and for exploring how we can act as citizens in order to enhance individuals' quality of life. My ambition is to contribute to this by elaborating on what I will call a public form of entrepreneurship which can create a new form of sociality in the public realm. The purpose by such a development is to re-establish the social as a force different from the economic rather than being encompassed by it. Entrepreneurship is then re-conceptualized as a sociality-creating force, belonging to society and not primarily to business. I also make use of an analysis of entrepreneurship as distinct from management, the latter being focused on efficient stewardship of existing resources and social control, while the former is animated primarily by creativity, desire, playfulness and the passion for actualizing what could come into being. Public entrepreneurship is a term thus meant to emphasize the creative and playful as central to entrepreneurial activity. (Hjorth, 2009, p. 207)

The similarities between public entrepreneurs and the broad view of entrepreneurship are obvious.

Citizenship is a composite concept that includes individuals and groups and discussions of citizenship always have to deal with rights and values and social practice in which forms of citizenship are practices (Petersen et al., 1999). Citizenship in today's society is less of an institution and more of an achievement. Citizenship is therefore a matter of identity.

Spinosa et al. (1997) is an example of an attempt to discuss the entrepreneurial aspects of citizenship. In their discussion, social changes are created by 'virtuous citizens' as well as by entrepreneurs. To become a public entrepreneur starts with what they call a 'virtuous citizen'. The point in this case is not a universal virtuousness, however, but a locally based praxis. To practice 'virtuousness' is in their opinion only meaningful if it is based on the ability to translate universal values to the local history–cultural context (Hjorth and Bjerke, 2006, p. 115).

Examples of public entrepreneurial activities are (compare Thompson, 2002):

- Remobilizing depleted social areas
- Setting up agencies for support and advice
- Re-utilizing of buildings and resources for social purposes

- Providing 'suitability training'
- Generating means for some common good issue
- Organizing voluntary operations
- Generating or supporting cultural activities that are not commercial
- Generating or supporting sports activities that are not commercial

The great entrepreneurial scholar (in his case discussing business entrepreneurs) Joseph Schumpeter claims that a person is a business entrepreneur *only* when he or she is building up a new venture and *stops* being it when this is done. He or she eventually changes into an administrator of his or her own venture. This is possibly even clearer for public entrepreneurs, that is, they are visible mostly in the beginning of a public entrepreneurial project. Also, when the public entrepreneur is gone, the public entrepreneurial activity in question may have problems surviving. This close connection between the public entrepreneur and his or her ambitions means that public entrepreneurship often goes on *as a project.*

Furthermore, public entrepreneurship is *often small scale and always local.* If it becomes too big, it may even be difficult to continue to be a public entrepreneur (it is, however, possible to continue by being an administrator in Schumpeter's sense).

Social entrepreneurs, and then public entrepreneurs as well, develop new organizational paradigms in order to involve more people in essential needs and they look at resources not only as financial ones (even if, like anybody else, they cannot live on air, of course). This can, for instance, be seen with Leadbeater (1997, p. 8) in his definition of social entrepreneurs:

> *Social entrepreneurs are identifying underused resources – people, buildings, equipment – and find new ways to use them to fulfil social needs.*

Thompson et al. (2000, p. 328) also supports this view in his definition of social entrepreneurs as:

> *People who realize that there is a possibility to satisfy some social need which the public sector does not want to or is not able to manage and who collect the necessary resources (in general people, often volunteers, money and facilities) and use them to achieve results.*

Concepts like 'social entrepreneurship' and 'citizen entrepreneurship' (and then probably 'public entrepreneurship' as well) are often criticized because:

- They are not clearly formulated.
- They are so dependent on support from outside.

I hope that this chapter has reduced the confusion in the conceptual brushwood.

Summary and conclusion

This chapter has discussed social entrepreneurs and its different varieties. Some space has been given to one type of social entrepreneur, which I think should have a more frontal role in discussions of our societies, that is, public entrepreneurs.

Think 6.1 How could an airline be more socially entrepreneurial?

Think 6.2 What advantages and disadvantages do you see in being a social entrepreneur?

Think 6.3 What is *not* social entrepreneurial?

Think 6.4 Formulate a social entrepreneurial project in the education sector.

CH 6 – CASE STUDY

Skate Malmö

Skate Malmö is a vision that has already been realized in its basic parts. It started with the so-called Building Berth Park, that is, the idea of building a youth park in an area that had previously been occupied by a shipyard, which had been closed. The champion of the project is John Magnusson, who is about 30 years old. His ambition is to build the best and most excellent skateboard outdoor arena there. He gained support from Malmö (the third largest city in Sweden) for his idea, which was to provide a model for cooperation between a city and its young citizens. John's ambition is characterized by involving young people in creating public places and to do this in a very democratic way. The physical part of the skate park is, by and large, finished today and it has become a great success.

John Magnusson is the archetype for a social entrepreneur, even if he is cooperating with enterprising people from the public sector as well as from the business sector. The Building Berth Park is nothing but a place, which is accessible to everybody.

The ambition in the long run is to position Malmö as a centre for skateboard activities in Sweden, even in northern Europe. They have come far with the outdoor skateboard arena and they had previously built an indoor arena in a building where a lot of youth activities, including a secondary school, are situated (today, John is its boss). They have also built several other outdoor skateboard arenas in the neighbourhood.

The most active power and the spider in the web is John Magnusson. Questions that he asks himself include:

○ What does the Building Berth Park stand for today and how can it be developed as a node for skateboarding?
○ How can the phenomenon 'skateboard culture' in Malmö be developed in a favourable way, considering factors like shortage of resources, common trade mark, many small actors, art, competitions, events, lifestyle and the combination of something financial and idealistic?
○ How can their outdoor and indoor arenas become a sustainable part of *Skate Malmö*?

 DISCUSSION QUESTION

> I look at John Magnusson as a public entrepreneur, but how can such a statement be justified?

To access the teacher's manual that accompanies this book, please use the following link:

http://goo.gl/DXQas.

7

Entrepreneurship and local development

Introduction

This chapter is about the necessity for local communities to achieve sustainable development, not only building on what they have already but always coming up with new ideas. This can only take place with the help of entrepreneurs of different kinds.

Local governments

The functions of the local government can be viewed differently (Herbert and Thomas, 1997, p. 123). Sharpe (1976) has identified three major functions of local governments as promoting liberty, participation and efficient service provision. Local governments provide liberty by countering a lack of local responsiveness usually associated with overcentralization. Participation in the local is also considered likely to be enhanced by some form of local elections. Finally, local governments are considered most likely to maximize the efficiency of service provision since they can assess local needs better by being close to the point of service delivery.

There have been several stages in development of local governments because urban systems have changed over the years (Herbert and Thomas, 1997, pp. 77–9)

The pre-industrial stage: an urban nucleus

In the period prior to large-scale industrialization, most cities were small. They normally had populations of less than 50 000 and a rudimentary form of economic, social and political organization. Their transport technology was equally rudimentary. Because of the limitations of transport facilities, influence in cities were either restricted to provide urban services for a relatively localized population and, even if the city also provided commercial, religious, social or political functions for a wider hinterland, the frequency of visits by long-distance travellers and the associated functional interrelationships between the city and the outer limits of its hinterland was still low. The city tended to be a distinct urban nucleus loosely related to a wider rural area and to other cities.

The industrial stage: urbanized area

In the early stages of industrialization, particular resources were localized. Some towns could grow in size because of the natural advantages that they possessed. Transport started to become more efficient due to canals being built and railways being constructed. They provided more efficient means of intercity contacts, principally for the transport of industrial materials and finished products. This increased the linkages between towns with complementary industrial structures as well as between industrial towns and market areas. Towns became much larger than their pre-industrial counterparts, although they retained their relatively compact form. Low status housing gravitated markedly to areas of industrial employment and new industrial areas and higher status residential suburbs tended to develop along the public transport routes radiating outward from the city centres, creating a distinctly tentacular urban form.

The post-industrial stage

The post-industrial period is characterized by a considerable increase in the speed and efficiency of communications. One special explanation for this was the development of the telephone. Also, the rapid growth in number of motor vehicles changed the emphasis of inter-urban transport to the private car. These changes reduced the constraint of distance on the development of economic and social linkages both between and within cities. A significant section of the more mobile labour force has gravitated to residential areas in more attractive areas at greater distance from their work. This has led to a suburbanization of often large areas of land around major cities. In effect, more dispersed forms of the 'urbanized region' have become more dominant features of the urban system.

It has frequently been asserted that Western urban centres are now being managed, organized and governed in different ways, leading some to proclaim the emergence of a 'new urban politics' (Cox and Mair, 1988; Kirlin and Marshall, 1988). According to Hubbard and Hall (1998, pp. 1–2), it appears that this new urban politics is distinguished from the 'old' by the ways in which the politics pursued by local governments are being steered away from the traditional activities associated with them. This reorientation of local government is characterized by a shift from the local provision of welfare and services to more outward-orientated policies designed to foster and encourage local growth and economic development. These policies are supported and financed by a diverse array of new agencies and institutions, as public agencies try to promote economic growth. Such cooperation with the private sector has seen local governments taking on entrepreneurial business characteristics – risk-taking inventiveness, promotion and profit motivation – leading many commentators to refer to the emergence of *entrepreneurial cities* (Mollenkopf, 1983; Judd and Ready, 1986; Gottdiener, 1987; Harvey, 1989).

However, with respect to local government entrepreneurialism, cities are very different from firms (Leitner and Sheppard, 1998, pp. 31–2). Local governments are defined by their territoriality: they are legally fixed in place, with boundaries that can be extended only with difficulty. In contrast, firms' ties to place are contingent, depending in the final instance on considerations of profitability. Furthermore, the political structure of local governments is very different. Firms are institutions governed by their owners, with a hierarchy of authority overlaying intra-firm networks. Local governments also have a hierarchical structure, but their corresponding urban centres are complex communities and networks of public and private institutions and civil society, in which lines of authority are not dictated from above but depend in the final instance on democratic processes; the ability of governing authorities to gain legitimation in the eyes of urban residents. Finally, firms may have relatively straightforward economic goals with profits often as the bottom line. Local states are not primarily responsible for making profits, but are supposed to be concerned for the welfare of their residents.

Most research in entrepreneurship concerns business. There are, however, distinct differences between business situations and local government situations, which are summarized in Table 7.1 (Westerdahl, 2001, p. 40).

Table 7.1 Differences between businesses and local communities

Businesses	Local communities
Economical, quantifiable values	Social values stressing meaningfulness (which cannot be measured quantitatively)
Clear organizations	Loose connections in networks, which have neither obvious extension nor form
Present standardized economic reports	Participate in bringing narratives into the open in order to strengthen local identity
Act according to general economic principles	Lean towards what is meaningful in the local context

Source: Westerdahl (2001, p. 40).

The increased interest in local governments

Some reasons for the *increasing interest in local governments* are:

1. The bases of central control of an economy have changed – it has become smaller (MacKinnon et al., 2002).
2. Small- and medium-sized communities have shown themselves better at managing the modern society in geographically concentrated areas – in spite of globalization in the world (Porter, 1998).
3. Nearness has proven itself to reinforce productivity and innovation (ibid.).
4. It is not that people come together in urban centres, the economy of a country continues to concentrate itself to specific areas and places – in spite of globalization. It seems like 'place' rather than 'space' is essential for economic life (Florida, 2003). More about 'space' and 'place' in Chapter 11.

Three developments have influenced local urban centres today, influences that should be seen as possibilities, not as threats (Hall, 2005):

- *Post-industrialization.* With Daniel Bell´s book *The Coming of Post-Industrial Society* (1974), the concept of *the post-industrial society* made a name for itself in the public debate. In this classic work, Bell describes how American society is changing from an industrial to a service society. Information and communication technology, knowledge and a new organizational paradigm ('the network society') constitute important parts of this society. It is in 'hot', urban places where ideas are created and disseminated (Sernhede and Johansson, 2005, p. 10). In these urban centres, however, in parallel with the growth of a well-situated middle class, which is adapting to the new knowledge-intensive economy, there are also new types of poverty and 'social exclusion'. The middle class is developing a demand for a number of new services (cleaning, gardening, painting, handicrafting, etc.). These are provided by the less educated workforce, which for different reasons has not been able to adapt to the new economy. The post-war welfare state is transformed, among other things, by new concepts as far as urban development is concerned, where in the beginning the expansive industrial suburbs were part of a national effort for modernization, inclusion and social cohesion. However, nobody walking around in a city today can avoid meeting people who are begging. To those who bring themselves out in the peripheries of the large cities, meeting other kinds of stigmatization and alienation is even more tangible (ibid., pp. 10–11). The reports about the conditions in many modern suburbs are not edify-ing. Many modern societies have developed to a situation where the most exposed groups are no longer positioned at the lowest rung of the ladder. They have been placed outside the very ladder itself (Sernhede and Johansson, 2005).

- *Globalization.* That form of globalization that we talk about here, and which is referred to in the contemporary globalization debate, is a new form of global economy (totally different from colonial times), which developed during the second half of the 1970s. This new form is based on multinational corporations, on new forms of communication and on the free flow of financial capital (Hall, 2005). The old relation-ship between periphery and centre is no longer valid in the same way as before. Yesterday's division between developed and less-developed regions at a global level is more complex today. Subordination, misery and hunger in the so-called developing countries exist today in urban centres in the Western world. This new order is neither less cynical nor less brutal (Sernhede and Johansson, 2005, p. 18).
- *Migration.* Migration, the global relocation of people, has caught and transformed most cities in modern countries. The migration processes during the latest decades have brought the Third World to all Western metropolises.

That post-industrialization, globalization and migration which has just been described are seen in cities and urban centres, among other things, in the following way (Sernhede and Johansson, 2005):

- ○ Newly rich people are getting together in attractive suburbs ('the new underclass') and that part of the population with money to spend settle down in the inner city (so-called 'gentrification').
- ○ It is more and more a matter of 'we' and 'they', that is, more of social exclusion for many groups of the population.
- ○ The city is transformed from manufacturing, work and trade to tourist attraction and exclusive apartments.

The new, post-industrial economy, globalization and migration has not only created new class constellations, tensions and interfacial conflicts but also led to new strategies for how the dominating levels maintain and reinforce the social order. In a similar fashion the subordinated and excluded develop new forms of resistance. All these tendencies are seen and are possible to read in the city space. (Sernhede and Johansson, 2005, p. 22; my translation)

Necessary *changes in local governments* today are:

1. From *service providers* to *leadership* ('community-ship'?).
2. From *administration* to *governance*.
3. From *office management* to *acting on arenas, where venturing citizens* ('public entrepreneurs') *participate in various action nets.*

It is increasingly clear that it is not possible in a local community or a city to achieve sustainable development by copying successes elsewhere but only by connecting to and building new networks locally and outwards and to base this on what is unique and organic in their own situations, pointing this out in all possible ways, so-called 'place marketing' (for more information on place marketing, see, for instance, Ekman and Hultman, 2007). What has become a classic centralized government programme in many countries should be replaced by attempts to create territorial specializations that cannot be copied in other places. They circle around a mix of specific local conditions which seen as a totality only exist in one place. Under such circumstances competitive advantages can be created continuously (Öhrström, 2005, p. 65).

The entrepreneurial city

Learning to be an entrepreneurial city involves, among other things (Painter, 1998, pp. 268–9):

- The acquisition of specific skills, such as those associated with place promotion, auditing, commercial accounting and negotiation with private part of the society (the business and the citizen sectors), when preparing funding applications from outside.
- The development of new self-understandings which might involve, for example, a subordination of the role of 'welfare provider' to that of 'business supporter', or the role of 'bureaucrat' to that of 'strategic leader'.
- Acquiescence (rather than active resistance) in the face of centrally imposed requirements to shift to more entrepreneurial practices of governance.
- The acceptance of change and of 'challenges' as inevitable or even desirable, in contrast with a previous expectation of stability.

Inspired by Soja (1996), it is possible to talk about three kinds of city places. The *first* place is the physical aspects of the city, like public spaces, amusement parks, shopping malls, gated communities as well as shanty towns or other islands of poverty. This place is perceived. The *second* place is rather conceived. It is a product of the creative artist, the artful architect, the utopian urbanist and the philosophical geographer, among others. This is a kind of imaginary city, constituted by an abundance of images and represen-tations (Hubbard and Hall, 1998). The *third* place is the *directly lived* place, an enacted city. This third place is the most interesting one in entrepreneur-ial studies, as I see it. To use Beyes' (2006, p. 170) words: 'A theatre of entre-preneurship has a lot more to offer than commerce and economic drive'.

A common trend in local government in many countries has been greater activism in promoting local approaches to local conditions (Dupuis et al., 2003). This is what was called place marketing above. Urban places may phe-nomenologically be regarded as potential 'directly lived places' – as potential sites for reorganizing the established and crafting the new. 'Communities have within themselves the ability to foster entrepreneurship by defining it at the level of every person and every interaction' (Steyaert and Katz, 2004, p. 191), or to phrase it differently, 'crossing research on entrepreneurship and entrepreneurial cities with thoughts on and observations of socially produced places' (Beyes, 2006, p. 255). However, researchers seldom con-sider the lived culture of entrepreneurial cities or the changing textures and rhythms of everyday life in their work (Hoggart, 1991, p. 184).

Traditionally, one perspective developed in Western industrial societies that local governments had a strong 'managerial' role in controlling land-use plan-ning and providing local services (Herbert and Thomas, 1997, pp. 124–5). This reflected a liberal-democratic and welfarist tradition associated with a strong Keynesian-type of state control over national economies. Since the mid-1980s, however, with the growth of global competition, the economic sovereignty of the nation-state has declined and most Western governments have had to be more mindful of market forces. Most local governments have moved towards a neoliberal mode of operation whereby 'unproduc-tive' public service expenditure has been cut in order to make more capital available for private investment. Also, local government is being replaced by a broader conception of 'local governance' where a kind of combination of common, private and voluntary agencies deliver services once provided by the local government. In this situation, local government becomes only one of many forces affecting the local environment and local service deliv-ery system, and local development in the modern urban centre is increas-ingly influenced by market forces and quasi-autonomous non-governmental organizations (NGOs).

In these complex new conditions relatively little is known empirically about the precise way in which the new forms of local governance is function-ing. However, we know somewhere local governments have been charac-terized as changing from 'provider' to 'enabler' and the 'managerialism' of the industrial era is being replaced by a post-industrial 'entrepreneurialism' (Davoudi, 1995; Mayer, 1995). Jessop (1996) suggests, for instance, that entrepreneurial governance has become the dominant response to urban problems because this discourse appears particularly attractive to those urban centres being caught in a seemingly downward spiral of deindustrialization and decline.

Similarly, the notion of urban entrepreneurialism currently enjoys wide popularity among academics, especially in urban geography, where the examination of urban politics and local socialization forms a logical outgrowth of the localities studies which came to prominence in the 1980s (e.g. Cooke, 1989). A huge interest in the emergence of entrepreneurial forms of urban politics has been displayed by planners, sociologists and cultural theorists, particularly as the reassertion of space in social theory has heightened awareness of the ways in which locality-specific factors mediate more general processes of economic and social change (Soja, 1996). More about the concepts of 'space' and 'place' in social research can be read in Chapter 11.

There appears to be a broad agreement that urban entrepreneurialism is essentially characterized by the proactive promotion of local economic development by local government in alliance with other private sector agencies (Hubbard and Hall, 1998, p. 4). Therefore, it seems that urban entrepreneurialism can be defined through two basic characteristics; first, a political prioritization of pro-growth local economic development and, second, an associated shift from urban government to urban governance.

The interest in this subject started by drawing attention to the increased involvement of the local state in the proactive encouragement of economic development. In this sense, entrepreneurialism has been described as distinctive political culture (Graham, 1995). The objectives of entrepreneurial policies are there described as inherently growth-oriented: creating jobs, expanding the local tax base, fostering small firm growth and by attracting new forms of investment. The aim of such policies is to promote the comparative advantages of the city relative to other cities that may be competing for similar forms of investment.

The current ubiquity of such entrepreneurial policies throughout the advanced capitalist world is now indisputable, and it is possible to conclude that an entrepreneurial attitude has infiltrated even the most recalcitrant and 'conservative' urban centres (Hubbard and Hall, 1998, p. 7). According to Eisenschitz and Gough (1993), what appears to have been crucial in encouraging this widespread adoption of entrepreneurial policies is that they apparently offer something for all local governments, irrespective of political ideology. 'In short, the idea of the internationalization of economic activity, the increased geographical mobility of production and investment, and the rising power of transnational corporations appear to have instilled an edgy insecurity at all levels of the urban hierarchy, with urban governors and representatives feeling obliged to adopt suitable policies to attract capital investment given their perception of an increasingly competitive global economy' (Hubbard and Hall, 1998, p.7).

The 'generic' entrepreneurial model of governance is reliant on specific boosterist policies. Local governments are allocating increasingly high budgets to advertising and promoting the centre as a favourable environment for business and leisure (Savitch and Kantor, 1995). Also, marketing a place seldom restricts itself to presenting the existing virtues of the city, but seeks to redefine and reimage the city, weaving in specific place 'myths' designed to erase the negative iconography of dereliction, decline and labour militancy associated with the industrial place (see Watson, 1970 [1991]; Barke and Harrop, 1994; Dunn et al., 1995).

In place marketing like in many other kinds of marketing it does not make much sense to distinguish between the 'myths' and 'realities' of the urban centre. The images of the place presented in the brochures, adverts, guidebooks and videos come to define the essence of the place as much as the place itself. This is even more evident in the promotion of various prestige projects, described as 'flagships' or 'megaprojects', which aim to improve on the perceived success of the rejuvenation of some other places.

These spectacular, large-scale urban projects have attracted attention when discussing entrepreneurial cities. Less substantial, but often highly publicized, some public art has also been fabricated as the entrepreneurial urban landscape is made increasingly playful, blurring the distinctions between entertainment, information and advertising (Hall, 1992; Miles, 1997). Place promotion is sometimes criticized by academics precisely due to a supposed dualism of image and reality implicated by projects of place promotion (see Burgess and Wood, 1988; Watson, 1970 [1991]).

As image assumes ever-greater importance in the post-industrial economy it is becoming increasingly apparent, however, that in the actual shaping and production of urban centres, it is necessary for them to present positive images of themselves to the outside world. Similarly, programmes of economic development are becoming driven more and more by image-enhancing initiatives. Narratives of entrepreneurialism often include place promotion.

It is in the context important to understand the differences between the processes of selling and marketing urban places. The distinction between 'selling the city' and 'marketing the city' is crucial in understanding the relationship of place promotion to urbanization.

In this light, 'the *cultural* transformation of urban centres into "spectacular" places of (and for) consumption, populated by a harmonious and cosmopolitan citizenry, has sometimes been hypothesised as perhaps the most important element of entrepreneurial forms of local politics' (Hall, 1998, p. 28). However, even if the conscious manipulation of city image is principally designed to make the city more attractive to *external* investors, it is important to realize that it also plays an *internal* role in fostering local support and civic pride, potentially gathering widespread support for entrepreneurial policies (ibid.). Perhaps the manipulation of urban place has become the most important aspect of activities among urban governors and their coalition partners in the modern entrepreneurial era.

The new type of urban policy does not only involve the state of the local place but also a large number of business and citizen actors (Leitner, 1990; Graham, 1995). Inevitably, the new type of speculative projects and initiatives, which is sometimes so central to the new type of entrepreneurial policy, is underwritten by actors outside the groups employed by the local government. The *rapprochement* between political and business communities, as manifest in the bewildering array of partnerships, networks and development corporations, is another reason for making it harder to detect the boundaries between the various sectors of the society. This convergence has resulted in a heightened control by new bourgeoisie and property interests, consisting almost exclusively of business*men* (Savage and Warde, 1993; Peck, 1995). However, this formation of coalitions or partnerships is seen as one of the principal means by which local governors achieve capacity to act.

In conclusion, new urban entrepreneurialism is perceived to be fundamentally different from the other forms of city governance that have preceded it. Many writers seek to stress the shift that has taken the interest among urban governors away from a concern with broad-based welfare and social policies to the adoption of a more outward-oriented stance designed to foster and encourage local development and economic growth (Hubbard and Hall, 1998, pp. 13–15). However, while urban governors are adopting a more proactive stance and spending more on local economic policies, this does not suggest that there has not been a wholesale abandonment of managerial policies, and that there are important continuities between the two modes, even if they are often depicted as polar opposites.

Savitch and Kantor (1995) argue that a dualistic model of managerialism and entrepreneurialism overshadows the way in which most local governments adopt a mixture of managerial (socially progressive) and entrepreneurial (growth-centred) policies. Furthermore, such ideas may mask the fact that local governments, to a lesser or greater extent, have always pursued entrepreneurial strategies and that they have always been part of local economic development. It is important to stress that there might be dangers in accepting the idea that entrepreneurial governance is distinct from other modes of governance in all respects.

Finally, in the short term, it might be that the new urban orientation may produce economic growth, neglecting the principles of social justice. 'There is little reason to suppose that the benefits of entrepreneurial policy will be fairly distributed' (Hubbard and Hall, 1998, p. 19).

There are many different meanings to '*the entrepreneurial city*' (Painter, 1998, pp. 260–1):

- *The city as a setting for entrepreneurial activity*. In this definition, the city is seen simply as a container or location for investment and risk-taking activities on the part of the private business. Therefore, if contemporary cities are more entrepreneurial than in the past, this must be simply because the nature of private business has changed (perhaps from a more monopolistic, corporate form to a form which is prepared to accept higher levels of risk for the prospect of very high returns).
- *Increased entrepreneurialism among urban residents*. In this case entrepreneurial cities would be those in which a large (or at least growing) proportion of residents were becoming entrepreneurs. This might be seen in the establishment of increasing numbers of small and medium-sized businesses.
- *A shift from public sector to private sector activity*. An entrepreneurial city could be defined as a city in which an (absolutely or relatively) increasing amount of urban economic activity is undertaken by the private sector, either through direct transfers from the public to the private sector, or by competition between the two.
- *A shift in the values and meanings associated with urban living in favour of business*. Here, an entrepreneurial city would be one in which urban life increasingly came to be associated with cultures understood to be somehow entrepreneurial.
- *A shift in urban politics and governance away from the management of public services and the provision of local welfare services towards the promotion of*

economic competitiveness, place marketing to attract inward investment and support for the development of indigenous private sector firms.

I would like to add another one to this list, a meaning that I prefer as far as an entrepreneurial city is concerned:

- *A place where all kinds of entrepreneurial activities can take place and where all parts of the community are seen in entrepreneurial terms.*

More about governance

The concept *governance* has been introduced to clarify that change of the political decision process which takes place today. Earlier, until the 1970s, the national states and the political authorities could at different levels, through their elected advocates, more or less decide on the politics themselves. Today, due to the economic globalization, due to the growth of EU, due to regions having more power and due to a demand for a deeper democratization process, government at different levels in a country that wants to keep up with the rest has no longer the exclusive power. Within the EU in particular, politics is shaped through different networks, where representatives at the EU-level as well as at the national level, non-profit organizations and business companies are made part of the process. More parties are consequently involved in different political decisions. One problem, experienced with governance by some researchers, for instance Blomgren and Bergman (2005), is that power becomes more blurred because politics are made in networks. This also makes political accountability more difficult.

According to Jessop (1997), governance is associated with a particular form of rule. Unlike the hierarchical rule provided by local state and the anarchy of the market, he argues that governance involves 'heterarchy', which might be defined as 'rule through diversity'. The change from 'government' to 'governance' also means a shift from an isolated public sector to a picture where the business and citizen sectors are part of and share responsibility and tasks.

> Urban politics is no longer, if it ever was, a process of hierarchical government in which decisions by local politicians are translated straightforwardly by public bodies into social and economic change. Rather it involves a complex process of negotiation, coalition formation, indirect influence, multi-institution working and public–private partnership. This diffuse and multi-faceted form of rule has come to be termed 'governance'. (Painter, 1998, p. 261)

> The new urban entrepreneurialism typically rests on a public–private partnership focusing on investment and economic development with the speculative construction of place rather than amelioration of conditions within a particular territory as its immediate (though by no means exclusive) political and economic goal. (Harvey, 1989, p. 9)

> We are probably moving from a welfare state to a new welfare mix where responsibility should be shared among public authorities, for-profit providers and third-sector organisations on the basis of strict criteria of both efficiency and fairness. (Defourney, 2001, p. 2)

Another way to phrase is to say that there is simply a smaller and smaller space to place all social activities in that part of society, which is financed by taxes (Öhrström, 2005, p. 53).

Local governments and various kinds of entrepreneurs

Local governments are in many ways in the centre of the development of a new entrepreneurial society. Also, they need all sorts of entrepreneurs within their area of interest. For a long time, they have tried to promote the immigration of business entrepreneurs in order to create employment and economic growth. Increasingly, however, they need to focus on other types of entrepreneurs as well. First of all, perhaps, they need to act over and above just being employed – not just to be and to act as if, as I have presented it.

Local government employees' intervention in their own development and employment growth could be called *municipal–community entrepreneurship* (Dupuis et al., 2003, p. 131). But another type of local entrepreneur central to 'community' often discussed is the 'ordinary' person as entrepreneur (Leadbeater, 1997; Thake and Zadek, 1997), that is, a 'new breed of local activists who believe that energy and organization can improve a community. They can be found organizing street patrols to liberate redlight districts, or running local exchange-trading schemes' (Rowan, 1997, p. T67). But they can also be some more or less prominent member of a local centre who acts entrepreneurially in the sense of attracting external investment, thereby improving the employment situation, without necessarily starting any business themselves. These people could be called *community business magnets* (Vestrum and Borch, 2006, p. 2). Being a community business magnet 'entails innovative community effort as a catalyst for the growth of local employment opportunities' (Dupuis and de Bruin, 2003, p. 115).

Table 7.2 Some entrepreneurs and other actors of interest to local governments

	Independent business entrepreneur	Corporate business entrepreneur	Public sector entrepreneurs	Community business magnets
Institutional setting	New business venture	Business venture	Public sector organization	Community
Role and position	Independent business people	Corporate executives	Politicians/ Common sector officers	Local public figure/Regional developers
Main activity	Create and grow business. Usually invest own cash aspiring to create wealth for them and their investor	Create values with an innovative project. No financial (but career) risk, but also less potential for creating personal wealth	Create value for citizens by bringing together unique combinations of resources. Career risk and no financial rewards	Facilitate and inspire entrepreneurship and renewal within their community. Limited focus on financial rewards

Source: Adapted from Zerbinati and Souitaris (2005).

Community business magnets could be defined as the mobilization of resources in order to create a new activity, institution, enterprise or an enterprising environment, embedded in an existing social structure, and for the common good of individuals and groups in a specific region (Johannisson and Nilsson, 1989; Paredo and Chrisman, 2006). The community is seen as an aggregation of people within a rural area that are generally accompanied by collective culture/or ethnicity and maybe other shared relational characteristics (Paredo and Chrisman, 2006).

Table 7.2 presents a summary of the differences between independent business entrepreneurs, corporate entrepreneurs, common sector entrepreneurs (or municipal-community entrepreneurs) and community business magnets.

Social entrepreneurship thereby becomes a way of re-imagining the role of individuals within communities, where a sense of community has been 'lost' following the embrace of the market and neo-liberalism during the 1980s (Taylor, 2003). Community-based business magnets or community business entrepreneurs can play a decisive role for depleted communities (Johnstone and Lionais, 2004). These business magnets or community business entrepreneurs have several similarities with the bricoleurs, a concept that I brought up in Chapter 5.

They use the term 'depleted community' to better understand the problems of communities affected by downturns in the local economy. To them,
depleted communities are manifestations of uneven development. However,
to Johnstone and Lionais (2004) depleted communities are more than
simply locations that lack growth mechanisms. They are also areas to which
people retain an attachment.

> A depleted community, therefore, continues to exist as a social entity because it is
> shaped by positive social forces as well as by negative economic forces. While the
> economic signals are for people to move, the ties to community, the emotional
> bonds and the social benefits of living there create a powerful resistance to leaving.
> A depleted community, therefore, maintains a strong and active network of social
> relations. This can be understood in terms of the distinction made in the literature
> between *space* and *place*. (Johnstone and Lionais, 2004, p. 218)

Johnstone and Lionais (2004) use Hudson (2001), who contrasts *space* as
an economic (capitalistic) evaluation of location based on its capacity for
profit with *place*, which is a social evaluation of location based on meaning
(more about space and place in Chapter 11). It happens that locations thrive
both as spaces for profitable enterprises and as places with a rich social fabric.
When this is the case, the location appears to combine the best of economic
and social life. Florida (2002) argues, for instance, that certain features of
place, such as tolerance to social differences, serve to attract highly creative economic actors who are drivers of wealth creation (Florida, 2002). In
such locations there is a synergistic relationship between space and place.
Depleted communities do not enjoy this kind of synergy, however, instead,
they suffer from economic stagnation and decline from social problems associated with economic decline (Johnstone and Lionais, 2004, p. 219).

Depleted communities may also be expected to have a diminished stock of
entrepreneurs especially if, in the past, those communities relied on a limited
number of growth mechanisms.

Community entrepreneurs and other actors working in depleted communities are likely to experience a number of obstacles to development, including venture-capital equity gaps (Johnstone and Lionais, 1999, 2000), labour
skills gaps (Massey, 1995a; Davis and Hulett, 1999) and a lack of business
and financial support institutions (Johnstone and Haddow, 2003), as well as
a lack of appropriate institutional thickness (Amin and Thrift, 1994; Hudson,
2000). Because of these obstacles, conventional private sector development
in depleted communities is less robust and less likely. As a consequence,
depletion could be something of a permanent condition there.

> Redevelopment in depleted communities is not likely to occur through traditional private industry-led mechanisms. If redevelopment occurs at all, it will probably be through less traditional means. This does not imply that the entrepreneurial process is irrelevant; on the contrary, in areas where capitalistic relations are less robust, the entrepreneurial process will, as it is argued here, manifest itself differently. Depleted communities will act as hosts to alternative forms of entrepreneurship that are adapted to their particular circumstances. (Johnstone and Lionais, 2004, p. 220)

Community business entrepreneurs do not look for personal profits. They evaluate wealth in terms of the benefits accruing to their own broader community. Traditional business entrepreneurs aim to provide personal gain and profits for themselves and for the shareholders of their business; community business entrepreneurs aim to create community benefits. Community business entrepreneurship can be distinguished from social entrepreneurship because it is focused on business organizations rather than charities, social ventures and purely social organizations. The process of community business entrepreneurship is neither entrepreneurship in the traditional business sense nor social entrepreneurship as commonly understood in the literature. It employs the tools of the former with the goals of the latter (Johnstone and Lionais, 2004, p. 226).

Although the barriers to development might be the same as those faced by traditional business entrepreneurs (finance gaps, labour skills gaps, lack of business support institutions, etc.), community business entrepreneurs can adapt in a variety of ways to overcome these obstacles. This is due to the fact that communities are not only the location of their entrepreneurial process. Some examples from Johnstone and Lionais (2004):

- Community business entrepreneurs can accept unconventionally low rates of return from their projects because personal profit is not then an objective.
- Community business entrepreneurs may also have a wider choice of organizational forms to employ when doing business.
- Also, once a project is undertaken, community business entrepreneurs have a different set of resources to call upon to achieve their goals. Among these resources is the access to volunteers. On top of that, not only do community business entrepreneurs have access to significant volunteer time, but also much of this may come from skilled technicians, professionals and business people.
- Another resource available to community business entrepreneurs is access to capital from neo-traditional sources. Community business

entrepreneurs can overcome this by convincing local people, who would normally not invest in private businesses, to invest in their community businesses and organizations.

- Similarly, community business entrepreneurs can attract customers who will buy from community-based organizations in preference to other (often non-local) organizations (Kilkenny et al., 1999).

A strong commitment to place enables community business entrepreneurs to marshal a number of financial, professional and labour resources around their projects that would not be available to other, more traditional, business entrepreneurs. That is, community business entrepreneurs use the assets of community to overcome the obstacles of depletion.

Studies show that there are four main arenas within which social entrepreneurs can have a potentially critical impact (Grenier, 2009, p. 183). Some of these presented here are valid more for social enterprisers than public entrepreneurs (another word for public innovators, as we know):

1. *Community renewal* (Brickell, 2000; Moore, 2002; Thake and Zadek, 1997). Social entrepreneurship is said to enhance social capital and build community. Moore (2002) identifies the impetus for social entrepreneurship in the UK as having its origin in community and neighbourhood renewal, in particular urban regeneration, issues that had been policy priorities for many years: 'it is the impetus for local regeneration and renewal that has provided one of the major driving forces of the social entrepreneurship movement' (Moore, 2002, p. 3). 'Community leaders and "social entrepreneurs" were to become the catalysts for overcoming the problems of run-down neighbourhoods' (Newman, 2001, p. 145).

2. *Voluntary sector professionalization* (Leadbeater, 1997; Defourney, 2001, 2003). Social entrepreneurship is identified in the UK context as essential to reform a sector that is 'slow moving, amateurish, underresourced and relatively closed to new ideas' (Leadbeater, 1997, p. 50). Defourney argued that there is a 'new entrepreneurial spirit' reflecting an 'underlying movement' which is impacting and reshaping the non-profit sector (Defourney, 2003, p. 1). In these accounts, social entrepreneurship appears as a kind of modernizing force within the UK voluntary and community sector, providing an impetus for change, new forms of voluntary action, and a professional edge that will take the sector forward to further expand its role as a mainstream provider of social services.

3. *Welfare reform* (Leadbeater, 1997; Thompson et al., 2000; Mort et al.,

2003). This is another envisaged social entrepreneurship as a timely response to social welfare concerns of the day and as an answer to the 'crisis of our welfare systems' (Defourney, 2003; see also Leadbeater, 1997; Thake and Zadek, 1997; Dees, 1998). Social entrepreneurship is claimed to 'help empower disadvantaged people and encourage them to take greater responsibility for, and control over, their lives' (Thompson et al., 2000, p. 329), and to counter dependence on welfare systems and charity (Leadbeater, 1997; Mort et al., 2003).

4. *Democratic renewal* (Favreau, 2000; Moore, 2002; Mulgan, 2006). Moore (2002) argues that globalization and the rapidly changing world had given rise to new philosophical debates, new notions of more socially and environmentally responsible economies, and basic questions such as: what kind of society would we like to live in? 'Social entrepreneurs and the social enterprises they create are one kind of response to a renewed search for the public good' (Moore, 2002). She argues that social entrepreneurship is 'producing a new form of citizenship, a new relationship between civil society and the state' (Moore, 2002). Along similar lines Mulgan (2006) describes social entrepreneurship as: 'part of the much broader story of democratization: of how people have begun to take control over their own lives, over the economy, and over society' (Mulgan, 2006, p. 94).

Some examples of how a local community could *act in public places in general*:

- *Create awareness*:
  ○ Participate in arranging a public entrepreneurship day.
  ○ Finance various publication in public entrepreneurship issues.
  ○ Institute a prize, 'The local public entrepreneur of the year'.
- *Participate in building public places more specifically*:
  ○ *Physically*: offer venues at a low rent; initiate 'Middle Age weeks'; arrange cultural exhibitions, music festivals and the like; open an 'entrepreneurship office' accessible to *all* kinds of entrepreneurs, not only in business.
  ○ *Virtually*: Present and discuss public entrepreneurs on the home page.
  ○ *Discursively*: Start a series of discussions and lectures on public entrepreneurship open to the public.
  ○ *Emotionally*: Participate in discussions about what it means to be a citizen in the local community in question.

Some more specific examples of how local governments can act in public entrepreneurial matters that I have come across in my research are:

- Visualize a place where citizen ideas are received and from where they can be assisted by the local government.
- To 'empower' the citizens: to teach citizens to create themselves.
- To create courage among employees to dare to break the 'budget pattern' and allow them to make mistakes.
- To assist in establishing a fund, meant to be used in public entrepreneurship.
- To let the citizens take part of the local government's network.
- To arrange a workshop to find out which public entrepreneurship project can be created and to inspire to more public entrepreneurship.

Haughton (1998) asserts that there are two different ways to run a local community development (Table 7.3):

I see three good reasons to *consider the citizen sector* more in local community activities:

Table 7.3 Two different ways to run a local community development

Through citizen entrepreneurs	Through a modification of previous ways or build bridges to the new
Made by people living in the community	Made with people living in the community
To maximize local control and decision-making	To use the local potential to attract external investments
Local ownership of the strategy	Local involvement in the strategy
To reduce economic leakage	To connect to the budget of the community
To build a local capital base	Community control of the expense decisions
Permanent regeneration and role for community investments	Programming per election period
To build an asset base with the members of the community in order to create income streams (for instance, work places which are owned and run by the members of the community)	Strategy to transfer certain activities to the business sector
Citizen entrepreneurs	An increased risk-taking with the community's decision-makers
'Alternative' projects	To modify the community budget
To build an alternative local economy	To build a stronger community economy
To evaluate through different social measurements	To modify traditional economic measurements

1. It constitutes a growing share of employment next to the public sector and the business sector.
2. It constitutes that sector in society that stresses meaningfulness the most, because it concentrates on needs not demands.
3. It provides different pictures of the society, which leads to more innovation and a more sustainable development. I have learnt to understand that innovation cannot be planned to any major degree, but is a result of different interfacing 'pictures'.

To *manage complexity* by a local government in their neighbourhood – *a summary*:

- The post-modern perspective stresses the unique characters in the local context as a contrast to other contexts (Healey, 1997).
- Society is to an increasing extent created by cultural communication in which people live in parallel, at work, where they live, where they enjoy their spare time (a kind of *'culture of the place'*) (Öhrström, 2005, p. 54).
- To support territorial nearness and the existence of regional specialization where key technologies (technology here consists of hardware and software as well as of human ware) build the platform for innovative abilities (ibid., p. 63).
- To create relations and coordination between 'reflexive agents' and organizations from all camps (including public entrepreneurs) with a high ability for continuous learning and de-learning (a necessity in a knowledge-based society).
- To think in terms of 'enabling' rather than 'planning' in the traditional sense (Guinchard, 1997). The increasing complexity in society is asking for more spatial coordination of living, work, service and entrepreneurial activities ('public places'), which in turn presumes strategies interested in a holistic thinking and in coordination between different activities.
- Planners who previously had a role as experts to the politicians now become coordinators in a co-acting process – they can no longer deliver the truth but rather become those who moderate different interests and contexts. They become more of experts on analyses of contexts and on initiating flows than on drawing plans (Öhrström, 2005).
- Politics become local as well as global at the same time, run by more or less temporary constellations (ibid.).
- There is more and more discussion about a shift from a linear view on planning as 'government' control to an orientation to be able to influence different networks and partnerships in more or less 'public' places

through 'governance' as a solution to the problem of managing the complexity in a local community.

Summary and conclusion

This chapter has discussed local development and the role of entrepreneurs in this context.

Think 7.1   What is the meaning of 'a more developed local place'?

Think 7.2   Describe a place that in your opinion has developed very favourably?

Think 7.3   Which five activities do you want to see in a local development first of all?

Think 7.4   How do you make local development more sustainable?

CH 7 – CASE STUDY

Development of a local community

Choose a local community that you know well and discuss how it could develop more favourably and sustainably!

To access the teacher's manual that accompanies this book, please use the following link:

http://goo.gl/DXQas.

8

Start-ups of entrepreneurial activities

Introduction

This chapter starts by discussing rational and natural starts of entrepreneurial activities and then goes on to looking at how intrapreneurial and social entrepreneurial activities are started. It then deals with the important role that networking is playing for entrepreneurship, provides my opinion about creativity and my view of (the lack of) relationship between entrepreneurship and growth.

Rational and natural entrepreneurial start-ups

The narrow view of entrepreneurship tends to build rational models. This has had the consequence when referring to starting entrepreneurial ventures of talking about *goals-rationality* (causation) or *means-rationality* (effectuation) (Sarasvathy, 2001). Goals-rationality looks at the establishment of an activity such that goals and ambitions with starting-up are rather explicit and that the entrepreneur looks for alternative possibilities to fulfil these goals and ambitions. He or she then chooses the means that seem to provide him or her with the best chance to achieve what he or she wants. This requires that the entrepreneur has great analytical skills, that he or she puts much time and effort into what he or she wants and that he or she has a reasonable ability to forecast the future.

A goals-rational person decides by trusting his or her ability to forecast the future and to achieve his or her goals by using that set of means which is available or which can be acquired. Much of the narrow view of entrepreneurship is based on this thought. Those who think goals-rational assert that 'if I can forecast the future, I can steer it'. Goals-rational entrepreneurial start-ups are illustrated in Figure 8.1.

Means-rational (effectuation) is rational as well, but the way to proceed is determined by those means that are available, not those goals one wants to

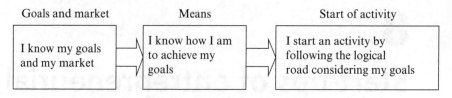

Figure 8.1 Goals-rationality (causation)

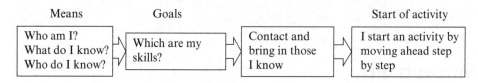

Figure 8.2 Means-rationality

achieve. Those who think means-rational assert that 'if I can steer the future, I do not need to forecast it'. Means-rationality is a rational logic, which new as well as experienced entrepreneurs can use in the very rough time of the start-up of an entrepreneurial activity. Means-rationality is illustrated in Figure 8.2.

According to *Wikipedia* (3 July 2012) means-rationality consists of four principles:

- *Birds in Hand Principle*. Start with your means. Do not wait for the perfect opportunity. Start taking action, based on what you have readily available: who you are, what you know and whom you know.
- *Affordable Loss Principle*. Set affordable loss. Evaluate opportunities based on whether the downside is acceptable, rather than on the attractiveness of the predicated upside.
- *Lemonade Principle*. Leverage contingencies. Embrace surprises that arise from uncertain situations, remaining flexible rather than tethered to existing goals.
- *Crazy Quilt Principle*. Form partnerships with people and organizations willing to make a real commitment to jointly building the future – product, firm, market – with you. Do not worry so much about competitive analyses and strategic planning.

There is reason to believe that entrepreneurial new business ventures emerge more often in a natural way than in a rational way (this does not mean, of course, that rational business ventures are completely unnatural or that natural business ventures are complete irrational). This can be discussed by using the concept *bricolage*, a concept I brought up in Chapter 5, which, as I see it, is the creation of something new through involving actors in the process of recombination and transformation of existing resources for old and for new purposes (Garud et al., 1998; Baker and Nelson, 2005). Lévi-Strauss, who revitalized the concept, offered no specific definition, but bricolage is often described as 'making do with whatever is at hand' (Lévi-Strauss, 1966, pp. 16–17; Weick, 1993; Miner et al., 2001) and the bricolage construct was further refined by Baker and Nelson (2005), where they defined it as a focus on resources at hand, using existing resources for new purposes, recombining existing resources and making do to provide break-through solution in creating emerging business firms. Lévi-Strauss (1966) offered no specific definition of bricoleur, but bricolage is often described as 'making do with whatever is at hand' (Lévi-Strauss, 1966, pp. 16–7; Miner et al., 2001; Weick, 1993).

Bricolage activities mean a set of actions 'driven by the pursuit of existing and often scarce resources that can be recombined to create novel and interesting solutions of value that affect their respective markets' (Kickul et al., 2010, p. 232). The concept of bricolage can help us understand how some emerging entrepreneurial ventures are embracing challenges under conditions of tight resource constraints.

While rational models of creating business ventures look at rent-seeking behaviour of prospective commercial entrepreneurs, bricolage instead focuses on more natural prosocial behaviour of entrepreneurs whose environments are typically resource constrained and essentially present new challenges without providing new resources. Bricolage is often about exploiting physical, institutional, social or other inputs that other firms reject or ignore. Realizing greater impact through innovation may depend on the extent to which entrepreneurs can apply and combine the resources they have to new problems and possibilities (Baker and Nelson, 2005).

Lévi-Strauss (1966) makes, as I mentioned in Chapter 5, a distinction between 'the engineer' and 'the bricoleur', which in my case can be taken as the difference between developing entrepreneurial ventures rationally or naturally. The two terms stand for two different ways of thinking, where the engineer always tries to make his or her way out of and go beyond the constraints imposed by the present, while the bricoleur by inclination or necessity always remains within them. One important difference between the two or between rational and natural behaviour in general is that the 'bricoleur' always puts something of him- or herself into what he or she is doing (Lévi-Strauss, 1966, p. 21).

The importance of the relationships between a business firm and its environment for the growth of the firm has been discussed for a long time. Penrose (1959) argued that firms having very similar material and human resource inputs may offer substantially different services to the market because of differences in their abilities to grasp possible uses of those inputs. Open systems models started to come forward at about the same time (Boulding, 1956), talking about the need for firms to act differently in different environments. These open systems models were later developed by Katz and Kahn (1978) and Scott (1998) among others. However, none of these models provides any useful explanation of *how* such firm-specific processes take place or, above all, how firms can create something from nothing. Theories of bricolage do.

'Orderly sequential processes may be the exception in entrepreneurship' (Baker and Nelson, 2005, p. 358). Bricolage, creativity and improvisation often appear tightly linked together. This differs from traditional linear social planning and focuses instead on social design processes and the frequency of connections between resources in the environment and resources within the firm. Bricolage is an important means of counteracting the organizational tendency to enact limitations without testing them. This suggests that a constructionistic approach to resource environments is sometimes more fruitful than objectivistic, rational views. An objectivistic, rational view of resource environments holds sway in much contemporary entrepreneurship research (Baker et al., 2005). The social construction of the resource environment involves reframing or outright rejection of prevailing definitions of resources is fundamental to the process of bricolage. This opens up new areas for entrepreneurship research. In the literature, action faced with limited resources has been studied in terms of finance, (for example, bootstrapping) and, to some extent, in terms of non-linear process design (Bhave, 1994). When defining resources at hand, we should also include resources that are available very cheaply or for free, even if others judge them to be useless or substandard, something which is rarely done in rational entrepreneurship research. This also means that creating value through bricolage does not depend on the Schumpeterian assumption that some assets are withdrawn from one activity to be applied in another, what he refers to as creative destruction.

It may seem like 'effectuation' and 'bricolage' are the same, but there are several differences:

- 'Effectuation' attempts to provide a more correct picture of how business start-ups take place by explaining them, using models; 'bricolage' attempts to understand business start-ups by interpreting entrepreneurs as agents in social constructions. (More about 'models', 'interpretations', 'explanations' and 'understanding' in Chapter 11).

- Somebody who is means-rational is cooking, using Sarasvathy's terms (2001), a meal by using what is at hand as ingredients and skills at the moment of cooking. A bricoleur 'starts' much earlier by collecting things, that he or she comes across – it might be an interesting ingredient or way of cooking which he or she adopts because it might be handy one day.
- A bricoleur can be very smart at improvising. To continue with Sarasvathy's picture about cooking a meal, a bricoleur, who looks at his or her situation not as factual but as a social construction and therefore questions what possibilities and limitations mean, may use an ingredient very shrewdly where it has almost never been used before.
- An effectual start means to know what is at hand as resources and skills and could, in principle, start with these means and skills anywhere anytime. A bricoleur is very tied to place and time and must keep these in mind in his or her ambitions.
- One example of how a bricoleur is tied to a time and a place (and at the same time one example of how he or she may be able to generate 'new' resources' from 'nowhere') could be that he or she is using flowers blooming at that time from his garden as decorations for the food (creating raw material) or that he or she is asking his or her guests, as good friends nearby, to come earlier and to participate in the pleasure of cooking the meal (creating labour).

Something from nothing is in many ways an extreme version of more from less. According to Baker and Nelson (2005), this can be done in three ways:

- Resources at hand
- Recombination of resources for new purposes
- Making do

Resources at hand

Lévi-Strauss (1966) observes that bricoleurs accumulate physical artefacts, skills or ideas on the principle that they may possibly come in handy rather than engineers, which he contrasts with bricolage, where resources are acquired in response to the well-defined demands of a current project. Previously learned skills and coping mechanisms are used as a pragmatic repertoire for dealing with challenging new situations. Prior or existing institutions or elements of failed institutions are buildings for new institutions – institutions not built *on* the ruins but *with* the ruins of the old regime. Above all, existing social network contacts are resources for building new businesses (Baker et al., 2005).

Recombination of resources for new purposes

Bricolage can mean to combine and reuse resources for different applications than those for which they were originally intended or used. System designers may 'paste together a few components into "something", see how it looks, play with it, check if it works, evaluate, modify or reject. This bricolage activity is not directed to any specific solution or configuration in general because [no one] knows in advance what the final configuration is going to be' (Lanzara, 1999, p. 337). Evolution is 'always a matter of using the same elements, of adjusting them, of altering here and there, of arranging various combinations to produce new objects of increasing complexity. It is always a matter of tinkering' (Jacob, 1977, pp. 1164–5). Bricolage means an 'ingenious reconciliation of existing organizational mechanisms and forms, picked by management according to subjective plans and interpretation' (Ciborra, 1996, p. 104).

Making do

Making do implies a bias toward action and active engagement with problems rather than lingering over questions of whether a workable outcome can be created from what is at hand. It also means by necessity a bias for testing received limitations. Many cases of bricolage are invoked during skilful acts of improvisation (Weick, 1993; Miner et al., 2001).

Bricolage always means resource limitations, at the same time as most entrepreneurial new ventures start small and local. Johnstone and Lionais (2004, pp. 227–8) provide examples of bricolage behaviour among entrepreneurs in so-called 'depleted communities', which succeed because of their local connections. I gave examples of this in Chapter 7.

A model of the bricoleurial way to start a business venture is provided in Figure 8.3. There are several differences between this figure and those in Figure 8.1 and 8.2, but the most important is possibly that the environment is not here seen as objective or factual, but as social constructions. The venture is emerging somewhat naturally from there. Another way to say this is that networking here truly becomes co-creation, not only an exchange of information (see later on in this chapter). (Baker and Nelson, 2005, p. 349) provides several examples of this:

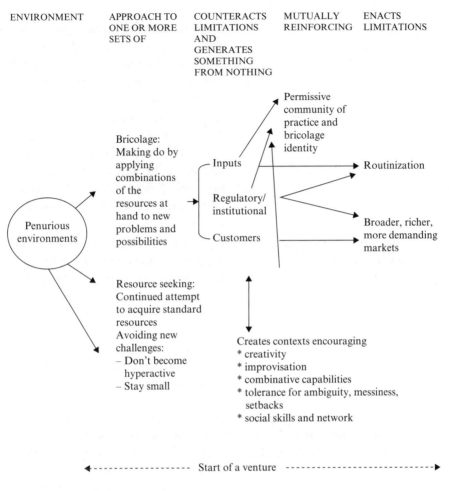

Source: Adapted from Baker and Nelson (2005, p. 353).

Figure 8.3 Bricolage

Environmental domain	Description of bricoleurial activity
Inputs: physical	By imbuing forgotten, discarded, worn or presumed 'single-application' materials with new user value, bricolage turns valueless or even negatively valued resources into valuable materials.
Inputs: labour	By involving customers, suppliers and hangers-on in providing work on projects, bricolage sometimes creates labour inputs.

Inputs: skills	By permitting and encouraging the use of amateur and self-taught skills (electronics repair, soldering, road work, etc.) that would otherwise go unapplied, bricolage creates useful services.
Customers/markets	By providing products or services that would otherwise be unavailable (housing, cars, billing system, etc.) to customers (because of poverty, thriftiness, or lack of availability), bricolage creates products and markets where none existed.
Institutional and regulatory environments	By refusing to enact limitations with regard to many 'standards' and regulations, and by actively trying things in a variety of areas in which entrepreneurs either do not know the rules or do not see them as constraining, bricolage creates space to 'get away with' solutions that would otherwise would be impermissible.

Bricolage notions of making do and using whatever is at hand links [*sic.*] with a fundamental social shift of developing smart, sustainable, projects that are integral to social change. This represents a shift from a consumption-based to a conservation-based way of doing things better than through an improved understanding of existing resources, their form, function, and fungibility, thereby developing a more clever, creative means of developing products and services aligned with market needs. (Kickul et al., 2010, p. 237)

Intrapreneurial start-ups

There are two classical models of how intrapreneurial activities (that is, entrepreneurial activities in existing business firms) arise, which seem to function fairly well even today. The first is a proposal from the person who coined the term 'intrapreneur'. He suggests in Pinchot (1985) that an intrapreneurial activity arises in four phases. These are:

1. *The solo phase.* In the beginning, the intrapreneur is building up the vision by and large on his or her own.
2. *The network phase.* When the basic idea is there, most intrapreneurs

can start to share it with some few friends in the place where they are working and with some trustworthy customers. From their reactions, they can get an opinion about the strengths and weaknesses of the concept. It is surprisingly easy to get others to contribute with their knowledge. To be asked for an opinion means still that you are seen as some kind of expert.

3. *The bootleg phase.* As the network phase goes on some people start to work closer with the intrapreneur in more ways than just giving encouragement and advice. Some kind of team is formed, but it still works 'underground', maybe at the intrapreneur's home or in some neutral place.

4. *The formal team phase.* Increasingly, it is required more of an intrapreneurial venture than just an idea with some individual(s) working with it. A formal intrapreneurial team, which eventually is established on the background provided by the intrapreneur, is hopefully functionally complete, acting independently and coming together in a commercialization possibly later.

This model fits well with those theories suggested by Donald Schon (Chapter 1) and with how the Post-It-notes product was developed with 3M (Chapter 4, Case study).

The second model of an intrapreneurial process was provided by Kanter (1983). She suggests three stages. This proposal does not contradict the first, but is in my opinion more operational and informative. The proposal is also not so individually oriented as the first one. Let me therefore present it in more detail.

Stage 1: defining the project

Before a project is started in an existing firm, the senior management must establish some principles for potential and possibly not yet started intrapreneurial projects. Those who work in the firm may have many contradictory opinions about suitable procedures to achieve an intrapreneurial goal. Clarifying the background to these contradictory perspectives can be decisive for success. In the beginning stages of an intrapreneurial project you need political information as much as you need technical data. Without political understanding it is not possible to pass the suggestion stage.

The culmination of the definition of the project comes when you sift through the information fragments from different sources and concentrate on a specific task. Then, the project leader must, in spite of the fact that the senior management team may have given a specific field as a mission, 'sell' the project that he or she wants to run.

Furthermore, the project leader, in order to move further, must attract interest from many more than just the senior managers, who eventually approved the mission in the first place. Several of these other persons can be independent actors who are not inclined to co-operate just because senior management seems to favour one intrapreneurial project among several others. Nor need subordinates automatically be willing to participate. Whatever position they have, they have a number of other tasks to practice and the right to make their own priorities.

In other words, even if one intrapreneurial project may start with an allocated task, it is usually supported only by general statements about results wanted, where the means, by and large, have not been specified. Sometimes the project leader initiates his or her tasks, but such initiations are rarely done in a vacuum. Constructive intrapreneurs listen to the flood of information that come from superiors and from colleagues and then identify the need perceived. In the first stages of defining an intrapreneurial project, its champion may spend more time talking to people outside his or her own function than with subordinates or with managers in their own functions.

Stage 2: building a coalition

The next step for intrapreneurial project leaders is to put together those resources and that support what is needed to make the project work. In order to succeed, these power-related means not only come from formal vertical sources but also from several other places within the organization.

Most successful intrapreneurial activities are a result of contributions from a number of different persons from several different areas. They constitute a kind of control and balance system for an activity which is not routine and therefore not exposed to normal controls. By building a coalition before a more extensive intrapreneurial activity is started, the project leader makes sure that there is enough support to keep a project going and guarantee its success. Sometimes the intrapreneur asks colleagues for 'contributions' in the form of time or personnel which can be collected later if senior management sanctions the project and provide general resources.

After having collected support from colleagues, the intrapreneur usually looks for support from higher up the hierarchy. Even if you find surprisingly few cases where the senior management directly supports a project, a general blessing from superiors is often crucial to put a team of well-meaning supporters together. Successful intrapreneurs learn whom or which individuals in the hierarchy have the power to influence their project (including material resources or critical introductory power to give an approval). Then they negotiate to gain support from these decision-makers by using formal polished presentations. While intrapreneurs can often sell their project to colleagues and other interesting peers by referring to their interests and reassuring them that the intrapreneur knows what he or she is talking about, he or she needs to provide senior management with better guarantees concerning the technical as well as the political appropriateness of his or her project.

Decision-makers in key positions tend to assess a proposal in terms of the possibility to sell it within *their own* domains. Sometimes, successful intrapreneurs provide their seniors with material and brief them about their own presentations to other people (for instance, members of the board), who have to approve of the project.

Usually, senior management expresses its general support, because many intrapreneurial projects, which originate from lower down the hierarchy, can manage to provide support at its own level or do not require financial means from higher up the hierarchy. However, support from senior management makes it possible to sell an intrapreneurial idea to the project's own personnel as well as to others.

Sometimes, a presentation at senior management level helps to bring up resources more directly. In some cases, successful intrapreneurs leave such presentations with promises of a larger investment or help to get personnel and facilities. Often, however, a promise of resources depends on the possibility of getting other individuals in the firm along. 'If you can get support and resources, get started' is a common directive to a successful intrapreneur.

With promises of resources and support, a successful intrapreneur can go back to his or her immediate superiors to plan how to proceed. Usually, these superiors are simply waiting for such signs in order to authorize a project to proceed. Often the managers in question are not completely involved or sold until the project leader has support from above. Usually the network of other supporters plays an active role during the stage of building a coalition. Their comments, criticism and objectives help the project to something which has a higher chance of succeeding. Another result of the stage of building a coalition is a set of reality controls which give some guarantee that a project, which will probably not make it, is moving on.

Stage 3: Action

The next step of the successful intrapreneur is to mobilize key persons to implement the project. Independent of whether these persons are directly subordinates or they constitute a special project group, the intrapreneur is building up a more or less formal team. Successful intrapreneurs bring people involved in the project together, give them instructions and tasks, encourage them to make the extra effort required, ask for their ideas and suggestions (both as a way for making them committed and for further adjustments of details) and give promises that the project is to be implemented. The technical details for the intrapreneurial project, that is, those tasks that actually are to be done, are now in the hands of the group. The project leader may possibly contribute with ideas and even involve him- or herself in practical issues, but his or her primary task is still mainly external and organizational, oriented towards defending the borders and the independence of the intrapreneurial project.

The first task of the project leader is to *handle disturbances* or criticism that might be risky to the project. Successful intrapreneurs do not face too much resistance – maybe because their previous coalition building determines whether the project starts in the first place. Resistance may however be expressed more passively – criticism of the details of the project, laziness, delayed responses to queries or arguments about allocation of time and resources among projects.

During this stage successful intrapreneurs may therefore have to spend as much time in meetings, formal as well as informal, as they did to launch the project. Intrapreneurial project leaders must prepare themselves carefully for these meetings so they can stand up to sceptical comments and objections with clear facts, persuasion and reminders of the positive outcomes that may be the result from reaching the project's objective. In most cases a clear presentation is enough. But not always.

When intrapreneurial project leaders need to counter challenges and criticism which can lead to disconnected power support and deliveries, they should try to keep other disturbances outside the borders of the project. In reality, the project leader defines a protection area for the work of the group. He or she goes him- or herself outside this area to fend off critics and to prevent people and rules provided by senior management to break off the project tasks. While the group itself is sometimes unaware of this contribution from the project leader, he or she is patrolling the borders. By acting as a disturbance filter, the project leader is protecting intrapreneurial projects by modifying the rules, by moving means from one account to another without having the approval to do so, by developing special award and stimulant packages, which make remuneration of achievements over and above the company's normal payments possible and by assuring that superiors stay away if necessary.

The second task at the action stage is to *keep momentum* and continuity. Disturbances come here from internal rather than from external sources. Delays and lack of activity is a constant danger, especially if the results lead to more work. In intrapreneurial projects, group members often complain about tendencies that routine procedures take over special activities and that they consume valuable time.

Furthermore, it is easier for project leaders to beat up the mood for a vision in the beginning than keep the objective in focus when facing the boring aspects of work itself. The project leader's group building skills are therefore crucial.

A third task for intrapreneurial leaders (and for several other members of the group as well) at the action stage is to get involved in *new reformulations* which are necessary to keep the project going. As they are necessary, intrapreneurial project leaders introduce new arrangements to co-operate with key tasks. When it may look like a project is about to get stuck – that is, when everything possible has been done and no new results are in sight – successful intrapreneurial project leaders often change structures or approaches. Such alternations may lead to a doubling of effort and a renewed attack on the problem.

The fourth task at the action stage, *external communication*, completes the circle. The project starts by collecting information, now is the time to spread information. It might be critical that colleagues and key supporters have an updated perception of the project and its progress. Constructive project leaders also give the benefit early to others who provide supporters with information. To do so will bring credibility to the project even before concrete results can be shown.

Intrapreneurship is an iterative process. One stage – say defining the project – is never completely passed. Even when manufacturing and marketing are approaching, circumstances may require corrections. This iterative character makes it difficult in any correct way to describe the intrapreneurial process in a number of independent stages. The same characteristics make it also the reason why the process is difficult to handle.

Social entrepreneurial start-ups

It is more difficult to see *natural stages* of a social entrepreneurial case compared to a business entrepreneurial case. However, there is one suggestion from Leadbeater (1997), which indicates the life cycle of a social entrepreneurial activity (Figure 8.4). This figure suggests three stages in the growth of a social entrepreneurial activity. Every stage has its demand and requires its own skills.

Stage one is where the organization tries to establish itself. It is consequently at this stage, which is, in my opinion, about the differences between entrepreneurship and management, the most entrepreneurial part of the start-up

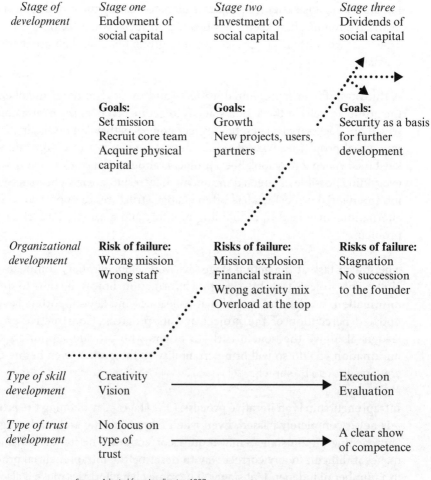

Stage of development	*Stage one* Endowment of social capital	*Stage two* Investment of social capital	*Stage three* Dividends of social capital
	Goals: Set mission Recruit core team Acquire physical capital	**Goals:** Growth New projects, users, partners	**Goals:** Security as a basis for further development
Organizational development	**Risk of failure:** Wrong mission Wrong staff	**Risks of failure:** Mission explosion Financial strain Wrong activity mix Overload at the top	**Risks of failure:** Stagnation No succession to the founder
Type of skill development	Creativity Vision		Execution Evaluation
Type of trust development	No focus on type of trust		A clear show of competence

Source: Adapted from Leadbeater, 1997.

Figure 8.4 Life cycle of a social entrepreneurial operation

and early development of an entrepreneurial project. The key question at the first stage is to formulate the foundation idea. But as the organization is established this idea must be reconsidered as the operation is expanded and possibly broadened. This formulation needs to be handled very sensitively having possible citizen users of the operation in mind. The whole thing is a matter of governance, which becomes more and more complicated as the operation grows.

As the social entrepreneurial activities widen they may need to change the need they satisfy due to changed citizen needs. Such changes can be very political if there is no awareness of how changes are made and in what direction they are going. This means that the organization must be very adept at how its own operation is to be evaluated – how to ask for accountability so to say. To be effective becomes more important as the operation moves on. The organization needs to build a good reputation based on what it does – in the commercial world this would be called branding. And the final challenge is the same as for the commercial entrepreneur – how to handle the fact that the champion is dying out?

We know very little about how social entrepreneurial activities are starting. Much research is needed to get some knowledge of this topic. My experience is that social entrepreneurial projects (in particular of the type I call public entrepreneurship) look more like natural start-ups than like rational start-ups of entrepreneurial activities (see earlier in this chapter).

Networking and entrepreneurship

Undoubtedly, networking plays an important role in entrepreneurial start-ups. Let us therefore consider this subject.

Some say that Piore and Sabel *brought in business networks* into entrepreneurship theories in their book of 1984 when they praised the industrial districts in northern Italy as an alternative economic model. They defined industrial districts as geographically concentrated operations that mainly consist of small firms which specialize in specific goods and services (often as part of an end product). *Today* there is a more fundamental view on the importance of networks.

> Networks have existed in all economic systems. What is different now is that networks, improved and multiplied by technology, have entered our lives so deeply that 'the network' has become the central metaphor around which our thinking and our economy is organized. If we cannot understand the logic characterizing

> networks, we cannot exploit the economic change which has now started. (Kelly, 1998, p. 10)

> The diversity of networks in business and the economy is mind-boggling. There are policy networks, ownership networks, collaboration networks, network marketing – you name it. It would be impossible to integrate these diverse interactions into a single all-encompassing web. Yet no matter what organizational level we look at, the same robust and universal laws that govern nature's webs seem to greet us. The challenge is for economic and network research alike to put these laws into practice. (Barabási, 2002, p. 217)

> Networks is the new sociomorphology and the extension of the logics of network influences to a high extent the way and the results of our production processes, experience, power and culture. (Castells, 1998, p. 519)

We could therefore, as mentioned in Chapter 2, rightly call our modern society *a network society*. It is the first time in history that the economic unit has been other than the individual, the organization, the region or the sector. Instead this unit is the network, where subjects and organizations are connected to each other and are constantly being modified and adapted to each other and to supporting environments and structures (Castells, 1998).

The network society is a more open society. A continuous search across the whole field of society is therefore necessary in order for the entrepreneurial actors of today not to be surprised. Through this search, relationships are built and maintained. 'The network economy is based on technology, but can only be built on relationships. It starts with chips and ends with relations' (Kelly, 1998, p. 179).

Consequently, the study of networks is popular today. However, there is considerable variation in what can be meant by 'network' and 'networking'. Competing definitions and perspectives often exist.

It is possible to talk about three important *parts* of a network (Hoang and Antoncic, 2003): (1) the content of the relationships, (2) the governance of these relationships and (3) the structure or pattern that emerges from the crosscutting ties.

Relationships (between people and between organizations) are viewed as the media through which actors gain access to a variety of resources held by others (Bjerke, 2007). Two such key resources for the actors are information and advice, which he or she can gain access to through his or her network.

In the uncertain and dynamic conditions under which entrepreneurial activity occurs, it is reasonable that resource holders (potential investors and employees) seek information that helps them to gauge the underlying potential of a venture, of which they are or want to be a part. Entrepreneurs, on the other hand, seek legitimacy to reduce possible perceived risk by associating with, or by gaining explicit certification from, well-regarded individuals and organizations. To be perceived positively based on your relationships in a network may in turn lead to subsequent beneficial resource exchanges.

The second construct that researchers have explored is the distinctive *governance mechanisms* that are thought to underpin and coordinate network exchange (Bjerke, 2007). Trust between partners is often cited as a critical element that in turn enhances the quality of the resource flows. Network governance can also be characterized by the reliance on 'implicit and open-ended contracts' that are supported by social mechanisms – such as power and influence or the threat of ostracism and loss of reputation – rather than legal support. These elements of network governance can give cost advantages in comparison to coordination through market or bureaucratic mechanisms.

The third construct is *network structure*, defined as the pattern of relationships that are engendered from the direct or indirect ties between actors (Bjerke, 2007). A general conceptualization guiding the focus on network structure is that differential network positioning has an important impact on resource flows, and hence, on entrepreneurial outcomes.

Similarly, Conway et al. (2001, p. 355) talk of four key components that should be investigated when studying human networks and human networking (discussion in this section follows Conway and Jones, 2006, pp. 308–10):

- *Actors* – individuals within the network;
- *Links* – relationships between individuals within the network;
- *Flows* – exchanges between individuals within the network; and
- *Mechanisms* – modes of interaction between the individuals within the network.

There is a large number of dimensions that can be used to categorize individuals within a network, from general dimensions such as age, sex, family membership, nationality, ethnicity and education level, to more specific dimensions such as functional background (for instance, finance, marketing or design) or sectorial background. The choice from this breadth of dimensions should be informed by the nature of the network and the purpose behind studying it.

The nature of the links or relationships between the members within the network varies also along a number of dimensions, of which the most relevant are the following (Conway and Jones, 2006, pp. 308–9):

- *Formality* – distinguishes between informal and personal links and formal links that are formulated in a contract, for example.
- *Intensity* – is indicated by the frequency of the interaction and the amount of flow or transactions between the two actors during a given time period (Tichy et al., 1979).
- *Reciprocity* – refers to the balance of the flow over time between two actors through a given link. The link is seen as 'asymmetric' or 'unilateral', when the flow is unbalanced (that is, by and large goes only one way) or 'symmetric' or 'bilateral', when the flow is balanced (that is, by and large goes both ways). Asymmetric links tend to lead to some kind of inequality in power relationships between two actors (Boussevain, 1974).
- *Multiplexity* – signifies the degree to which two actors are linked to each other through several role relationships (for instance, as friend, brother and partner); the greater the number of role relationships there is between two actors, the stronger are the ties (Tichy et al., 1979). Boussevain (1974, p. 30) also argues that 'there is a tendency for single-stranded relations to become many-stranded if they persist over time, and for many-stranded relations to be stronger than single-stranded ones, in the sense that one strand role reinforces others'.
- *Origin* – this dimension refers to the identification of the event that leads to the origin of a link. It intends to incorporate facts such as the context in which the relationship arose and who initiated it.
- *Motive* – the functional significance of networking does not qualify for providing a convincing explanation of why it happened. When they discuss this issue, Kreiner and Schultz (1993, p. 201) mean that 'one must determine the motives and perspectives of the actors who reproduce such patterns'.

Tichy et al. (1979) distinguish between four types of flows within a network, often named 'transaction content' in the network literature:

- *Affect* – the exchange of friendship between actors.
- *Power* – the exchange of power and influence between actors.
- *Information* – the exchange of ideas, information and know-how between actors.
- *Goods* – the exchange of goods, money, technology or service between actors.

Individuals may 'exchange' any of these types of transaction content for another, for instance, goods for money or information for friendship, even if in many cases, like in the last one, this can be more implicit than explicit. It is also worth pointing out here that the estimated value of the flow or flows between two actors within the network can vary widely between 'sender/provider' and 'receiver' as well as between other members within the network.

There is a number of ways in which individuals can interact with each other, for instance, talking to each other on the telephone, e-mail, documents or meetings face-to-face. Kelley and Brooks (1991) dichotomize these interaction mechanisms into 'active', which refers to a personal interaction, either face-to-face or on the telephone, and 'passive', which, by and large, refers to documents and other text material, where there is no direct relationship between 'provider' and 'receiver' of information. 'Networks do not emerge without considerable endeavour' (Birley et al., 1991, p. 58); consequently I am not only interested in the mechanisms for exchange of information and goods and services in a network, but also in those mechanisms and forums through which entrepreneurs build and maintain their network.

Networks in general may also vary along a number of dimensions. The most relevant network dimensions of interest are often (Conway and Jones, 2006, pp. 309–10):

- *Size* – this dimension simply refers to the number of actors participating within the network (Tichy et al., 1979; Auster, 1990).
- *Diversity* – this network characteristic often refers to the number of different types of actors within the network (Auster, 1990), which as I mentioned above can be seen along a number of dimensions like age, sex, education, etc.
- *Density* – the density of a network refers to 'the extensiveness of the ties between elements [actors]' (Aldrich and Whetten, 1981, p. 398), which can be seen as the number of existing links within the network divided by the number of possible 'links' (Tichy et al.,1979; Rogers and Kincaid, 1981). Boussevain (1974, p. 37) claims however that 'it must be stressed that network density is simply an index of the potential not the actual flow of information', that is to say, it is a measure of the network structure and not of the network activity. Boussevain (1974, p. 40) also asserts that 'there is obviously a relationship between size and density, for where a network is large the members will have to contribute more relations to attain the same density as a smaller network'. Furthermore, the network density tells us nothing about the internal structure of the

network in itself and as Boussevain (1974, p. 40) points out, 'networks with the same density can have very different configurations'.

- *Openness* – in the entrepreneurship literature there is often a distinction made between strong and weak ties. Strong ties are found in cliques and are associated with dense networks (that is, relationships between individuals who are linked to each other more closely), whereas weak ties also link people outside the clique and consequently create 'openness' in the network, that is to say, they are boundary-spanning relationships or links spanning 'structural holes' (Burt, 1992).
- *Stability* – Tichy et al. (1979, p. 508) define this dimension as 'the degree to which a network pattern changes over time'. Auster (1990) develops this further by talking about frequency as well as magnitude of the changes of members and links within a given network.

One important aspect of networks is that it is possible to separate *four levels in network* (Fyall and Garrod, 2005, p. 154):

1. Exchange of information
2. Adaption of activities
3. Sharing resources
4. Co-creation

The further down you go in these levels the more is asked of the members within a network. Networking often stops at the top level.

Networks have been found to assist small entrepreneurial operations in their acquisition of information and advice (Birley, 1985; Carson et al., 1995; Shaw, 1997, 1998), in supplementary acquisition of internal resources (Aldrich and Zimmer, 1986; Jarillo, 1989; Hite and Hesterley, 2001), in their ability to compete (Brown and Butler, 1995; Chell and Baines, 2000; Lechner and Dowling, 2003) and in their development of innovative activities and results (Birley et al., 1991; Rothwell, 1991; Conway, 1997; Jones et al., 1997; Freel, 2000). Gibson (1991, p. 117–18) claims that 'the more extensive, complex and diverse the web of relationships, the more the entrepreneur is likely to have access to opportunities, the greater the chance of solving problems expeditiously, and ultimately, the greater the chance of success for a new venture'. It may seem like a paradox that at the same time as entrepreneurs are seen as autonomous and independent, they are also 'very dependent on ties of trust and cooperation' (Johannisson and Peterson, 1984, p. 1).

So, 'networks' and 'networking' are important entrepreneurial tools to establish, develop and improve on small businesses and other operations in society. However, we see a difference between discussing networking as a way to improve on existing operations (a discussion in terms of 'space') and networking as a necessary part of human existence (a discussion in terms of 'place'). Discussions of the first kind often lead to technical issues like what is a good and a bad network, what makes a network more functional, and so on. Typical discussions of networks in terms of 'space' are:

- A more developed network is more valuable to a person who starts an entrepreneurial operation than to somebody who is running an ongoing operation.
- The advantages of being members in networks are there for large as well as for small entrepreneurial operations, but membership of a network is more important for survival of a small entrepreneurial operation.
- Networks make it possible for small entrepreneurial operations to gain access to resources that is not possible elsewhere.

There are those who claim that *if* these were no networking, there would be no venturing. There are even those who want to conceptualize the entrepreneurial process to *organize oneself through personal networking* (Johannisson, 2000).

Some results that I have found valid for networking by social entrepreneurs are:

- Networks are more important for social entrepreneurs than for business entrepreneurs, if for no other reason the former do not offer goods and/ or services that can speak for themselves. They constantly need to justify their social entrepreneurial operations.
- The differences between strong (emotional) and weak (calculative) ties are not at all so clear or even necessary to separate for social entrepreneurs as for business entrepreneurs.
- A champion in social entrepreneurship is partly more difficult to be and partly more difficult to replace than is the case in business entrepreneurship contexts.
- Confidence and trust are decisive for social entrepreneurs. Contacts alone are not enough, which could sometimes be the case for business entrepreneurs.

During the 1990s a new concept of capital, *social capital*, came into general use alongside the established concepts of financial, real and human capital. The idea of social capital came from sociology, not from economics, and it has proven particularly useful when analysing small firms and entrepreneurship (Westlund and Bolton, 2003, p. 77). The very term 'social capital' is commonly attributed to Jacobs (1961). As their main interest, analysts of social capital are concerned with the significance of relationships as a resource for social action (Nahapiet and Ghoshal, 1998). This reflects the growing concern over the role of social relationships in explaining or understanding business activity. A deeper view is that an actor's embeddedness in social structures endows him or her with social capital (Portes and Sensenbrenner, 1993; Oinas, 1999). In the literature, social capital is defined as the asset that exists in social relations and networks literature (Burt, 1997; Leana and Van Buren, 1999). Social capital can be described as a consequence of how social processes work, where lack of cooperation leads to a decreased flow of information and resources. Furthermore, social capital can reduce transaction costs (Putnam et al., 1993) or as Dosi (1988) puts it, lower the transaction costs by using middlehands that cannot be bought or sold on a market. Social capital can also reduce uncertainty (Fafchamps, 2000). To have access to social capital can be described as a catalyst for a useful social and economic interaction. All in all, social capital offers a way to understand how networks are functioning.

The social capital approach has developed in two ways. First, to demonstrate that the personal network among citizens who start a new business venture allows them to gain access to resources that they cannot raise on their own (Ostgaard and Birley, 1994) and, second, to illustrate the influence of social embeddedness and associated dynamism on economic exchange (Portes and Sensenbrenner, 1993).

In other words, networks have an economic as well as a social content. They consist, which has been mentioned above, of *weak* ties (a space concept) as well as *strong* ties (a place concept). In the latter case, the term *embeddedness* is sometimes used. Some important aspects of embeddedness as far as small firms are concerned are:

- The embedded nature of them is not only made up of economic transactions but also concrete social relationships that are built up by participating actors.
- A social relationship between the company's owner/entrepreneur must exist in business contacts before an economic transaction can take place.
- A moment of lack of trust, opportunism of a negative kind and disorder is always possible in all business transactions.
- It is difficult to discuss a single business activity without considering its predecessor and its follower.

Social capital can be seen as a *glue* as well as a *lubricant* (Anderson and Jack, 2002). When seen as a glue, it ties people harder together. When it is seen as a lubricant, it facilitates actions within a network. In the former case social capital may consequently have a binding effect, prevent deviants from acting and thereby have a negative effect on development. Powell and Smith-Doerr (1994, p. 368) express it such:

> Sociologists and anthropologists have long been concerned with how individuals are linked to one another and how these bonds of affiliation serve as both a lubricant for getting things done and a glue that provides order and meaning to social life.

Social capital could also be called *network capital* (Anderson and Jack, 2002, p. 196). Social capital is a productive asset, making certain specific results which, where social capital does not exist, would be impossible or more difficult (Coleman, 1990). From this perspective, social capital is created within the embeddedness process, that is to say both as a 'result' (a product of network) as well as a means (to facilitate what is going on). That embeddedness that takes place becomes an inevitable part of the social structure. But, as mentioned, social embeddedness can also have negative consequences because of the group's expectations. Networks can provide a mechanism for trust and legitimacy, but networks can also function to exclude or include – they can consolidate power without spreading it (Flora, 1998).

I see social capital mainly not as a 'thing' but as a process. It is a process that is created to facilitate an effective exchange of information and resources – an artefact, which can only be studied considering its effects.

It is not difficult to think of a close connection between development of social capital and corresponding growth of the third sector and number of citizen entrepreneurs. The organizations of the third sector have sometimes been called 'the organizations of the civic society' (Salomon and Anheier, 1997). It is in fact possible to talk about *civic capital* instead of social capital (Evers, 2001). If social capital is seen as civic capital it highlights the role of a wider group of political factors, both in terms of their general role in creating confidence and cooperation as in terms of their in building orientation and behaviour of groups and associations in the society. Social capital is then seen both as an indicator of the development of the civic society (built by social as well as political action) and a way to debate civic engagement with an eye on economic development and governance (Evers, 2001, p. 299).

> Social capital constitutes a resource that may be mobilized to a greater or lesser degree within a production process so as to improve its performance. But it is also an end in itself because it is a 'civic' capital contributing to a democratization process. Social capital is present in groups, networks and the local social fabric.

> Inasmuch as it is – at least partly – indivisible and thus cannot be appropriated by any single individual social capital constitutes a local quasi) public good. (Laville and Nyssens, 2001, p. 317)

A comment on creativity

There is an increasing amount of literature written about creativity. In this book there is neither space nor reason to give more than a personal comment on the subject.

It is, in a way, surprising that in spite of all that has been written on the issue, it is possible to ask whether what creativity really is has been clarified by all that has been written about it. It still seems that we (the same way as we understand entrepreneurship) understand it when it appears, but that we still have problems grasping it. This is, in my view, because it is not really possible to limit it in a definition, at the same time as we read too much into it. We can, as I see it, look at the phenomenon on three levels. The first is to admit that there is creativity through thinking inside the box. We could call this *creativity inside the box* (Figure 8.5).

Figure 8.5 Creativity inside the box

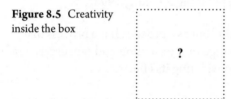

We have seen that this kind of creativity exists. A bricoleur does not go 'outside the box', as discussed earlier in this chapter.

We get a more radical kind of creativity by thinking outside the box. We may call this *creativity outside the box* (Figure 8.6). Many researchers of entrepreneurship talk about this type of creativity as necessary when they talk about successful entrepreneurs.

Figure 8.6 Creativity outside the box

Figure 8.7 Creativity   **?**
without a box

I believe, however, that there is nothing in the real world that we could call to mind without a box (Figure 8.7). This is, in my opinion, what too many theorists of creativity dream of – but in vain!

> A thing like absolute creativity is probably not possible. You are always creative in relationship to a idea complex – a theory (Sahlin, 2001, p. 45; my translation).

Entrepreneurship and growth

The narrow view of entrepreneurship sometimes asserts that the founder of a new firm should have a growth ambition in order for him or her to be seen as an entrepreneur. I see it is a requirement which is too rigid as well as meaningless. It is a fact that most business start-ups do not achieve any major growth; nor do all entrepreneurs have the same ability to handle growth. It is possible, as do Sexton and Bowman-Upton (1991), to ask a number of questions like: what is it with the business starter that makes him or her put his or her business into a growth cycle that takes place with fewer than 10 per cent of the companies of a country? Why is the typical business starter oriented towards change and growth and is this something that separates a manager from an entrepreneur? Are these factors in place already when the business starts? If this is the case, is this then seen in decisions and actions that take place in order to start the business or do all businesses start the same way, where later the happy ones survive and grow? Sexton and Bowman-Upton (1991) claim that growth is not automatic. It must, in their opinion, be planned carefully in order to take place and actions taken in order for it to be reached. They look at growth as a controllable factor. It is a decision to be made by some to act forcefully to achieve, for others to achieve more slowly and for some to avoid.

It *is* possible to separate the entrepreneur from the ordinary small firm on the basis of growth orientation (Sexton and Bowman-Upton, 1991, p. 8). Growth orientation can be measured in terms of the owner(s) purpose when the firm is starting, his or her (their) inclination to further growth and to come up with strategic plans to encourage the growth of the firm. It is also worth pointing out, that growth-oriented managers in big firms share these orientations. So, growth orientation *can* be seen as a way to separate an entrepreneurial firm from any small firm, but note that this does not separate the entrepreneur from growth-oriented persons in their own company and in larger firms. Based on this assumption, Sexton and Bowman-Upton (1991, p. 14) propose the following matrix (Figure 8.8).

High Marketing orientation Low	Managerial Growth	Sustainable Growth
	Marginal small firms	Low-growth entrepreneurial firms

Low　　　　　　　　　　　　　　　　　　High

Entrepreneurship orientation

Figure 8.8 Small firms in terms of growth mode

My view, however, is that an entrepreneur does not have to have growth ambitions and still be called an entrepreneur, neither when he or she starts a firm, nor later. One reason is that most of the time successful businesses after start-up grow to an 'adequate' level and then stay there. Another reason is that I see difficulties in separating some specific traits from other traits that you could call 'growth orientation' and claim that only entrepreneurs have those. I assert instead that, when firms grow it *may* take place in an entrepreneurial way, but in most situations where growth takes place it is because of successful *management*! Because I believe that an entrepreneur is not the same as a manager.

Summary and conclusion

This chapter has discussed different cases of entrepreneurial start-ups. Issues discussed have been rational and natural entrepreneurial start-ups, start-ups of intrapreneurial and social entrepreneurial activities, the role played by networking for entrepreneurship, creativity and that lack of relationship, which in my opinion exists between entrepreneurship and growth.

Think 8.1 Which are the three most important factors in entrepreneurial start-ups in your opinion?

Think 8.2 Which factors limit the size of an entrepreneurial operation in your opinion?

Think 8.3 Which are the three most important members of a network when you start a business in your opinion?

Think 8.4 Must a successful entrepreneur be creative?

CH 8 – CASE STUDY

www.netflix.com

(Adapted from Barringer and Ireland, 2006, p. 121)

While cleaning up your living room, you discover a 3-week-overdue DVD from a local DVD-renting shop. When you return it the next day, you find out that with the late fees you have incurred, you could have bought the movie. To add insult to injury, you do not even remember watching it!

When Reed Hastings returned a copy of *Apollo 13* to a video store and was charged $40 in late fees, he thought, 'There must be a better way', and started *Netflix*.

When it was founded in 1997, *Netflix* was similar to the traditional movie rental model, except that customers selected their rentals online and movies were delivered to their homes. After watching a movie, a customer would return it in a prepaid envelope via the postal service. Reed had not eliminated late fees, but he did limit them to $2 per week.

Two years later, *Netflix* changed its approach to a subscriptions service that offered unlimited DVD rentals with no late fees. For a flat monthly fee of $17.99, you get three DVDs. Here's how it works. On the *Netflix* website, you list the DVDs you would like to watch, choosing from *Netflix*'s menu of over 12 000 movies. The DVDs are mailed to your home. You can keep these DVDs as long as you want, with no late fees. When you return one, the next selection on your movie priority list is mailed out. You are always entitled to have three DVDs as long as you are willing to pay the monthly fee.

The result of *Netflix*'s new approach has been rapid subscription growth, particularly among customers who hate paying late fees. *Netflix* could now claim to have over 2 million active subscribers and is adding new subscribers every month. To minimize risk and reduce overhead, the company has a number of interesting twists to its business model. One is that it does not pay for much of its inventory. Instead, the company has risk-sharing alliances with the major movie studios, including *DreamWorks SKG*, *20th Century Fox*, *Universal Studios* and several others, in exchange for a share of the rental revenues and a stake in its business. In return, 80 per cent of the 3.3 million DVDs in *Netflix*'s inventory were acquired from the studios without any up-front payment. These partnerships with the studios also allow *Netflix* to offer its subscribers movies within 90 days of release, which is quicker than traditional video stores.

Netflix raised $82 million in an initial public offering (IPO) of shares of its stock in May 2002. The IPO, which was led by *Merrill Lynch*, was one of the most successful of the year. Despite its success, however, and its ability to go public, several questions linger about the strength and ultimate viability of *Netflix*'s business model. Some observers still aren't sold on *Netflix*'s ability to achieve a sustainable competitive advantage and believe the viewers will eventually tire of paying $17.99 per month. In addition, other observers believe that *Blockbuster*, *Hollywood Video* or even *Wal-Mart* will eventually imitate what *Netflix* is doing and will squash the smaller rival.

CH 8 – CASE STUDY *(continued)*

 DISCUSSION QUESTION

How would you like to characterize *Netflix*'s network and how would you like to improve it?

To access the teacher's manual that accompanies this book, please use the following link:

http://goo.gl/DXQas.

9

Women as entrepreneurs

Introduction

This chapter is about a somewhat neglected part of entrepreneurship, women as entrepreneurs.

Some facts

Research about woman entrepreneurship (then in business) did not start until the 1970s with some breakthrough studies done by Schreier (1973) and Schwartz (1976). Today the number of businesses being run by women is estimated at around half as many as those being run by men (Global Entrepreneurship Monitor, 2007). Most woman business entrepreneurship takes place in developing countries, but this is a result of necessity if nothing else (ibid.).

In the United States, it is estimated, however, that 48 per cent of all private business today are owned by women, defined as businesses where women own at least half of them (Carter and Bennett, 2006, p. 178). In the UK, it is estimated that 15 per cent are owned by women, 35 per cent by men and that 50 per cent of businesses there are co-owned by men and women (Small Business Service, 2004). The number of women who run a business varies in Sweden depending on the study, but by and large the share is 22–28 per cent ('Jämställdhet för tillväxt', 2011). Within the EU (15 countries) on average 15.5 per cent of men and 8 per cent of women are self-employed (Franco and Winqvist, 2002).

A strong segregation of genders also exists in terms of choice of trade or industry selected by business start-ups. It is obvious, for instance, that construction work is much more common among men, for instance. Among women, it is relatively more common to start businesses managing personal services (including taking care of children and the elderly) (Holmquist and Sundin, 2002, p. 18). In the United States more than half of all women businesses are in the service sector (Kuratko and Hodgetts, 2004, p. 647). In

Sweden, one major reason for the large number of women's businesses focusing on personal service is that the public sector has recently transformed greatly there.

The share of women among start-ups in the business sector is increasing everywhere, however (Kuratko and Hodgetts, 2004, p.645; Carter and Bennett, 2006, p.176). The extent to which women start a business in the United States is, as a national average, twice as high as that for men (Kroll, 1998) and the share of businesses run by women there has been much faster than in most other countries (Carter and Bennett, 2006, p.178). In Sweden, the increase as far as woman start-ups in the business sector increased from 19 per cent to 30 per cent between 1990 and 1999 (Holmquist and Sundin, 2002, p.14). More enterprising women should mean a higher degree of employment and higher growth in a country like Sweden. The whole thing is, however, a matter of equality and democracy – which does not always appear in the debate ('Jämställdhet för tillväxt', 2011).

One reason why fewer women are business entrepreneurs compared with men could be that women sometimes feel that they are discriminated against and not always taken seriously when they want to start a business (Hisrich and Brush, 1986). This has also been confirmed in later studies (Bridge et al., 2009). Female start-ups and female senior managers also tend to experience more obstacles to success than their male counterparts (Chell, 2001). In order to understand the differences in male and female start-ups, we probably have to dig deeper, however.

Female and male enterprising – a social construction?

Even if the number is increasing, there are, according to Spilling and Gunnered Berg (2000), few studies that actually consider entrepreneurship among women compared to entrepreneurship among men. Those studies that have been conducted have in many cases been quantitative and documented differences of the factual kind, presented in the last section (Gatewood et al., 2003). Ahl (2002) claims that these studies overestimate the differences between men and women, at the same time as they ignore several similarities. Feminist researchers of entrepreneurship have taken into consideration, and critically looked at, the invisibility of woman entrepreneurs (Sundin, 1988; Sundin and Holmquist, 2002). This is the case in academic research (Ahl, 2002) as in statistics and among business advisors (Sundin and Holmquist, 2002). A feministic perspective can visualize woman entrepreneurship more. To apply a feministic perspective means to problematize constructions and representations of gender in, for instance, texts, research and praxis as far as entrepreneurs and entrepreneurship are concerned. This means not only to question that marginalization which woman entrepreneurship has, but also to question and to problematize the ruling male entrepreneurship position (Pettersson, 2004, p. 20). Among others, Holmquist (2002) is claiming, that questions about *what* and *who* are important in entrepreneurship in order not to make woman entrepreneurship invisible. One way to do this is to apply theories of social constructions of reality.

Constructionistic feministic research is based on the theory that gender, like many other constructions in our world, is social (compare Berger and Luckmann, 1966 [1991]), that is, created in and through those construction processes which are built into language (Nilsson, 2004, p. 47). As social category in language, gender is something which has been created in different negotiation processes. Gender has in this view no *essence* in itself, that is, not as any natural sets of 'male' or 'female' inherited in men's and women's bodies, respectively, but it is created and maintained in different negotiation processes through language between people (ibid.). Gender is then not seen as 'any natural fact' (Flax, 1987, p. 627). (Gender does not necessarily have to be seen as a social construction in other views, of course. The surgeon, for instance, is probably not doing so most of his or her time at work; nor is it adequate to see love between man and woman as just a social construction.) Our understanding of gender then gets in the social research perspective a meaning as a social and cultural praxis because it does not then reflect social categories but constitutes forms of how these are to be understood (Ehrlich and King, 1994). With theories of social constructions as a basis we must in research as well as in practical work of change take language as a start for the discussion, not only see language constructions as a result of our efforts (Nilsson, 2004, p. 47).

To look at gender as an ongoing social construction means, as mentioned, to delete from the cause list any essential differences between women and men, but it means at the same time that the perceptions of what is masculine as well as feminine is not changed in any simple way (Nilsson, 2004, p. 48). The spoken and written word is easier to change in a local context, but it may get a very structural meaning in a wider social context (ibid.). According to Magnusson (1996, p. 43; my translation) this means that language 'at the same time means autonomy as well as a repetition of earlier patterns. The person, who speaks, is controlling the language at the same time as she is caught by it.'

Entrepreneurs are generally stereotyped as men (Sundin, 1988; Sundin and Holmquist, 1989; Holmquist, 1997; Gunnered Berg, 1997; Lindgren, 2000;

Ahl, 2002). It is generally understood among feminist researchers that entrepreneurship in general has a masculine bias.

Gnosjö is, for instance, one place in Sweden which is in general associated with active and successful entrepreneurship and which has a large number of self-employed. The entrepreneur in Gnosjö, however, is most often seen as a man dressed in blue overalls with tools in his hand. This is the case even though 33 per cent of the entrepreneurs in Gnosjö are women (Pettersson, 2004, p. 177). Even if women entrepreneurs are rarely mentioned in relationship to Gnosjö, this place is seen as interesting as an entrepreneurial place, but this is questionable just for this reason (ibid.). What is seen as knowledge concerning Gnosjö is, no doubt, excluding one-third of its entrepreneurs, that is, women!

Holgersson (1998) asserts that the social construction of entrepreneurship to a large extent makes women invisible, that they function only as a necessary periphery when constructing the man.

One of the reasons why the entrepreneurs (implicitly) are represented by men is that the concept of entrepreneur has masculine connotations (Sundin, 1988; Sundin and Holmquist, 1989; Holmquist, 1996; Ahl, 2002). The same goes for concepts like 'business person' and 'small business manager'. The word 'entrepreneur' comes, as we know, from French and is a masculine word. The corresponding feminine word, 'entrepreneuse' is rarely used, if ever (Javefors Grauers, 2000). The symbolic representation of an entrepreneur is consequently a man (Sundin, 1988), who is usually running a business in manufacturing (Danilda, 2001). At the same time, manly or masculine are rarely used. If gender is mentioned in connection with entrepreneurs or entrepreneurship, it refers to women (Javefors Grauers, 2002).

According to Gunnered Berg (1997) theory and research in the field of entrepreneurship is characterized by a kind of 'gender blindness', as it is focused on businesses owned by men and the masculine entrepreneur (Pettersson, 2004, p. 186). Empirical studies of entrepreneurship are centred around men in an unreflecting way, which in turn means that entrepreneurship theories are constructed along the same lines (Mulholland, 1996; Javefors Grauers, 2000).

Women as social entrepreneurs

There are many factual circumstances whereby women 'are well suited' as social entrepreneurs:

- It is more common among women as business entrepreneurs than for men to look at the local market as more important (66 per cent of women compared to men) (Holmquist and Sundin, 2002, p. 16).
- Among women it is relatively more common, as already mentioned, to start a business within the personal services sector (Holmquist and Sundin, 2002, p. 18).
- It is more common among women than among men to choose part-time as a working option (Coulter, 2001, p. 300; Holmquist and Sundin, 2002, p. 18).
- Women have as enterprisers a higher social motive and a lower growth ambition than men (Holmquist and Sundin, 2002, p. 12).
- A smaller number of women fail as entrepreneurs compared with men. One explanation could be that women are better than men at handling people (Kuratko and Hodgetts, 2005, p. 648).
- One early study of woman entrepreneurship (Watkins and Watkins, 1984) came to the conclusion that women's choice of business to a large extent is determined by which area is showing the least resistance to their success and where technical and financial demand for starting a business are low.

The risk, of course, is that choosing the social entrepreneurial alternative, women will continue to be invisible as entrepreneurs. Even if social entrepreneurs are important, not to say decisive, in building a fairer and more loyal society, they hardly get the great headlines or the limelight as technically skilled inventors, as pathfinders in breaking new markets or as successful people in business!

Summary and conclusion

This chapter has discussed women as entrepreneurs, partly from a factual empirical perspective, partly from a social constructionistic perspective.

Think 9.1   Why, generally, do twice as many men as women start businesses?

Think 9.2   If Steve Jobs had been a woman (and had a different name, of course), what could Apple have become?

Think 9.3   What is implicitly placed in the following expression: 'This company is very feminine'?

Think 9.4   Imagine starting an entrepreneurial operation with homosexuals as a major customer target group. How could such a company been designed?

CH 9 – CASE STUDY

Catherina Ronsten (2act Important Meetings)

Catherina Ronsten is a Swedish entrepreneur. 2act Important Meetings is a company building up a case bank of stories told by people of how they experience important meetings. These stories are used for various coaching and educative purposes.

'To start my own – that was not in me, it must have been for somebody else. Somebody who can. But then, a sunny autumn day 16 years ago I stepped into the office of Internal Revenue in Stockholm. I signed the form and became an unlimited-liability firm. But don't imagine that I had plans to involve myself full-time in this firm. No, my world was not about creating a business firm but possibly to make some extra money apart from being employed full-time elsewhere.

It did not turn out that way, however. It became more than part-time in the firm. Jobs just came in. At first, I worked as a consultant with ethics, public relations and marketing. The mid-1990s were good times for me, but after a few years, on a whim, I educated myself as a journalist; I suddenly felt that I had found my home.

After my exam I did not do what most of my fellow students did, took a position at some local newspaper to learn the job. No, I thought I was too old for that. At that time I was 30+ and had more than 10 years of experience at the leadership level of one Swedish political party. I also had, apart from my journalist and marketing exam, a number of other professional qualifications and lots of exciting work experience in my rucksack.

So I did what I had done many times before: I followed my heart. I lived well as a free-lance journalist for a number of years. To have a profession in writing is fantastic. To get paid for learning new things, meeting people and asking them all you want to know is just incredible. I know that many people say that it is hard to make a living as a freelance journalist, but for me it was easy. I think it is because I had the advantage of daring to and to actually make contacts. To sell is not difficult or intangible for me and I thought that I offered the paper good content with my articles.

If you had asked me whether I was an entrepreneur during my first year running a business of my own I would quickly and definitely say: No! But today I am. A proud entrepreneur; a social entrepreneur. So what happened between then and now?

I became a company, I began to run a business and I realized that what I wanted to do with my business was to contribute. To lift something into the society that I considered was not there and something that I could contribute in order to improve things. A product, a service – something that was missing from society and which I could add to it. I wanted to give something that could improve things for many human beings. The idea did not come just like that; it did not whisper but it screamed and throbbed eagerly at my heart. Not one day passed without me facing it.

The articles, the black articles – all with a focus on crisis, disaster and breakdown at Swedish schools. The words were strong and they fed themselves indefatigably and directly

CH 9 – CASE STUDY *(continued)*

into my consciousness. I defended myself, I cut off and I went on long detours with pop music drumming from my CD player. I did not want to hear, I did not want to see. I did not want to know. But the words came in and pounded constantly in my consciousness. 'Do something now! Take it on now!' and it had just taken down the barricades where I had been standing for over 10 years and ordered me to create an increased awareness of the environment and climate issue.

I was not tired, rather fed up. Now life should be lived and I should be able to take time for family, friends and interests outside work. I was supposed to have a job where I could go home at 4 o'clock. But then they came again, the placards, the articles, the news broadcasts, misery, disaster.

Only a few years after I had taken the step into politics in the mid-80s, I had turned off TV as soon as it was time for a news programme. I simply could not stand listening to all misery. I even had a correspondence with the person in charge of the major news programme on TV, where I questioned their focus, which I saw as a 'total misery focus'. And with the motivation that there should be some good news to find somewhere, shouldn't there? I do not want to tire you with the answers, just summarize with a few words the feeling I got after having read them. Hopelessness. Total hopelessness. Darkness.

Then came an early summer day in 1999. I knew it was coming, but I did not really want to. However, I woke early that morning and knew exactly what I had to do to be an active part of some positive change. How I should use my time and my firm to be an assisting power, a co-creator of positive change. I was to use my pen and my curiosity and I was to work with assisting power. Because, think what might happened if we, instead of focusing on what did not work in our society, directed our searchlights on what did work. What could we then achieve?

I wrote a proposal, a short PM and then made a few telephone calls that same morning. The area I wanted to focus on was completely new for me, for school and for education. I had really no knowledge. No children going to school and no direct connection to school. Experience I had, of course. I had been to school myself, I had even been mobbed a couple of years by our teacher and had shirked through most of upper primary school. But this was not what I was to talk about. It was the light and the meeting between teacher and pupil that had become of importance, what had made a positive difference. I wanted to investigate and ask the following question: Who had been of importance to me? When did it happen? What did he or she say? What did they do and in what way had the meeting influenced me today?

I wrote quickly and directly from my heart and started with the words: 'There are teachers who I hated like a plague and teachers who I loved most of all . . .'. This short PM was sent with my fingertips that sunny morning. The same afternoon, around 3 p.m., my telephone rang and the woman at the other end said: 'What a marvellous idea, it suits us perfectly. Let's go for it!!' It became the start of the largest adventure of my life. An

CH 9 – CASE STUDY *(continued)*

adventure, which has grown to a fantastic business company and contributed to really giving me the feeling and insight about that I am a real entrepreneur. Somebody, who wants and can contribute to society with my competency, experience and desire.

I did not know it then, but this also became the start of *2act Important Meetings*, which through the years has given me so much joy, wonder and expectation. We work with story-telling and have collected stories about important meetings at school, in nursing, in sports, in the business world and in politics. And there are more collections going on. We build from scratch using important meetings between many people. In our story bank, we have today more than 3000 stories and more are to come and we will collect stories from around the world. *2act Important Meetings* has a business concept to add value to, improve and mediate stories in an interesting and instructive way. In a way that makes your meeting become worth more than if you had kept it for yourself.

Your meeting and your lesson can become somebody else's bridge – to create something new, to help you grow as a human being and to live more and better. This is what *2act Important Meetings* does. We work with assistant power. Add value to, improve and transmit knowledge. Be the change!

The years before I took a formal journalist education, I had with interest and with much commitment dedicated myself to work making the environmental issue a central issue. Together with others who were there 'early' (the issue had in a way already gone far already and it was late . . .), I was part of and made sure that we brought in the environmental issue as a natural part of decision-making, on the political as well as the business agenda. At the beginning of the '90s I worked as the person in charge of an environmental institute in Sweden, which operated as a limited liability company, which early and with great success cooperated with other companies to promote environmental issues. This was done through distributing knowledge about and cooperating with senior management, environmental education, environmental auditing and through effectively as well as out in organizations distributing knowledge about environmental issues in some of the largest companies in Sweden, like *IKEA, McDonald's, Scandic Hotels* and more. They showed the way and went first.

After a few years with this environmental institute, I was headhunted by the Swedish Church to start what was later named Fairtrade in Sweden. This was a new and completely unknown occupation, but also a pleasant challenge to take on and to create something which did not exist in Sweden. Again I stood behind the barricades against something which was wrong in my opinion and which needed to be corrected. This social injustice and that exploitation of poor people which we, in the rich countries, completely out of ignorance were (and still are) doing. Now we have become more aware of the threat to the environment and there are a lot of people dreaming about being part of the new environmental movement. Not only those with bicycles and saddles decorated with flowers. No, fresh power has come, hungry young people who can see something important in this

CH 9 – CASE STUDY *(continued)*

movement. Eager with great confidence to be able to be just that person who can make a difference. Change the world. For the better!'

 DISCUSSION QUESTION

> What is specifically feminine about what Catherina Ronsten is doing as an entrepreneur?

To access the teacher's manual that accompanies this book, please use the following link:

http://goo.gl/DXQas.

10

Entrepreneurial activities in different national cultures

Introduction

After having summarized two quantitative studies concerning the magnitude of entrepreneurial start-ups in different countries in the world, this chapter provides a more detailed picture of the culture for business and entrepreneurship in five major cultures in the world.

GEM and GEDI

There is reason to consider the fact that entrepreneurs, even if you stick to business entrepreneurs, exist everywhere, *not only in the business world or in modern society* and that entrepreneurs in other parts of the world partly think and act differently from the way we do and that we can learn something from this.

During the last 10 years or so, an international research project has been going on, which indicates the mission to *measure the business formation process in different countries*. This, so-called GEM-project (GEM stands for Global Entrepreneurship Monitor) is a larger research project, which is interested in understanding economic development. The business formation process is an important aspect of how different 'carrots' and institutions are cooperating to produce innovations and deliver new products and services to the society.

The GEM reports (which are annual) indicate the level of business start-ups based on a combined index, which is called the Total Entrepreneurial Activity (TEA) index, which measures the percentage of the adult population (between 18 and 64 years of age) that is involved in setting up a business, of which they attempt to own at least a part. The TEA index consists at the same time of two kinds of initiatives, depending on which stage the business project is in: nascent initiatives or start-up (SU) businesses which have not been going for more than 3 months and new initiatives or baby businesses (BB), businesses that have been active more than 3 months but less than 42 months (Sánchez et al., 2010, p. 131).

The five countries which had the highest TEA during 2007 (Global Entrepreneurship Monitor, 2007) were:

1. Thailand   26.9 per cent
2. Peru   25.9 per cent
3. Colombia   22.7 per cent
4. Venezuela   20.2 per cent
5. Dominican Republic   16.8 per cent

China was positioned in 6th place with 16.4 per cent, the United States was positioned in 13th place with 9.6 per cent and UK in 28th place with 5.5 per cent (among 42 countries that participated that year).

Another global study started in 2011 and it is called the Global Entrepreneurship and Development Index (GEDI). It is somewhat broader than GEM. The purpose of GEDI is to contribute a more total understanding of economic development in different countries. The index calculated in this study is a tool to measure how fast 'the future' is spread around the world. Similar to a global positioning system, GEDI can point out the time and the place and identify strengths and weaknesses in different countries in comparison with other countries. It also offers a measurement of the quality and extent of the business formation process in these countries. GEDI captures the contextual aspects of entrepreneurship by focusing on entrepreneurial attitudes, entrepreneurial activities and entrepreneurial aspirations – what the constructors call the three As.

GEDI is part of a long-term research project that aims to measure global development. It is an annual evaluation which through the centuries is supposed to provide us with a valuable database containing most countries in the world. The objective of GEDI is to include most countries (Ács and Szerb, 2011, p. 2).

So, GEDI is composed of three blocs or sub-indexes – the 3 As: entrepreneurial attitudes (ATT), entrepreneurial activities (ACT) and entrepreneurial aspirations (ASP). Those three indexes are based on 14 pillars, where every one of them contains an individual and an institutional variable, which represent micro and macro aspects of entrepreneurship. The 14 pillars according to Ács and Szerb (2011, pp. 4–7) are:

Related to entrepreneurial attitudes (ATT):

- Pillar 1: Opportunity perception
- Pillar 2: Start-up skills
- Pillar 3: Nonfear of failure
- Pillar 4: Networking
- Pillar 5: Cultural support

Related to entrepreneurial activity (ACT):

- Pillar 6: Opportunity start-up
- Pillar 7: Tech sector
- Pillar 8: Quality of human resources
- Pillar 9: Competition

Related to entrepreneurial aspirations (ASP):

- Pillar 10: New product
- Pillar 11: New technology
- Pillar 12: High growth
- Pillar 13: Internationalization
- Pillar 14: Risk capital

The five first countries (71 countries were included in the study) according to GEDI 2011 were:

Position 1: Denmark
Position 2: Canada
Position 3: United States
Position 4: Sweden
Position 5: New Zealand

GEM and GEDI sometimes come to radically different results. But here is not the place to discuss different methods to measure the degree of entrepreneurship in different countries and the quality of these methods but just to realize that there are differences in different countries in this respect. It is my definite opinion that such differences can, at least partly, be understood by the culture ruling in those countries.

To understand culture

When discussing culture, it is commonly about answering two questions:

1. Is behaviour part of culture or is culture only those values governing behaviour?
2. Is culture something clear in the mind of everybody or something which is more or less unconscious?

Based on the answers to these questions, it is possible to set up Table 10.1 (Bjerke and Al-Meer, 1994, p. 177). This table presents different ways of looking at what culture could be seen as.

Table 10.1 Four different ways to look at culture

Culture as	Something clear in mind	Something which is more or less unconscious
Behaviour	e.g. An annual budget routine (A)	e.g. How people sit down at a meeting (B)
Values	e.g. The business concept of a company (C)	e.g. To take for granted that planning is always good (D)

That definition on which this chapter is based is Alternative D, that is

> *Culture = Basic norms of behaviour, values and beliefs, which have developed interactively between people, which have been interpreted and been given a meaning, which by and large are unconscious but which govern behaviour without being behaviour in themselves.*

Some comments on this definition:

- You are born with a culture; culture is something you learn your whole life (but mostly in the beginning). There are many sources of this learning, for instance, parents, friends, school and place of work.
- Every human being has a unique culture in the sense that his or her kind is a unique mix from different sources. Every group, however, develops a more or less joint culture, of which people are part, which, except for the group's common behavioural norms, values and conceptions, also have their own aspects of life, taken from other places.
- Culture in a group consists of behavioural norms, values and conceptions, which, even if they are learnt by its members, still gradually become more or less unconscious.
- Culture is something which, even if it is mainly unconscious, still is felt as something meaningful by those who take part in it.
- Culture among people and groups has a crucial influence on how it expresses itself as artefacts, art, literature, language and everyday

behaviour, etc. I want to refer to this as *cultural manifestations without being culture itself*. It may, for instance for a nation, be its architecture, its flag and its language. For a company it may be its logotype, its interior fittings or its vocabulary.

> Culture is an intriguing concept. Although we can easily read a definition of it, when we begin to consider that definition and what it implies, culture becomes a prodigious and commanding notion. Culture manifests itself in patterns of language and in forms of activity and behaviour that act as models for both the common adaptive acts and the styles of communication that enable us to live in a society within a given geographic environment at a given state of technical development at a particular moment in time. It also specifies and is defined by the nature of material things that play an essential role in common life. Such things as houses, instruments and machines used in industry and agriculture, forms of transportation, and instruments of war provide a material foundation for social life. Culture also helps dictate the form and structure of our physical realm, and it encompasses and specifies the social environment permeating our lives. (Samovar et al., 1981, pp.24–5)

A language is something of *a mirror of culture*:

> Some linguists have posited that language may actually influence certain aspects of culture. Language, they suggest, establishes the categories on which our perceptions of the world are organized. According to this theory, language is more than a system of communication that enables people to send and receive messages with relative ease. Language also establishes categories in our minds that force us to distinguish those things we consider similar from those things we consider different. And since every language is unique, the linguistic categories of our language will never be identical to the categories of any other. Consequently, speakers of any two languages will not perceive reality in exactly the same way. (Ferraro, 1994, p.49)

I have worked outside Europe for about 20 years. I have functioned every-where as an academic (visiting professor), taken notes and read what I came across about those countries I lived in, in particular to understand the culture in which I lived. The rest of this chapter is a summary of my experiences of this matter as far as business activities and entrepreneurship in five different culture groups are concerned. These are:

- The American
- The Arab
- The Chinese
- The Japanese
- The Scandinavian

This order of presentation is nothing else but alphabetic and does not reflect any kind of priority.

When I speak of 'the American' I mean the United States and by 'the Scandinavian' I mean those countries that speak a Scandinavian language, that is, Denmark, Norway and Sweden. I worked in the United States for a year, have often been in that country since then and have an academic education in Business Administration from Lund University built on American principles, I have lived and worked in the Arab world for 3 years, I have lived in countries dominated by Chinese for 8 years, I have worked intimately with Japanese for 4 years and I was born in Norway but have had Swedish citizenship for many years. With this as a background I think I have a relatively deep knowledge from which to explain how I look at culture's consequences for business activities in general and the entrepreneurial activity in particular in these five contexts.

Culture exists between members of a group, small or large. It can be found in families, in cities, in business firms, in nations and more and it is partly different between these levels. I 'paint with a broad brush' so to say by leading culture discussions at the level I do. Four comments, before I go into the five cultural contexts:

- My pictures should not be seen as average in any statistical sense, not as typical (in the sense of 'most common'). They should be seen as 'typifications' or 'ideal types' in Weber's sense (a concept which I touched upon under 'To be involved over and above the usual' in the Introduction). There is probably not any living single individual in any of the five cases that perfectly matches my picture and there is, in practice, nothing but discrepancies from these pictures.
- I look at how a culture of a country influences its business style, not vice versa.
- I can only bring up here some of all the material that I have collected.

Those who want to read more on what I am talking about can read my book *Business Leadership and Culture. National Management Styles in the Global Economy* (1999).

American business culture

People in the United States tend to be future-oriented rather than oriented to the present or the past. It is generally thought that with this concentration on the future – together with a high value placed on action and work – it is not only possible, but mandatory, to improve on the present. The future is then anticipated to be bigger and better (Samovar et al., 1981, p. 72). The United States fosters a cult of progress, and belief in progress involves accepting change and the progress can be steered. Progress in America is often measured in materialistic possessions, and is associated with technological control of the environment. In short, Americans assume that environment can be subjugated to the human will, given enough time, effort and money. And this should be done – in the service of humankind.

This suggests an active and dynamic orientation and a willingness to make risky decisions. Growth is seen as a vital need in the United States in its own right (Humes, 1993, p. 112), but also to grow bigger:

> Big has always been the American calling card. In fact, I bet you can't drive more than seventy-five miles in any direction, from anywhere in the United States, without running into a 'biggest in the world' of some sort. (Peters, 1989, p. 13)

Some outsiders see American companies obsessed with mergers, acquisitions and short-term gains (Kobayashi, 1990, p. 8).

Controlling today (for the future) means to control time. In the United States, 'time is money'; it should be carefully used, properly budgeted and should not be wasted.

> Thus, time becomes a major concern, and in fact, plays a central role in the everyday life of the typical North American. The majority of adults in the United States have strapped to their wrist a device that divides hours into minutes and minutes into seconds, so that no matter where we are we will always know the correct time. We punch timeclocks to determine the quantity of our work. We measure how long it takes a sprinter to run 100 meters in hundredth of a second. Even the biological function of eating is done in response to the clock, for we often eat because it is lunchtime or dinnertime. Several years ago a major US watch company spent millions of dollars on an advertising campaign that claimed that their watches were guaranteed to lose less than two seconds per month. Clearly, the company would not have spent that much money to convey that particular message if it was not what the American consumer wanted to hear. (Ferraro, 1994, pp. 91–2)

Cultures with a sequential view of time, such as the United States (and Britain), are usually short term in their business strategies. Cultures with a synchronic view of time, for instance in Japan (or in Germany), are typically long term strategically (Trompenaars, 1995, p. 174). On the other hand, promptness in American society is highly valued. To be kept waiting is often taken as an insult or a sign of irresponsibility and, if late for an appointment, an apology is expected to be offered (Ferraro, 1994, p. 92).

There was a time when the United States took the ethnocentric view that they were the greatest, and that everybody else was trying to reach their standard. One example (according to Humes, 1993, p. 141) is an American business management professor who said: 'The only difference between the American way of doing things and the way the rest of the world does things is that the rest of the world hasn't caught up yet'.

The United States, as a superpower, is naturally highly criticized (as well as praised), for instance, because of overcommercialization or because of a society breaking up, going from *Gemeinschaft* to *Gesellschaft* (a distinction introduced by the German sociologist Tönnies more than 100 years ago). Occasionally, US firms successfully use American themes abroad (Koontz and Weihrich, 1988, p. 238). However, phenomena such as McDonald's and Coke in a society may mean that it has adopted a foreign cultural manifestation without necessarily having changed its own (deeper) cultural values, which is, as mentioned before, an important distinction to me.

Americans live in a society where youthfulness is appreciated (Ferraro, 1994, p. 109). Americans tend to emphasize what is new and young by maintaining a youthful spirit. The American free enterprise system has encouraged this love affair with all things new. As part of their future orientations, Americans prefer to conform to standards that are momentarily current and up to date rather than old-fashioned (Samovar et al., 1981, p. 79). Old-fashioned, however, is not the same as conservative. Even if there is a tendency in the American type of societies to be less conservative (Hofstede, 1984, p. 140), it may be fashionable to be conservative – particularly if an aspect of the American way of life is threatened!

On the business scene, American managers endorse 'modern' management and try to be up to date (Hofstede, 1984, p. 174). The American business style has truly been popular (and in many parts of the world still is).

Americans see it as almost a right to be materially well off and physically comfortable. They expect convenient transport, a variety of clean and healthful foods and comfortable homes equipped with labour-saving devices.

> Materialism is a major force behind the American genius for devising and employing machines to provide efficiency and convenience in daily life. Americans

> are famous for taking all kinds of gadgets and machines with them on their trips abroad. They exhibit a strong tendency to perceive their tasks as requiring the use of machines, tools, and equipment. (Samovar et al., 1981, pp. 68–9)

The high value placed on materialism in the American culture in the sense of 'using various mechanical and electronics tools to accomplish a task' is sometimes reflected in the ethnocentric attitude towards other individuals, groups and societies as being 'underdeveloped' or 'poor', if they do not have the high standard of living expected by many Americans. Achievement is defined according to Hofstede (1984, p. 200) in terms of personal recognition and wealth.

Unlike many cultures in the East, the West has developed separate institutions with separate spheres of influence for the spiritual life and for the material aspects of life for human beings. This means that the spiritual and social life of humankind in Western thinking is outside work (Pascale and Athos, 1982, pp. 17–18). One of the most important distinctions in American life is to separate work from play. American culture is very doing-oriented. The country is almost a perfect example of a culture that stresses activity and work. Americans also believe that individuals can influence the nature by hard work and customers by heavy advertising. Promotion and pay in the United States is also based on performance, not seniority. The stress on efficiency in the United States has always impressed observers.

> *Efficiency* is a word of high praise in this society that has long emphasized adaptability, technological innovation, economic expansion, mass production, standardization, up-to-dateness, practicality, expediency, and 'getting things done'. The mere listing of these words and phrases reveals how the multiple extensions of efficiency are used as a standard against which activity is judged. American concern for efficiency at once sets this society apart from others that place greater emphasis upon aesthetic, contemplative, ritualistic, mystical, or outer-worldly concerns. (Samovar et al., 1981, p. 70)

Time orientation is also, as mentioned earlier, very intensive in the American culture. So, when an American manager complains that 'I've spent the whole damn day on the phone', he or she is giving voice to the image that a precious resource – time – may have been wasted (Johnson, 1988, p. 42).

It can even be said that American problem-solving is scientific instead of traditional. Logic and scientific methods have been internalized as the means of solving new problems and solutions are perceived as progress or improvements. Science, as it is being practiced in the United States, is based on the assumption that reality is and can be rationally ordered by humans, thereby being predictable and manoeuvrable.

Americans are, in principle, very informal. They also tend to be on the expressive side. North Americans also frequently assume that informality is a prerequisite for sincerity. Conflicts in American organizations are consequently rather normal. Deviant behaviour is not felt like a threat; people have greater tolerance and preparedness to trust others. Americans tend to exhibit emotion, yet separate it from 'objective' and 'rational' decisions (Trompenaars, 1995, p. 66). This could be seen as a result of the clear distinction between work and pleasure in the United States.

There are no generally recognized social classes in the United States, income and achievement act as the main differentiators, and the American culture emphasizes equality in social relations. If we were to choose the hallmark of American culture, this should probably be the value of the individual (Hofstede, 1984, p. 158; Humes, 1993, p. 113; Ferraro, 1994, p. 109), that is, reliance on the individual initiative, self-assertion, personal achievement and responsibility.

> The ideal of the individual is deeply rooted in American social, political, and economic institutions. Although historians, philosophers, and social scientists don't always agree on its origins or its more recent forms, there is a general understanding that the value of the individual is supreme and it is the individual who has the capacity to shape his or her destiny. (Ferraro, 1994, p. 88).

Some fundamental characteristics of individualistic cultures are (Samovar et al., 1981, pp. 75–7; Hofstede, 1984, pp. 92, 132–3, 153, 154, 166–7, 171, 173–4; Schwind and Peterson, 1985, p. 71; Arvonen, 1989, p. 102; Bjerke, 1989, p. 41; Ferraro, 1994, pp. 91, 109; Trompenaars, 1995, pp. 51–4, 142–4):

- Nuclear families and independent children
- Private lives and opinions appreciated
- Self-orientation and self-motivation
- Freedom and variety are important
- Education promotes independence
- Individual initiative is encouraged
- Stronger ambition for individual advancement and leadership
- Individuals do the job and are rewarded as such

- Cosmopolitan outlook
- Strong feelings against collectivism

Though the American culture appreciates other kinds of achievements as well (actors, entertainers, statespeople, scientists and generals, to name but a few), promotion in business serves as the main path for moving up the ladder for most people in that society.

Closely associated with the American preference for individualism, freedom and achievement is the emphasis placed on competition. The status of the individual in a country like the United States is tied to education and knowledge and in the American type of culture, experts are treated with great respect and loyalties to a profession are greater than loyalties to the company. Even the 'profession' as manager is looked at as being a specialist and an expert.

The American business culture can be typified as in Table 10.2. This gives, among other things, the following prerequisites for entrepreneurship in the United States:

- Strength is measured by size
- Do not stand still – always move forward and renew what you are doing
- Gain control of your situation
- You can always make it if you work hard enough – and the opposite
- Take a 'scientific' approach to things
- There are always solutions even if they are less sometimes possible
- Success in business is a dream and it is admired
- Rewards are given individually and kept individually
- What you are doing is your own business

Table 10.2 American business culture

⇨ Progress and growth
⇨ Modernity
⇨ Materialism
⇨ Activity and work orientation
⇨ Informality and equality
⇨ Logic, efficiency and pragmatism
⇨ Individualism and achievement
⇨ Freedom and competition
⇨ Knowledge and specialization

Arab business culture

One word is paramount in understanding culture throughout the Arab world. This word is religion. Religion relates to more aspects of life there than in few other places. It also has an impact on Arab thinking in business. Islam holds that the world is built up by two realities: one divine and one created (Samovar et al., 1981, p.93). Allah, the divine, created the world as we know it for the pleasure of mankind. The created world is available to everybody, but the divine reality is revealed only to a few. To gain access to this divine reality there are many rules to follow for a Muslim. Religion becomes part of a Muslim's daily life, and a visitor to the Arab world who shows respect for the Islamic religion will gain a favourable reception almost everywhere. Generally, speaking, religion can be a way of coping with an uncertain future and religion can reinforce differences in uncertainty avoidance between cultures (Hofstede, 1984, p. 137).

In modern times, the dominating factor in the consciousness of most Middle Easterners has been the impact of the West (it started historically with Europe) and the transformation – some say dislocation – which it has brought. Most cultures in the Middle East are traditional and Muslim and caught in the midst of conflict and change. Some Arab political leaders feel, therefore, that:

> there is no need for the Arabs to choose between alien ideologies, such as capitalism or socialism, conservatism and liberalism, democracy and authoritarianism. Instead, they feel that these choices are unnecessary if only the tenets of the Islamic Shari'a [Islamic law] are applied as the guiding principles of economic, governmental, and community law. (Muna, 1980, p. 15)

The desire to maintain both the Arabic and the Islamic identity is prominent not only in political circles, but also among Arab academics and businessmen (to Westerners, few women are seen in business). There is therefore much emotional resistance to change the Arab type of culture (Hofstede, 1984, p. 132) and problem-solving procedures follow precedents or adapt old procedures to new situations without any major change. Departure from tradition is generally presumed to be bad until proved otherwise. The Arab world is a clear example that modernization is not the same as Westernization.

As a consequence of traditionalism, nationalism and a lack of trust in foreign management principles, joint venture is a common approach for foreigners who want to start a business in the Arab world (Bjerke and Kazi, 1990, p. 1).

> [Arab culture] has its own special breed of entrepreneurs, who, with a mixture of innate desert cunning and Western sophistication, have managed to build their own business empires, both at home and in Europe and elsewhere. The oil boom provided dramatic examples of highly successful businessmen who moved from investing in industrial development projects to buying controlling interests in Western banks and on to financing petrochemical plants and shipping fleets (even amusement parks). Some [Arab] businessmen started off as importers or exporters, or both. They developed an ability to locate deficiencies in their own national economy and seeked [sic.] to fill the gaps with imported skills and finished goods. (At-Twaijri, 1989a, p. 7)

Cultures vary in terms of how explicitly they send or receive verbal messages. Arab culture is a high-contextual culture. This means that communication between people relies heavily on hidden, implicit, contextual cues such as non-verbal behaviour, social context and the nature of interpersonal relationships. To a foreigner, communication between Arabs may sound very inexact, implicit and indirect. This means that in a high-contextual culture such as the Arab one, non-verbal communication is very important and there is a lot of it there. Arabs 'speak' very much with their hands and use facial expressions extensively. Details are important in such an 'intense' and 'all-penetrating' culture as the Arab one. Middle Easterners are excellent interpreters of contexts and good psychologists, including skilled negotiators. Negotiation and bargaining is an art in the Middle East (as well as in other high-contextual cultures like the Chinese one and the Japanese one).

In one sense, Arabs are very social and informal. For instance, titles are not a general cultural manifestation, except for royal families, ministers and high-level military officers. Arabs are also generally very generous and hospitable. One can say, however, that the Arab culture is also very ritualistic. They score very high in uncertainty avoidance (Bjerke and Al-Meer, 1993, p. 32). And as much as social informal rules are not to be broken, neither are rules in a business setting (Hofstede, 1984, p. 133). Rituals play many roles in the Arab world.

Arab culture manifests a definite class structure. The Arab class is based on the family (tribe) and its background. In the Arab type of culture, people are born into extended families or clans. Children are socialized in this kind of family structure and become closely identified with family and kin. Among Arabs, like the Chinese, there is a deep commitment to family honour, loyalties and responsibilities. People are motivated by security and belonging (Hofstede, 1984, p. 256). There is an intrinsic satisfaction in being loved and respected (Trompenaars, 1995, p. 160). To live in a collectively oriented culture as the Arab one means that individuality is a negligible value (Sitaram and Cogdell, 1976, p. 191). Care is more important than individual freedom (Trompenaars, 1995, pp. 47–8). It means also that social relationships are predetermined and people think in terms of ingroup and outgroups (Hofstede, 1984, p. 167).

It is easy to understand that values like friendship and trust play a major role in the Arab type of culture. In fact, policies and practices are based on loyalty and a sense of duty in such a culture (Hofstede, 1984, p. 173). Loyalty is seen as a virtue and considered more important than efficiency (Muna, 1980, p. 80). The latter may even be ranked as a tertiary value (Sitaram and Cogdell, 1976, p. 191).

The low stress on efficiency among Arabs is associated with the fact that their sense of time is less strict than among Westerners. Punctuality is of tertiary value (Sitaram and Cogdell, 1976, p. 191), and it may take a long time for a visitor to see the host at his office, even if an appointment is made. A Middle Easterner does not assume nor exercise control over his time. Issues and actions are triggered by whether the time is right, not on schedule or by reference to a mechanism. Patience is a virtue among Arabs (Harris and Moran, 1987, pp. 62 ff).

This fits well with what I have said about Arab culture so far that organization pyramids are very steep – steepest of all in an international comparison made by Trompenaars (1995, p. 114). They are tall and centralized (Hofstede, 1984, p. 107). What usually follows from such steep pyramids – and maybe particularly so in the Arab culture – is that top-down communication is dominant and that authoritarianism becomes a primary value (Sitaram and Cogdell, 1976, p. 191). This could be called 'management by subjectives' instead of 'management by objectives' (Trompenaars, 1995, p. 160).

One interesting aspect of the Arab culture is that the distinction between formal and informal is not very useful as far as organizations are concerned. (The same thing is the case for many other seemingly clear Westerner classifications when attempting to characterize Arab organizations). It may appear on the surface that superior–subordinate interaction is very formal and restricted and that informal discussions with subordinates are avoided. The Arab organizational type has been characterized as 'full democracy', that is, relations between people as well as work processes are rigidly prescribed (Hofstede, 1984, pp. 215–7).

However, the point is that these prescriptions are not uniform. The Arab organization does not work as a bureaucracy in the Max Weber sense! Arab executives conduct business in a leisurely way. They dislike, in fact, foreigners' 'business-is-business' impersonal notion (Muna, 1980, p. 85–6), but that is not all. Arabs are truly more person-oriented than role- or task-oriented. Their management approach is even personal and pragmatic to the extent that procedures may differ from one occasion to the next, even if the two occasions are similar and even if in both cases rules being applied could be very strict! One estimate is that public rules and regulations are applied only about 20 per cent of the time (ibid., p. 83).

I have heard visitors saying that Arab bureaucratic organizations do not work, but they do! However, this is understandable only if you are able to untangle their complicated web of power play and get inside their high-contextual daily life. Some authors call it 'organized chaos'. I invented the impossible concept 'formal informality' (which Arabs became very fond of).

The Arab executive is, like executives in other cultures, influenced by the structure of the society outside his firm and by the values, norms and expectations of its people. One consequence of this in the Arab case is that he sees himself as a father figure:

> The [Arab] executive's role within his community and organization is shaped to a considerable extent by the expectations of relatives, friends and employees. The top executive, by virtue of his position in the organization, sees himself as the head of a family: employees are seen as members of that family. (Muna, 1980, p. 1)

It is a common opinion that Arabs are fatalists:

> Arab behaviour is greatly influenced by the belief that destiny depends more on the will of a supreme being than on individual behaviour. A higher power dictates the outcome of important events, so individual action is of little consequence. This thinking affects not only individuals' aspirations but also their motivation. (Hodgetts and Luthans, 1991, p. 37).

There are at least two objectives to this view:

1. There are within Islam as many precepts exhorting initiative, rationalism and activism as there are precepts which encourage fatalism. The Hadith (interpretations of the holy Koran) admonishes man first to think and plan ahead, then put his trust in Allah (Muna, 1980, p. 95).
2. It is too simplistic to generalize that most Arabs (Muslims or non-Muslims) are fatalistic regardless of their socioeconomic and educational background. My experience from the Arab world is that this

pattern is much more complicated. The category of people of interest in my studies, that is, business leaders, do not, in general, fit into this stereotypical mould.

It is perhaps the frequent use among Arabs of the phrase *Insha'Allah* ('if God is willing') that flavours the opinion of many expatriates and foreign visitors. However, instead of interpreting this phrase as a sign of resignation and inactivity, a person should (perhaps particularly in business circles) see it more as a sign of Arabs' view of patience as a virtue (which I have mentioned earlier) and that the expression has the approximate meaning 'Let us see. I hope it will be so'.

Middle Easterners act on emotion; in contrast, Americans are taught to act on logic (which was mentioned in the last section). Emotional expressions are common among Arabs. Because they act so intuitively and spontaneously, some say that they are conflict-prone. Being very temperamental, Middle Easterners may try to avoid arguments at first, but once in a discussion, there is a lower readiness to compromise with opponents (Hofstede, 1984, p. 133). Peace, in the general sense of it, is of negligible value in Muslim cultures (Sitaram and Cogdell, 1976, p. 191).

Arabs have, however, developed a unique mechanism for settling disputes, that is, 'the mediator'. Mediation has for centuries been the traditional method of settling disputes on the tribal and village level, and it has been adapted to the modern world. The mediator, who is a person in a higher social position than the feuding parties, has as a task to separate and restrain them. These parties are supposed to restrain themselves out of respect for the mediator. The greater prestige of the mediator, the higher the chance of him being successful. Reconciliation, not judgement of (legal) right or wrong, is the purpose of mediation. The mediators mediate. They do not arbitrate or act as any kind of judge. A compromise through mediation in Arab societies means that the personal values of the parties are compromised. Arabs also believe that mediation is rooted in a certain realism, that is, all problems do not have neat solutions.

The Arab business culture can be typified as in Table 10.3. This gives, among other things, the following prerequisites for entrepreneurship among Arabs:

- Always think of Muslim rules – also in business
- What is new must be adapted to the society
- There are long-established rules for how things are to be done
- There are many rules and, operatively, I decide because I am the boss

Table 10.3 Arab business culture

⇨ Tradition and religion
⇨ A trader's mentality
⇨ High-context and symbolism
⇨ Social but ritualistic
⇨ Loyalty and belonging
⇨ Authoritarianism and formal informality
⇨ Paternalism
⇨ Fatalism
⇨ Caring but conflict-prone

- Do not try on your own if you are outside the top layer in the firm or the society
- Industrial democracy – what is that?
- Access to finances only if you have a higher social status
- Low (imported) labour costs

Chinese business culture

Everyone in China is at least half philosopher (Chu, 1991, p. 187). Also, Asian culture has no clearly defined division between religion, philosophy and business. Faith and philosophy are lived every day as a way of life. To understand the Chinese, for example in the context of business styles, it is important to understand the principles by which they live and to what extent the teachings of their philosophers are applicable today.

Chinese religion has no direct equivalent to Western or Middle Eastern scriptures, but there are mythologies as well as moral and ethical philosophical writings. The oldest and most complete book of Chinese mythology is the *Mountain Sea Scriptures*. This is a combination of several works, some of which are over 4000 years old. This book maintains, among other things, that creation and development is a process of combining *Yin* and *Yang* forces, the female and male aspects of energy. This concept of a positive and a negative side of all things influences many aspects of Asian life and thought (Chu, 1991, pp. 175–6).

Philosophically, there are several major influences affecting Chinese thinking, including Confucianism, Buddhism and Taoism (Harris and Moran, 1987, p. 309; Hoon-Holbauer, 1994, p. 84). Of these, Confucianism turned out to be the most viable. Confucius' teachings on personal ethics have been established among Chinese as a set of pragmatic rules daily life (Hofstede and Bond, 1988, pp. 7–8; Lasserre and Schütte, 1995, p. 131; Naisbitt, 1995, p. 80). These rules, or values, include hard work, thriftiness, obedience, patience and perseverance. They are to be achieved through strict respect of traditional hierarchical relationships and the importance of acquiring skills and education.

It is a common belief that the Chinese interest in philosophy also includes an interest in strategy:

> Since Asians believe that the marketplace is a battlefield and that life is a series of battles, they also believe that mastering military strategy is essential for success, as well as for survival. Asian rules have always placed great importance studying the classical Chinese treaties on military strategy, the *Bing-Fa*. The common people have also studied them and continue to study them in order to apply their principles to the affairs of daily life. (Chu, 1991, p. 12)

This should mean that modern business strategies applied by Asians can be seen as updated versions of old Chinese texts on military strategy.

This is a nice thought, but I believe it is a myth, at least as far as Chinese business *applications* are concerned. I have experienced these people as having many adequate business qualities. They are extremely good at exploiting opportunities and at deal-making; they are masters of financial, in particular cash, management; in short, they are a result of a long series of opportunistic tactical moves. They are persistent, enduring and may survive in business for a long time by simply accumulating slim short-term gains, but perseverance and long-term existence is not the same as strategic thinking!

Characteristics of a Chinese business enterprise include an autocratic, centralized type of management. The Chinese type of culture implies (Hofstede, 1984, p. 92):

- Managers are seen as making decisions autocratically and paternalistically, but also pragmatically;
- Employees fear disagreeing with their boss;
- Weaker perceived work ethic; more frequent belief that people dislike work;
- Employees reluctant to trust each other.

Personal bureaucracy could be a good word for characterizing Chinese organizations and leadership style. Unlike Western firms that are supposed to concentrate on 'core competencies' (what they are best at), in Chinese firms, managers want to have a hand in most things connected with their business (*The Economist*, 1995, p. 27). The Chinese way is to control everything (*Business Week*, 1995, p. 31). And everybody who is not a key individual (a member of the extended family (a member of the extended family, functioning more on trust) is supervised (Redding, 1993, p. 217). 'Business leaders are control freaks' (*Business Week*, 1997, p. 52). 'The search for control was held by a number of people (interviewed) to be a basic instinct, somehow a natural part of being Chinese' (Redding, 1993, p. 88).

By being pragmatic (often corrupt in Western eyes) and sometimes by copying (occasionally illegal in the same eyes), many Chinese business millionaires (sometimes billionaires) have started from a humble trading position or an intermediary background (not very innovative professions), building up conglomerates concentrating on businesses such as property, shipping, hotels and telecoms. Because they find it hard to separate management from ownership, they tend to 'avoid industries that require the complex integration of many different skills' (*The Economist*, 1996c, p. 70).

Power is very important to the Chinese (Jansson, 1987, p. 15) and the Chinese culture is a very power-centred culture. One way to show 'class' is through money and material possessions. The Chinese culture is generally very materialistic. The old Chinese principle of avoiding excesses to keep a proper balance between the opposite forces of *Yin* and *Yang* often seems to be neglected in our modern times. The Chinese have difficulties in letting go of money (Jansson, 1987, p. 26); there is a worship of power and money according to some (Yang, 1991, p. 111). It is not greed, however, that drives Chinese to be so money-oriented; it is fear – and the yearning for the protection that money will give you (*The Economist*, 1996a, March, p. 12).

The Chinese are very secretive. They like to keep information to themselves; they do not want to expose anything about their business outside the inner family. But what is shown to the environment is that success is measured in numbers and that marketing is limited to sales. Western inventions such as advertising and sales promotion hardly exist at all (except in the networking sense). The Chinese seem to deliberately avoid entering the world of mass marketing and brand name goods (Redding, 1993, p. 229). They have also no sense of after-sales service. Once a deal is done, it is done.

Concentrating so much on sales and sales numbers may occasionally mean that quality becomes of less significance. Lack of quality control is also often a problem in the Chinese workplace.

The one thing the Chinese are good at, however, is financial control. Chinese entrepreneurs 'have an excellent mastery of financial levers' (Lasserre and Schütte, 1995, p. 106), and in their daily business dealing, they pay close attention to cash management. In order to always have cash available to be ready for any profitable deal that may turn up can lead a Chinese to selling his or her goods at a lower price (even at a loss) in order to move money faster and even to borrowing money in a bank and then saving it at the same bank again to increase his or her assurance of access to ready cash, even if the bank is changing its credit policy (Limlingan, 1986, pp. 86–91).

As long as the Chinese make money, they feel that time is on their side, thinking in terms of sales and financial outcome makes the Chinese prone to short-term thinking (Jansson, 1987, p. 23; Lasserre and Schütte, 1995, p. 131). However, foreign firms trying to do business with the Chinese should not think short term. A lot of time is involved in acquiring experience and cultivating relationships for an outsider. Laboriously established connections can easily break down. The point is not to work with the Chinese in the sense of a complete strategic package, but accumulating trust, one step at a time. Time is not equal to money for the Chinese, as it tends to be in the West. In the Chinese culture, time is time, and money is money.

Asian tradition puts the right of the group ahead of any individual (Seagrave, 1996, p. 367). In Asian cultures, individuals have a very deep attachment and sense of belonging to social groups (Hoon-Holbauer, 1994, p. 85; Lasserre and Schütte, 1995, p. 270). Asian countries score very low on individualism (Hofstede, 1984, p. 158). The importance of the family and of strong family ties has been certified by many (Harris and Moran, 1987, p. 311; Chau, 1991, p. 161; Chu, 1991, pp. 200–201; Hoon-Halbauer, 1994, p. 89).

The Asian business environment can best be described as a series of interlocked networks (Lasserre and Schütte, 1995, p. 124). It is a key element of Chinese business (Hoon-Holbauer, 1994, p. 85). The distinctive feature of the Chinese business model has never been the individual firm, but the network of them (Rohwer, 1995, pp. 240–1). In Chinese this is called *guan-xi*, which is similar to what we refer to as social capital and it can be translated as 'relationships' or 'connections'.

Everywhere in the business world contacts are needed, but their importance must be magnified many times to understand *guan-xi* (Chu, 1991, p. 199). Hundreds of books have been written about *guan-xi*, but it takes a lifetime to master. Every society in Asia is built around relationships and it is more than a matter of degree compared with the West. The Chinese carry around their relationships as part of their person. This philosophy has deep roots.

> *Guan-xi* grew out of an agricultural society in which people swapped favours with neighbours, relatives and friends of friends. Like fishermen, Chinese make nets of *guan-xi* in which knots are tied with marriage, school, clubs, secret societies, both forward and backward in time. You can collect *guan-xi* built up by your mother or grandfather. It can be inherited or conveyed. Under communism, business was not arranged for profit but for *guan-xi*, a different kind of collateral that bypasses official channels. *Guan-xi* eases pain. It stops bullets. Feuds are ended by calling in someone obliged by *guan-xi* to both parties, who negotiates a settlement. Some Chinese keep records of *guan-xi* in ledgers. A Singapore programmer has developed software to keep track of *guan-xi*. (Seagrave, 1996, p. 341).

In the West there is networking as only an aspect of ongoing business; in Asia, networking comes first, then comes business (*The Economist*, 1997, p. 73).

Culture may stress various parts of the body. For a Westerner, the 'heart' is important (that is where our feelings are supposed to be); for a Japanese, it is the 'stomach' (the centre of harmony). An important aspect of Chinese culture is 'face' (Hoon-Holbauer, 1994, p. 85).

The fear of losing face is nothing else but the fear of having one's ego and one's prestige deflated. It can be caused by a broad range of things: having an expected promotion fall through; a child failing an examination; a daughter marrying a poor man; a brother working in a lowly position; receiving an inexpensive gift and so on (Chu, 1991, p. 197).

The logical counterpart to 'losing' face is 'gaining' face. The prestige of a Chinese may be inflated by working in a large company, by being surrounded by 'influential' friends, by showing off materially or so on.

Asian cultures stress 'shame' and Western cultures stress 'guilt'. Shame is associated with public disgrace and loss of prestige and guilt carries a sense of individual responsibility and conscience (Lasserre and Schütte, 1995, p. 273). The importance of shame for a Chinese person makes it difficult for him or her to admit a mistake (Jansson, 1987, p. 17; Yang, 1991, p. 14) or to ask for help (Lasserre and Schütte, 1995, p. 273). Also, they are not happy to be told how to do things, especially in public (Jansson, 1987, p. 17).

Most Asians are extremely superstitious. When the Chinese person is faced with an important decision, they may seek auspicious signs or consult oracular books or fortune-tellers. They may also give special significance to colour, generally favouring red (for life) and gold (for prosperity) (Chu, 1991, pp. 162–3). Being superstitious is one way of 'cushion oneself' against failure in the face of risk (Wong, 1995, p. 144).

> The prevalence of certain traditional mystical or superstitious practices in China and South-East Asia may come as a surprise to the unprepared Western manager. Even in the more industrialised and Westernised Chinese societies, notably Hong Kong, Taiwan and Singapore, certain traditional practices still prevail and should not be overlooked. To cite one example: geomancy, also known as *feng shui*, or the divination and interpretation of certain landscape features and sacred sites, is still widely practiced in the Chinese world. In practical terms this means that real-estate purchases and building sites must first be approved by a geomancer. Whether Western expatriate managers approve of this process or not, they should not disregard the fact that their Asian staff and colleagues will consider it an important procedure. (Lasserre and Schütte, 1995, p. 276)

On the other hand, taking decisions directly, relationally and specifically as the Chinese often do, gives them a trust in themselves and in common sense, plus a high willingness to take risks and an ability to face uncertainty. The Chinese score low on uncertainty avoidance (Hofstede, 1984, p. 122) and they excel in risk taking (Jansson, 1987, p. 22; Chen, 1995, p. 108).

The Chinese business culture can be typified as in Table 10.4. This gives, among other things, the following prerequisites for entrepreneurship among Chinese:

Table 10.4 Chinese business culture

⇨ Philosophy and strategy
⇨ Autocracy and pragmatism
⇨ Power and materialism
⇨ Sales and quick results
⇨ Familism
⇨ *Guan-xi*
⇨ Face and prestige
⇨ Superstitious but risk-willing

- Material gain = own success
- Always be prepared for a negotiation
- Commit yourself quickly, if it looks promising; backing from the environment comes (eventually) later
- Play the role that looks suitable – do not care about who is 'really' you
- To be secretive is a strength; keep in within the family
- Control everything
- Always think of your 'face'
- Contacts, contacts, contacts
- Take risks (if the signs are right)

Japanese business culture

The 'core' of Japan is the bureaucracy, parliament and big business. On top of that, there is a high degree of cooperation between Japanese business and government. This close relationship has deep historical roots and has been going on for a long time (Namiki and Sethi, 1988, p. 61).

> Government and business representatives tend to work and plan closely together. Objectives are usually formed by the two groups in collaboration. When the government makes a policy statement, business has had a hand in formulating it. The large trading companies are economic leaders and work directly with the government in setting economic policy. The Bank of Japan reviews the impact of any agreements that might influence the domestic economy. Their evaluation and recommendation are then sent to other concerned government agencies. Government involvement is essential in any major negotiations that affect either the national interest or those of an entire industry.
>
> It is prudent to be aware of appropriate government channels, as the achievement of national objectives is a mutual aim of both business and government. Both the Economic Planning Agency and the Ministry of International Trade and Industry (MITI) establish guidelines for all international transactions. Guidelines are enforced not by the agencies themselves, but by individual agents who act as intermediaries between the public and private sector.
>
> Yet it would be wrong to assume that business and government in Japan have a single compatible goal in mind at all times. Conflict does arise, both within different government ministries, as well as between competing economic sectors. Unlike many Western nations, the Japanese government enjoys a proportionately small ownership of industry. This private industry maintains a very powerful voice in Japan's economic direction. (Moran, 1988, p. 44)

It could be claimed without exaggeration that Japan is a planned economy (*The Economist*, 1993, p. 12). Japan Inc. is actually an expansion of the corporate culture idea on a national scale (Deal and Kennedy, 1988, p.5). Today's bureaucracy at senior levels in Japan is like the old political class from its history in a new guise – 'leadership by an intelligent élite with moral obligation to guide the people' (*Business Week*, 1991, p. 18).

Japan remains at heart a feudal society (*The Economist*, 1990, p. 11). This is, for instance, shown in the fact that democracy is practiced more in form than in substance (Namiki and Sethi, 1988, p.64). The Japanese are highly rank-conscious. Higher-ranking persons expect respect from those below (At-Twaijri, 1989b, p.35). Because the position and status of a person play such a big role in Japan, the Japanese have developed a complicated system to draw attention to such matters (Pascale and Athos, 1982, p. 120).

Maybe Japan's greatest strength is loyal, hardworking people. It has been referred to as its 'only national resource' (Peters and Waterman, 1982, p.39). Japan's culture inspires workers to excel (Waterman, 1982, p.70), and this type of culture has strong superegos and an inner urge to work hard (Hofstede, 1984, p. 140).

The Japanese have learnt to live with scarcity. Physical and geographic density in Japan has made its people not only reinforce groupism, interdependence and a sense of debt and obligation, but also to excel in material handling, transportation, quality control, cutting out waste, energy conservation and convertibility (McMillan, 1985, pp.20–1).

There is an age-old passion in Japan for smallness and craftsmanship. The folding fan, miniature gardening, the tea ceremony and other ritual staples of the Japanese life all stem from this (Peters, 1989, p. 15). Its emphasis on quality fits nicely with its skills, in particular its bent for craft (nonspecialized) labour and its use of the worker as the primary means of adding value to a product (ibid., p. 13). The repertoire of Japanese management practices generally includes quality circles (QCs) and zero defect movements fully implemented (Johnson, 1988, p.35). And the Japanese understanding of quality is all-inclusive (Nadler, 1984, pp.50–1).

I mentioned earlier that the Japanese have a synchronic view on time, not sequential. This means, for instance, that the Japanese do not use the word 'strategy' the way it is understood in the West. They have, rather, a method of coevolving with customers (Trompenaars, 1995, p. 174). This means, also, that 'decision-making' as an act at a specific point in time does not make sense in the Japanese culture. Decision process and implementation overlap without any precise moment of decision in between (Söderman, 1983, p. 8). The Japanese language does not even have an equivalent for 'decision-making' (Hofstede, 1984, p. 27).

The Japanese have a mixed attitude to the future. On one hand, they hate uncertainty (Hofstede, 1984, p. 122). However, on the other hand, the Japanese can accept more uncertainty, ambiguity and incompleteness. Certain things simply *are* and should be accepted as such (Pascale and Athos, 1982, p. 88). The Japanese do not think, for instance, that it is worth trying to control nature (Trompenaars, 1995, pp. 126–7).

What complicates the picture is that the Japanese commonly believe in *karma* (Sanskrit = 'deed'), which is a Buddhist understanding that the sum of a person's acts is a link between his or her different existences in the wheel of reincarnation. These acts are not given from outside. There is, at least partly, a choice. In the context of business, Japanese see the future as full of complications and the idea is not to explore possibilities, but to solve problems (Sallivan and Nonaka, 1988, pp. 7–8). This can be explained historically. Some of Japan's worst disasters are constant reminders of the link between geography and nature's peril (McMillan, 1985, p. 24). The idea is not to create the future, as in American culture, but to dominate a selected section of it, to prepare the battleground through a thorough information intelligence operation (Dedijer, 1991). 'It is a known fact that Japanese military thought and strategies have tremendous influence on Japanese management practice' (Wee et al., 1991, p. 4).

The Japanese conquest of world markets is very much like a well-directed military campaign.

Several studies show that Japanese culture is one of the most high-contextual cultures there is (competing with the Arabs and the Chinese for this position) (Czinkota et al., 1994, p. 231; Ferraro, 1994, pp. 51–2). Verbal communication in Japan is implicative, that is, comprehending the subject of communication through linkages to its environment or other events, relying on analogies, symbolisms and indirect statements. To announce something is, for the Japanese, only half the truth. The other half is who the announcer is and what is going on behind the stage (Pascale and Athos, 1982, p. 92).

The Japanese appreciate mild, undemonstrative and humble attitudes. They are extremely anxious to avoid unpleasantness or confrontation, like the Chinese, 'saving face' is a key concept (Pascale and Athos, 1982,

p. 99; Moran, 1988, p. 43). Exhibiting emotion is not acceptable in Japan (Trompenaars, 1995, pp. 63–4). Aggressiveness is a tertiary value (Sitaram and Cogdell, 1976, p. 191). The Japanese are therefore not likely to say 'no' directly lest it offends someone. With the Japanese, too, a 'yes' at first is not to be taken as a firm 'yes'. It may be just a polite 'yes' which keeps the door open for further discussions, which later on may lead to 'no' (Moore, 1982, p. 538). A 'yes' (or rather a non-'no') may contribute to a pleasant atmosphere (Kawasaki, 1984, p. 6). So a 'yes' can mean many things and should be interpreted contextually (Ferraro, 1994, pp. 52–3). Along the same lines, how something is said could be more important that what is said in Japan. Tactfulness and indirectness are highly valued.

A Japanese person has relations with many different kinds of groups with strict roles to be played and well-defined obligations in each, that is, the household instils the sense of ordered hierarchy where the father and the eldest son are very close; the group guided by a mentor transmit loyalty and attachment or the rice paddy community with its collective norms or obligations and status (McMillan, 1985, p. 37). The group is also the basic unit at work (Pascale and Athos, 1982, p. 123; Humes, 1993, p. 112; Trompenaars, 1995, pp. 51–2). The group takes decisions, assumes responsibility, does the job and is rewarded (Arvonen, 1989, p. 132). But the Japanese do not only value a group higher than its members but also order and harmony among people in a group more than the characteristics or the personal traits of any member (Harris and Morgan, 1987, p. 27).

To the Japanese businessman, organization *really* means people:

> When the Japanese say that organization is people, they really mean it. They know that a great many contemporary corporate problems fall outside the scope of organization or planning in a paperwork sense. Only active and alert organization members, working as an integrated team, can properly address and resolve them. (Ohmae, 1982, p. 227)

Another way to express this is to say that Japanese companies are run for the benefit of their employees – of, by and for its people (*Business Week*, 1991, p. 11). Japanese business leaders also have traditionally kept a low profile and operated as facilitators.

> Many Japanese chief executives, when asked what they consider their main responsibility, will say that they work for the well-being of their people. Stockholders do not rank much higher than bankers in their list of concerns. Most Japanese chief executive officers (CEOs) are in fact employed in much the same

way as factory workers, having climbed the corporate ladder starting in their early twenties and having been members of the company union before becoming *kacho* (section chiefs) in their mid-thirties. (Ohmae, 1982, p. 219)

As a consequence (but also a cause of) Japanese groupism, dedication and synchronous view of time, they have a long-term view (Humes, 1993, p. 112). The Japanese approach to business has also stressed harmony and cooperation more than speed (ibid, p. 117). There is a strong need for agreement among the Japanese and decisions are commonly made not by formal leaders, but built up by growing consensus called the *ringi* system.

> The concept of consensus in natural to the Japanese, but it does not necessarily mean that every decision comes out of a spontaneous group impulse. Gaining consensus in a Japanese company often means spending time preparing the groundwork for it, and very often the consensus is formed from the top down, not from the bottom up, as some observers of Japan have written. (Morita, 1986, p. 198)

Decision-making by consensus encourages initiatives for change from the lower rather than the upper management, diffuses a sense of responsibility to all members involved, and makes top management perform an essential role in the *ringi* system, of course. The system is effective only if the middle management is competent in bridging the gap between lower and higher levels of management. In Japanese firms middle managers acquire this skill partly through a system of job rotation from one function to another (Namiki and Sethi, 1988, pp. 79–80).

Due to all group pressure and orientation in Japan, performance appraisals are not very common there. If they exist, they are implicit and infrequent.

The Japanese business culture can be typified as in Table 10.5.

Table 10.5 Japanese business culture

⇨ Government-business connections
⇨ Feudalism, rank and work
⇨ Scarcity and quality
⇨ Domination and *karma*
⇨ Sensitivity and tactfulness
⇨ Groupism and harmony
⇨ Organization as people and facilitating leaders
⇨ Long-termism
⇨ Consensus

This gives, among other things, the following prerequisites for entrepreneurship among Japanese:

- Think long term
- Collect as much information as you can before you take the plunge
- Build on your strength
- It can be difficult to get around the establishment
- Use your resources as efficiently as possible
- Together we are strong – as Japanese
- Avoid conflicts – seek consensus

Scandinavian business culture

Scandinavians live in very egalitarian countries, where there is equality among sexes, among professions, among generations – among everything (Phillips-Martinsson, 1992, p. 19). The social norm in the Scandinavian type of culture is that inequality in society should be minimized (Hofstede, 1984, p. 94). There are no generally recognized social classes; one even has 'to work hard to "spot differences"' among people there (Lawrence and Spybey, 1986, p. 58). There are also smaller generation gaps. Kinship is relatively weak and parents put less value on children's obedience.

However, there is not only a feeling of equalitarianism in Scandinavia. There is also justice for all, a 'passion for equality', which goes far back in history (Andersen, 1984, p. 110). All should have equal rights, and laws and rules apply to all; privileges are not considered acceptable (Hofstede, 1984, pp. 94, 259). In modern terms, it can be said that there is a strong commitment to democratic values in Scandinavian countries (Lindkvist, 1988, p. 53), and 'a strong feeling for fair play' (ibid., p. 3).

However, Scandinavians do not score extremely low in individualism. They can accept rules and regulations (as long as they are fair) (Daun, 1989, p. 129).

> The researchers and management consultants interviewed find that the Nordic management culture, as a result of our history and religion, among other things, rests on equality and consensus. Cooperation between individuals is deeply rooted within the Nordic social democratic parties. Strong cooperation and high degree of unionization have framed our society. Within the Nordic countries a higher degree of altruism exists than is the case in the USA for example. But, at the same time, no affiliations with the clan exist as they do in Japan and Southern Europe. Thus, the

conclusion is that the Nordic countries are characterized by *collective individualism*. (Lindkvist, 1988, p. 27)

In the Scandinavian type of culture, hierarchy means inequality of roles which are established for convenience only. There is more communication in organizations and employees are less afraid of disagreeing with their boss (Hofstede, 1984, pp. 92, 94). Egalitarianism means co-determination at work in Scandinavian firms (Lawrence and Spybey, 1986, p. 123), and a democratic decision-making style. Industrial democracy fits well with the Scandinavian type of culture (Hofstede, 1984, pp. 268–9). The deeply entrenched egalitarianism of the Scandinavian culture has made it easier to introduce less formal, more delegating styles of management (*Business Week*, 1982, p. 79). It also means less centralization and flatter organization pyramids (Hofstede, 1984, p. 107; Trompenaars, 1995, p. 144).

People in the Scandinavian countries have an ingrained respect for rules, unlike, for instance, the Chinese (Yang, 1991, pp. 28–9). I do not mean that there is less crime in Scandinavia than elsewhere, only that the severity of legal punishment is not the main deterrent to breaking the law, cultural training is. This might be *one* reason why, in an international comparison, legal penalties are relatively mild in Scandinavia:

> As part of its initial backwardness, [Scandinavia] missed out of the feudal system and the economic structure that went with it. The peasants were never suppressed to the degree that they were in the rest of Europe, and to a large part were owners, under the Crown, of their own Land (Tomasson, 1970). On this basis they were consistently represented in the parliaments called by the King. It is difficult to avoid the impression that this was a solid foundation for the high level of involvement in and enthusiasm for government, engendering an ingrained respect for the law, for which [Scandinavia] has become so renowned. (Lawrence and Spybey, 1986, p. 2).

In one study (Phillips-Martinsson, 1992, p. 19), Scandinavians (in this case Swedes) describe themselves as 'well organized' and 'structured'. Scandinavians love tidiness and cleanliness, but are described as 'dull' (Lawrence and Spybey, 1986, pp. 20–1). Some call them 'uniform', 'inflexible', 'rigid' and 'bureaucratic' (Phillips-Martinsson, 1992, pp. 60, 62–3, 75).

In the same study (ibid., p. 19), Scandinavians describe themselves as 'reliable', 'honest', 'ethical', 'loyal' and 'correct'. Honesty among Scandinavians is certified by others as well (Lindkvist, 1988, p. 29; Daun, 1989, p. 56).

Scandinavians adore privacy. Privacy is a prime feature of the Scandinavian character (Tomasson, 1970). People do not 'drop in' on each other (unless you are very good friends) and there is a strong preference for a private office among white-collar workers (Lawrence and Spybey, 1986, p. 25) as well as among students in their accommodation (Daun, 1989, p. 100).

The Scaninavian style of leadership does not include being responsible for the employees' private sphere (Steinberg and Åkerblom, 1992, pp. 38–9). Four characteristics of the Scandinavian type of culture are (Hofstede, 1984, pp. 171, 200–201):

- Everyone has a right to a private life and opinion;
- Company interfering in private life is rejected;
- Work is less central;
- People prefer shorter working hours to more pay.

The strict line put up by Scandinavians between work and private life can be a handicap in contact with or working with other cultures, where this line is less clear. On the other hand, a Scandinavian can be described as independent (Daun, 1989, p. 56). A successful upbringing in this culture leads to responsible and independent young men and women, who will take their place in the collective (Sjögren, 1985, pp. 40ff), that is, this collective individualist that was mentioned before.

One aspect of the 'collective' part of the Scandinavian collective individualist is that, among themselves, individual Scandinavians are not supposed to stand out in a crowd. It is not socially tolerated to be uppity as a Scandinavian; this is very much frowned upon. The important thing is to have what it takes but not more. This is also so at the national level. Scandinavians do not like to present themselves as set above other countries – this is something they shrink away from; they are, however, very proud of the country they live in, when they feel it is needed, they are happy to defend it.

To see oneself as not better than anyone else is known within Scandinavia (and to some extent, abroad as well) as the Jante Law. This 'law' was formulated by a Norwegian author, Aksel Sandemose, when he was talking about the conditions in a specific Danish village (Jante). It could have been Sweden (Klausen, 1984). Levelling, that is, not trying to be better than others, is a general characteristic of the Scandinavian type of culture (Hofstede, 1984, p. 205).

> It is bad to act 'uppity', to set yourself apart from others; displays of wealth are frowned upon, and styles tend to be national rather than segmented or stratified.

> Associated with the egalitarian norm is the norm of accessibility. If you recognise the minister of transport in the airport lounge you can complain to him about the delay. (Lawrence and Spybey, 1986, p. 59)

Associated with the norm of not standing out is also the Scandinavian's moderation –people are supposed to take and use just enough of what they need, not more (Phillips-Martinsson, 1992, pp. 19–20).

It is a general impression among foreigners that Scandinavian decision-making is slow (Lawrence and Spybey, 1986, p. 50; Lindkvist, 1988, p. 55; Phillips-Martinsson, 1992, p. 59; Brewster et al., 1993, p. 30). There are also critical voices heard about the Scandinavian style of decision-making. Some say that Scandinavian managers are indecisive (Brewster et al., 1993, p. 30), that they are excessively careful (Phillips and Martinsson, 1992, p. 59), that they are scared of the decision-making limelight due to a 'natural' shyness and fear of 'acting uppity' (Lawrence and Spybey, 1986, p. 50), or that they do not feel comfortable taking risks (*The Economist*, 1996b, Nov. 23, p. 16).

The rationality and practicality of a Lutheran background comes through in present-day Scandinavia:

> What emerges from any consideration of the development of [Scandinavia] is a strong impression of the commitment to secular rationality. A Weberian view, linking the 'spirit of capitalism' and associated scientific and technological advancements with the 'protestant ethic', would associate this with the early establishment of the Lutheran Church as the universal state church in [Scandinavia]. This must in turn be linked with the characteristic of the [Scandinavians] to put less emphasis on the individual whilst producing a secure social structure that enables the individual to go out and do things. (Lawrence and Spybey, 1986, p. 39)

Scandinavians appreciate sensibility and matter-of-factness (Daun, 1989, pp. 162–3). Managers see themselves as practical in the Scandinavian type of culture (Hofstede, 1984, p. 92), and Scandinavian business people describe themselves as 'efficient' and 'rational' (Phillips-Martinsson, 1992, p. 19). The strong emphasis on matter-of-factness may give an impression of a lack of feeling among Scandinavians, but is closely related to the importance of reasonableness and moderation in their culture, which I mentioned earlier.

Top managers in Scandinavia impress some foreigners as seeming to know what they are doing, not in the simple sense of being resolute rather than indecisive, but in the broader view of having a knowledge of the practical side of business (Lawrence and Spybey, 1986, p. 49). There is a high degree of product-mindedness in Scandinavian companies (ibid.) and a high amount of service in the sense of applying technical systems to satisfy customers' needs, such as the right to return products bought or cancel a hire-purchase agreement (if customers change their mind) and unconditional warranties (Lindkvist, 1988, p. 44). When comparing American and Scandinavian management development programmes, it is also found that the latter use outside resource persons much more, and revolve much more around discussions based on practical experience (ibid., pp. 61–2).

There are many factors behind the rational and practical orientation in the Scandinavian culture. Two more basic factors are:

1. Scandinavian culture is a low-contextual culture;
2. There is a strong emphasis on education in Scandinavia.

Scandinavians have a low-contextual culture (Ferraro, 1994, pp. 50–2). This means, for instance, that people are what they seem to be; paradoxes and surprises are few, and there is not a great need to interpret other people, their thoughts, purposes and so on. The spoken and written word is enough to understand each other. The Scandinavian low-contextual culture also shows in the fact that Scandinavians, when talking, are quite reserved in using their hands and maintaining a good amount of personal space.

Education is highly valued in Scandinavia (Lindkvist, 1988, p. 53). There is even what may be called 'a cult of competence' in Scandinavian culture (Lawrence and Spybey, 1986, p. 61). Lower strata in the society are also highly qualified and managers characterize themselves, and are characterized by others, as 'better trained and educated' (Brewster et al., 1993, p. 113).

Scandinavians are not only serious, they also take their job very seriously. Those who get to the top must want to be there for intrinsic rather than extrinsic reasons. They are less likely to be there for money. Financial incentives are quite low in Scandinavian companies by international standards. Also, taxes are high and there are hardly any fringe benefits, so there must be factors other than remuneration motivating Scandinavian managers. One such factor could be to be a more central part of the process of learning and of progress. These are important values to a Scandinavian.

Scandinavia has a remarkable record of innovations. Since World War II, it has also gained an international reputation as a 'shop' for social experiments. Scandinavian managers are change-centred (Brewster et al., 1993, p. 113).

Scandinavians are, in general, extremely willing to accept change (Frykman, 1987) as long as change will not jeopardize their national values and the feeling of security (Daun, 1989, p. 166). The Scandinavian way of thinking and learning is characterized by a focus on the learning process as such, creativity, being *ad hoc*, and inspirational (Trompenaars, 1995, p. 159). Even the problem itself is open to redefinition. Ways of changing are by improvising and attuning (ibid.).

Scandinavians are recognized as good at problem-solving and they like to experiment (Lawrence and Spybey, 1986, pp. 27–8). They have a strong belief in learning through experimentation (Lindkvist, 1988, p. 53). This is possible within companies because there is an optimism about people's initiative, ambition and leadership skills (Hofstede, 1984, p. 133), and employees are interested and involved in innovations (Lindkvist, 1988, p. 53). One author, Fons Trompenaars, has characterized relationships between employees in the Scandinavian type of organizations as 'diffuse, spontaneous relationships growing out of a shared creative process' (1995, p. 160).

Egalitarianism leads to patience, restraint, moderation and emotional control, which are all seen as Scandinavian virtues. In spite of interest in change and experimentation, however, Scandinavians do not like direct confrontation and forceful interpersonal challenges. In their opinion, problems should be solved by open discussions leading to a compromise, not by force (Lawrence and Spybey, 1986, p. 59). Aggressive behaviour is frowned upon in the Scandinavian type of culture (Hofstede, 1984, p. 140). Even the term 'aggressiveness' has negative connotations in Scandinavian languages.

Evading conflicts can be seen as a tendency to stay away from direct confrontation. Typical for many Scandinavians engaged in a discussion is they try not to raise topics which are strongly emotional and where opinions may differ widely (Daun, 1989, p. 102). This is a clear tendency in Scandinavian companies as well (Forss et al., 1984, p. 15; Steinberg and Åkerblom, 1992, p. 36).

The Scandinavian business culture can be typified as in Table 10.6. This gives, among other things, the following prerequisites for entrepreneurship among Scandinavians:

- Do not present yourself as better than others
- Go slowly – involve everybody, they all have a right to have an opinion
- Think about everything, be careful

Table 10.6 Scandinavian business culture

⇨ Equal and democratic
⇨ Ordered and honest
⇨ Privacy
⇨ Not standing out
⇨ Careful and slow
⇨ Rational and practical
⇨ Process, continuity and change
⇨ No aggression or confrontation

- Be sensible and practical
- Be honest
- Do not commit yourself too early
- Do it during working hours
- Change – but not too quickly and not too drastically
- Aggression leads nowhere

Five different entrepreneurial types associated with five different cultures?

If we typify five different entrepreneurs *who would fit with* those five cultures that have been discussed in this chapter, it might look like this, if I allow myself to speculate a bit:

- *In the American culture*: the growth-oriented, driving niche-thinker
- *In the Arab culture*: the well-established, business-oriented man
- *In the Chinese culture*: the negotiator with a fair amount of contacts
- *In the Japanese culture*: the well-established proponent of the culture
- *In the Scandinavian culture*: the careful equilibrist

But these are just speculations, of course. Maybe it is so that the most successful entrepreneur is the person who is with his culture *at the same time* as he or she points at the future. To be an entrepreneur means, after all, *to divert from what is established*, at least in some respect.

Summary and conclusion

After having presented some quantitative results concerning the extent of business start-ups in different parts of the world, this chapter has discussed five different 'national cultures' and their consequences for entrepreneurship.

Think 10.1 Provide examples of culture and cultural manifestations in your country.

Think 10.2 What would a national culture look like promoting entrepreneurship?

Think 10.3 What would a national culture look like preventing entrepreneurship from happening?

Think 10.4 Why is there so much entrepreneurship in China and India?

CH 10 – CASE STUDY

Three cultural clashes

(Adapted from Ferraro, 1994, pp. 39, 40, 61–2)

Sam Lucas, a construction supervisor for an international engineering firm, had the reputation of being tough but fair-minded. Personally he was very forceful, confrontational individual who always spoke his mind. He never hesitated to reprimand any worker who he felt was performing poorly. Even though during his 6 years with the company Sam had never worked outside of the United States, he was chosen to supervise construction on a new hotel project in Jidda, Saudi Arabia, primarily because of his outstanding work record. On this project, Sam supervised the work of about a dozen Americans and nearly 100 Saudi labourers. It was not long before Sam realized that the Saudi labourers, to his way of thinking, were nowhere as reliable as the workers he had supervised in the United States. He was becoming increasingly annoyed at the seeming lack of competence of the local labour force. Following the leadership style that held him in such good stead at home, he would reprimand any worker who was not doing his job properly, and he would make certain that he did it publicly so that it would serve as an object lesson to all the other workers. He was convinced that he was doing the right thing and was being fair, for after all, he reprimanded both Americans and Saudis alike. He was troubled, however, by the fact that the problems seemed to be growing worse and more numerous.

What advice might you give Sam?

A Danish fertilizer manufacturer decided to venture into the vast potential of Third World markets. The company sent a team of agricultural researchers into an East African country to test soils, weather conditions and topographical conditions in order to develop locally effective fertilizers. Once the research and manufacturing of these fertilizer products had been completed, one of the initial marketing strategies was to distribute, free of charge, 100-pound bags of the fertilizer to selected areas of rural farmers. It was thought that those using the free fertilizer would be so impressed with the dramatic increase in crop productivity that they would spread the word to their friends, relatives and neighbours.

Teams of salespeople went from hut to hut in those designated areas offering male heads of households a free bag of fertilizer along with an explanation of its capacity to increase crop output. Although each head of household was very polite, they all turned down the offer of free fertilizer. The marketing staff concluded that these local people were either disinterested in helping themselves grow more food and eat better or so ignorant that they could not understand the benefits of the new product.

CH 10 – CASE STUDY (continued)

Why was this an ethnocentric conclusion?

Heinz Hopf, an up-and-coming executive for a German electronics company, was sent to Japan to work out the details of a joint venture with a Japanese electronics firm. During the first few weeks Heinz felt that the negotiations were proceeding better than he had expected. He found that he had very cordial working relationships with the team of Japanese executives, and in fact, they had agreed on the major policies and strategies governing the new joint venture. During the third week of negotiations Heinz was present at a meeting held to review their progress. The meeting was chaired by the president of the Japanese firm, Mr Hayakawa, a man in his mid-40s, who had recently taken over the presidency from his 82-year-old grandfather. The new president, who had been involved in most of the negotiations during the preceding weeks, seemed to Heinz to be one of the strongest advocates of the plan that had been developed to date. Also attending the meeting was Hayakawa's grandfather, the recently retired president. After the plans had been discussed in some detail, the octogenarian past president proceeded to give a long soliloquy about how some of the features of this plan violated the traditional practices on which the company had been founded. Much to Heinz's amazement, Mr Hayakawa did nothing to explain or defend the policies and strategies that they had taken weeks to develop. Feeling extremely frustrated, Heinz then gave a fairly strongly argued defence of the plan. To Heinz's further amazement, no one else in the meeting spoke up. The tension in the air was quite heavy and the meeting adjourned shortly thereafter. Within days the Japanese firm completely terminated the negotiation on the joint venture.

How could you help Heinz better understand this bewildering situation?

To access the teacher's manual that accompanies this book, please use the following link:

http://goo.gl/DXQas.

11

Some philosophical and theoretical foundations

Introduction

This chapter discusses in more detail three philosophical and theoretical foundations, which have been of importance when writing this book, that is, differences between behaving and acting, between explaining and understanding and between space and place.

Behaviour and action

To behave

If a human activity is seen as *behaviour* it is looked at as observable, that is, it can be perceived empirically according to classic behaviourism. 'Behaviour' is used by many social scientists as an umbrella term for all human activities. This may lead to confusion, however, if it is not clear whether 'behaviour' or 'action' is referred to. I therefore suggest 'activity' as an umbrella term and 'action' and 'behaviour' as two ways of looking at human activities.

When looking at a human activity as behaviour, all non-observable aspects of this activity are neglected, as it then is necessary to try to explain what is going on using observable 'stimuli' and observable 'responses'. Every object in the environment then represents a potential 'stimulus'. In empirical research an object is described as a 'stimulus' if it gives a behavioural reaction. 'Response' is then defined as 'something a human person does' (Watson, 1970, p.6). To reduce human activities to observable processes should, according to the behaviourist Watson and his followers, make a consistent application of (natural) science methods to society possible. The ambition with behavioural science is then to define behaviour causally within the framework of scientific theories such that, given specific 'stimuli', corresponding responses from a human being can be predicted in a deterministic and general way.

Theories for cognitive behaviour constitute a development of classic behaviourism, because behaviour is then no longer described only in terms of stimuli and responses. 'Stimuli' are here transferred *through* reflection, cognition and awareness and are not until then seen as behaviour. The cognitive (motives, needs, attitudes, levels of aspiration etc.) is seen as a perceptual filter for 'stimuli'. Stimuli are now in turn described in terms of information. In these theoretical terms human behaviour is explained as responses to stimuli, which are chosen selectively in the social and environmental milieu and which are passing through cognitive processes and become information.

I do not want to go into any extensive analysis of the consequences of the behaviouristic view for entrepreneurship here. It is enough to say that its basic scientific orientation is to see the environment as a cause. In this view entrepreneurs live in a *world full of circumstances* so to say. Bodies react in a more or less deterministic way and their reactions are determined voluntarily only to some extent. Those who represent this view note *that* the subjective perception of environment sometimes differ from 'objective' facts. The reasons for *why and how* different perceptual filters appear are, however, not studied any further.

To act

From an 'action' perspective the situation is seen in a different way. 'Action' can generally be defined as a reflecting and intentional activity: a 'freely' performed activity which is goal-directed. It takes place as a mental activity. An action can be defined in its simplest form as 'intentionally effecting or preventing a change in the world' (von Wright, 1971, p. 83). An action can also 'designate the outcome of this ongoing process, that is, the accomplished action' (Schutz, 1962, p. 67). If a human activity is to be denoted an 'act', is this not only one aspect of 'reflexivity' which can be found in cognitive behavioural theories, but as a *purposeful* result.

I do not mean that there are any human activities which lack a conscious intention at the time one acts. It is necessary here to decide whether a conscious and free act becomes so routinized that it is no longer necessarily planned consciously. If this is the case, the activity can be described as a kind of 'quasi behaviour'. I simply claim that behaviour (physiologically and biologically conditioned reflexes) is hardly relevant in a social context in general or an entrepreneurial context in particular.

'Quasi actions' are, on the other hand, described by Habermas (1984, p. 12) as the 'behavioural reaction of an externally or internally stimulated organism, and environmentally induced changes of state in a self-regulated system'. By this Habermas means processes which can be described 'as if they were expressions of a subject's capacity for action', which in reality can be described as activities of a mechanism which itself is not capable of providing any cause of its actions. This can be compared with the von Wright's distinction between 'quasi causal' (causal descriptions of intentional action) and 'quasi teleological' (intentional descriptions of causal processes in the sense of functional explanations) activities (1971, pp. 84–5 and 58).

An action involves four *processual sequences* (often not very explicit and not necessarily following each other):

1. *Action project,* that is, formulating/creating the purpose. This is often a preparatory and foresighted process in a given situation. During this process the subject is considering suitable means to reach his or her goals and sometimes the general and justifiable expectations from other members of the society that must be met, etc.
2. *Definition of the situation*: a thinking sequence in terms of the intended goal. A certain situation is structured. Accessible means (physical and social) relevant for the purpose are determined and chosen here. Non-accessible elements relevant to the purpose constitute 'limitations'. The situation is interpreted according to specific values and norms. Sometimes, when the meaning of the elements of the situation is problematic, a rationalization of their significance is necessary.
3. *Realization of action, or realization of the 'subjectively imagined goal'* (Girndt, 1967, p. 30). This is the applied sequence of the action, through which a situation is changed or prevented from being changed. Sometimes even the technical component (the goal–means relationship), the legitimacy of the action and even the meaning component may be problematic at this stage.
4. *The consequences of the action*: the intended and non-intended consequences of the action constitute the new situation. This new situation is relevant to the agent and for other agents. This changed situation can be relevant to come up with a 'new' goal-means relationship and to reinterpret evaluations and norms as other prerequisites. There is a discussion whether, in order for an action to be worth its name, its consequences should be part of the action itself, which in von Wright's and Schultz' definitions above are included in 'application', or whether the consequences should be seen as a result of the action.

These sequences might not be observable by others (as an intellectual attempt to solve a problem) or they might be 'open, directed at the external world' (Schutz, 1962, p. 67). Behavioural theory explains the human activity as determined by stimuli, while action to action is purposeful and meaningful. The entrepreneur lives, in the latter case, in a world full of *meaning*, so to say (not circumstances as in the case of behaviour). When concentrating on individuals' mental processes, cognitive behaviourism is not very adequate for conducting research in a social milieu, because it assumes that the meaning context for socially relevant activities can be reduced to individual stimulus-behaviour. It consequently cuts off the social context. Problems do arise there, at best, in terms of individual cognitive dissonance. The meaning context in the social world can only, as I see it, be considered if we look at the members of society as purposeful and not just as 'responses'. Action theory provides a frame to do this. Behavioural theory does not.

The basic structures for action have been taken up and developed by Max Weber. He constructed conceptual distinctions which cover the different forms that purposeful action can take. 'Action' is seen by him as the basic units in the socialization process and can therefore be seen as the 'atoms' of a social universe. Those are the smallest units that be studied in the society, in the social world. With this view, sometimes the most interesting units for the social scientists could be the actions themselves, not the agents, the actors or the individuals. The agents are then the prerequisites for action to take place, but not the units to be studied as such.

Lately, a group of theories has come up which deals with how action in network is done. Those theories are labelled *Actor Network Theories (ANT)*. They have had some influence in criticizing the market as a fundamental arena for economic behaviour and might seem to be of some interest when discussing entrepreneurship activities. It started with Kuhn (1962) and his devastating critique of the naïve opinion of the relationship between natural scientific knowledge and nature (that is, the view that such knowledge reflects the true state of nature) and backed up with the assertion, for instance Winch (1958), that social science is fundamentally distinct from natural science. It led a group of sociologists to venture into the citadels of scientific activity – laboratories – to watch scientists at work (Murdoch, 2008). Their ambition 'was to create a legitimate space for sociology where none had previously been permitted, in the interpretation or explanation of scientific knowledge' (Shapin, 1995, p. 297). The resulting ethnographic studies dealt a further blow to the generally accepted simple correspondence between natural science knowledge and nature. They showed that scientists used a number of means to bring nature 'into order' in the laboratory (Hacking, 1983). Such means were technological instruments, such as 'inscription devices' (Latour and Woolgar, 1979), which transform material substances into figures and diagrams; literary techniques of persuasion, used within, for instance, scientific papers (ibid.); and political strategies, which might include coalition building in order to mobilize resources (Knorr-Cetina, 1981).

Researchers come up with new knowledge. So do entrepreneurs, because they come up with something new. One could therefore question if it is adequate to see any of these two categories as rational agents in the sense that they in an objective way select the most effective roads forward to reach a clearly formulated goal or that they constitute some kind of 'invisible hands' in Adam Smith's sense (1776 [2007]). They should be rather seen as business driven (business entrepreneurial) or idea driven (social entrepreneurs) 'visible hands'.

Explaining or understanding

To claim a clear difference between 'explaining' and 'understanding' may seem of little interest to some. However, it has become customary, though by no means universal, to distinguish between trying to get a picture of *events* or *behaviour* and trying to get a picture of *acts*. It is suggested that the term *understanding*, in contrast to *explaining*, ought to be reserved for the latter.

Since the inception of the disciplines of social science, lines of controversy have been drawn between those who do and those who do not make a principal distinction between two presumed alternative modes of thought, in the beginning represented by natural sciences and social sciences. Theorists rejecting any fundamental distinction between those modes have traditionally been called *positivists*. I call them *researchers interested in explaining*. They assume that the methods which have proved their unparalleled value in the analysis of the physical world are applicable to the materials of social sciences, and that while these methods may have to be adapted to a special subject matter, *the logic of explanation* in physical and social sciences is the same. Theorists, who draw a distinction between 'understanding' and 'explaining', are labelled *anti-positivists*. I call them *researchers interested in understanding*. The critical element in anti-positivism is the insistence that the methods of physical sciences, however modified, are intrinsically inadequate to the subject matter of social sciences; in the physical world knowledge is external and empirical, while social sciences are concerned with interpretations and with various kinds of experience.

Many methodological and theoretical discourses within social sciences since the late nineteenth century have concerned modes of thought of 'understanding' and 'explaining' (Bottomore and Nisbet, 1979). These discourses reached a high point in the period immediately before World War I, and they have been part of social sciences ever since.

The controversy between explaining and understanding is deeply rooted in Western thought. In its most elementary sense it is based on a presumed intrinsic difference between mind and all that is non-mind. The controversy cannot be eliminated by choosing between explaining and understanding, because, basically, these two cannot be compared. Most explaining-oriented researchers, for instance, claim that everything, in the natural world as well as in the human world, can be explained, at least in principle; while understanding-oriented researchers claim that understanding is only for humans. Furthermore there is no neutral position where you can choose between explaining and understanding in a business-like and impartial way. One has to 'choose' at the same time as, by necessity, being positioned in either the explaining or the understanding camp – which is really no choice at all! Furthermore:

- The purpose of explanations is to depict a factual (objective and/or subjective) reality in order to better predict its course from outside; the purpose of understanding is to develop means in order to better manage human existence from within.
- One explanation can replace another explanation; one understanding can replace another understanding. However, an explanation cannot (according to understanding-oriented researchers) replace an understanding (which it can, according to an explaining-oriented researcher). Understanding-oriented researchers claim that these are two different scientific approaches.

According to von Wright (1971) and Apel (1984) the German philosopher of history J. G. Droysen (1808–84) was the first, within science, to introduce the difference between 'to explain' and 'to understand' (in German, *erklären* and *verstehen*, respectively), to ground historical sciences methodologically and to distinguish them from natural sciences. He did this in *Grundrisse der Historik*, which was published in 1858 [1897]:

> According to the object and nature of human thought there are three possible scientific methods: the speculative (formulated in philosophy and theology), the mathematical or physical, and the historical. Their respective essences are to know, to explain, and to understand. (Droysen, 1858 [1897], p. 13)

Droysen's term 'verstehen' can be traced back to the modern founders of hermeneutics, F. Schleiermacher (1768–1834) and A. Boeckh (1785–1867) and was made more generally known through M. Weber (1864–1920). A historically significant form of the debate between understanding and explanation began with W. Dilthey (1833–1911). He utilized the dichotomy between understanding and explanation as the terminological foundation for distinguishing between natural sciences and *Geisteswissenschaften* (the humanities) as a whole. Initially understanding gained a psychological character, which explanations lacked. This psychological element was emphasized by several of the nineteenth-century anti-positivist methodologists, perhaps above all by G. Simmel (1858–1918), who thought that understanding as a method characteristic of the humanities is a form of *empathy* (von Wright, 1971). But empathy is not a modern way of separating understanding from explanation. Within hermeneutics, for instance, understanding is today associated with *language* (Gadamer, 1960 [1997]), within anthropology with *culture* (Geertz, 1973) and within phenomenology with *intentionality* in a way which explanation cannot.

Generally we can say that natural sciences require concepts which permit the formation of testable laws and theories. Other issues, for instance, those deriving from ordinary language, are of less interest. But in the social sciences another set of considerations exists as well: the concepts used to describe, explain and/or understand human activity must be drawn at least in part *from the social life being studied*, not only from the scientists' theories (Fay, 1996). Scientific concepts then bear a fundamentally different relationship to social phenomena from that which they bear to natural phenomena. In social sciences, concepts partially constitute the reality being studied, in relation to natural phenomena concepts merely serve to describe and explain (ibid.).

> It is possible to explain human behaviour. We do not try to understand an area of low pressure because it has no meaning. On the other hand, we try to understand human beings because they are of the same kind as we are. (Liedman, 2002, p. 280; my translation)

No one claims today that only natural sciences should aim for explanations and that only social sciences should aim for understanding. In practice, both attempts are made in the two scientific areas. Researchers normally separate the two approaches, although in everyday usage it is harder to distinguish between what is meant by 'explain' and 'understand'. While it seems relatively clear that 'explain' means, by and large, to figure out the external circumstances around what has happened or what is happening, there is, however, a wide variety of opinions in everyday language as to what we could mean by 'understand':

- 'To understand' means to find out more details.
- 'To understand' means to get access to subjective opinions.
- 'To understand' means to get a picture of the larger context in which a phenomenon is placed.
- 'To understand' means to get a picture of relevant circumstances that have taken place earlier in a specific situation.

To me, none of these equates to understanding; they are each just more detailed, more circumstantial or deeper aspects of explanation. As I see it, the crucial difference between explaining and understanding is that explanation sees language as *depicting* reality and understanding sees language as *constituting* reality!

Thus, researchers interested in explaining:

- look for factual (objective and/or subjective) data and use a depicting language
- want to find cause–effect relationships
- build models

While researchers interested in understanding:

- deny that factual and depicting data exist (at least in the human world)
- want to look for actors' view on meaning, importance and significance and use a constituting and forming (even performing) language
- come up with interpretations

In this, *models* are deliberately simplified pictures of factual reality; and *interpretations* are deliberately problematized pictures of socially constructed reality. It is natural for explaining-oriented researchers to build models and for understanding-oriented researchers to come up with interpretations! An interpretation is a theory-laden observation (Rose, 1999, p. 125). (Table 11.1 offers a summary.)

Researchers interested in understanding see some problems in explanatory knowledge:

- Data never speak for themselves. They must always be interpreted by the researcher.
- So-called 'facts' are always theory-laden.
- Human beings (including researchers) are never objective but members of a culture. They can even be seen as those who are contracting the culture.
- Explanations of phenomena can be very shallow – they lack depth.

Table 11.1 Explanation and understanding

Explanation	Understanding
Is using a depicting language	Is using a constituting language
Believes in a circumstantial world	Believes in a meaningful world
Sees behaving human beings	Sees acting human beings
Aims to depict a naturally complicated reality in models, that is, comes up with patterns in the law-bound reality by finding the most crucial circumstances in a situation and neglect those circumstances which are of less importance	Aims to problematize a socially constructed reality by using interpretations, that is, to construct pictures (maybe as metaphors) which can contain that meaning and those significances which are experienced in a situation and which, furthermore, provide openings for further construction of a meaningful social reality

Researchers interested in understanding assert that understanding is of interest only

- when people are studied
- by people.

As a representative of the broad view of entrepreneurship, it is my opinion that an understanding approach to studying entrepreneurship seems interesting because:

- We have a new kind of society which needs new solutions. Maybe an understanding-oriented research can offer better 'solutions' to the problems in this society.
- Language based, symbolic and culturally oriented research is to a large extent underutilized in social sciences and hardly used at all within social entrepreneurial research, where it seems very promising.
- Social entrepreneurship is built up by very human activities. It may be difficult to catch these activities by trying to explain them.

It can be said generally, that the narrow view of entrepreneurship attempts to explain entrepreneurial behaviour (Chapter 4 in this book) and that the broad view of entrepreneurship attempts to understand entrepreneurial actions (Chapter 5 in this book).

Space and place

The concepts of 'space' (*Raum* in German; *espace* in French) and 'place' (*Ort* in German; *lieu* in French) are basic components of the lived world and we take them for granted. We notice the absence of space when we are pressured and the absence of place when we are lost (Tuan, 1977). And just because we take them for granted, we normally deem them not worthy of separate treatment. Also taken for granted is the fact that we are 'put in a situation' in space and place to begin with, that space and place existed a priori of our existence on Earth. Just because we say that we cannot choose in this matter, we believe we do not have to think about such basic facticity to start with (Casey, 1997). However, when we think about the two concepts, they may assume unexpected meanings and raise questions we have not thought to ask (Tuan, 1977). In fact, space as well as place can be very complicated concepts, which is all the more confusing because, at first glance, they appear so obvious and common sense. After all, it is impossible to think of the world without the two (Cresswell, 2004, p. 124). To look at the world as space and/or place is to use dimensions to characterize the world into a special fashion and, like using any criterion, a special way to talk about and to understand the world. According to Cresswell (2004, p. 27), 'by taking space and place seriously, we can provide another tool to demystify and understand the forces that effect and manipulate our everyday life'.

Looking at the world as a world of places, for instance, we see different things:

> Looking at the world as a set of places in some way separate from each other is both an act of defining what exists (ontology) and a particular way of seeing and knowing the world (epistemology and metaphysics). Theory is a way of looking at the world and making sense of the confusion of the senses. Different theories of place lead different writers to look at different aspects of the world. In other words, place is not simply something to be observed, researched and written about but simply part of the way we see, research and write. (Cresswell, 2004, p. 15)

Space is normally seen as the more abstract one of the two concepts. When we speak of space, we tend to think of outer-space or possibly spaces of geometry (Cresswell, 2004, p. 8). Space is something deterritorialized (de Certeau, 1984). It can be discussed without considering that it might contain any social life, inhabited by actual identifiable people. It is an opening and a result of possibilities, for instance, from a business point of view. Spaciousness is closely associated with the sense of being free. Freedom implies space, enough room in which to act (Tuan, 1977).

Space is generally seen as being transformed into place as it acquires definition and meaning. Brenner (1997, p. 137) expresses it such: 'Space appears no longer as a neutral container within which temporal development unfolds, but, rather, as a constitutive, historically produced dimension of social practices'. Considering antonyms to place, we refer to words such as 'remove', 'take away', 'dislodge', 'detach' and 'take off' (Rämö, 2004). When space feels familiar to us, it has become place (Tuan, 1977). In other words, place is then a meaningful location, to which people are attached (Altman and Low, 1992).

Places are significant to human life. We might even say, like Cresswell (2004, p. 33), that 'there was no "place" before there was humanity but once we came into existence then place did too'. Places are being made, maintained and contested. All over the world, people are engaged in place-making activities (ibid.). Nothing we do is unplaced (Casey, 1997, p. ix).

However, places are not isolated. Cronon (1992) argues that we must pay attention to their connections. Places are something we occupy. The relationships between people and places are at least as complex as relationships between people, but of another kind. As mentioned, places give meaning to people. This is where people learn to know each other and themselves. Places become points which stand out in every individual's biography and a set of feelings for different places develop through social interaction (Ekman and Hultman, 2007). Altman and Low (1992, p. 7) phrase it such that 'the social relations that a place signifies may be equally or more important to the attachment process than the place qua place'.

Even though the term *homo geographicus* has been coined (Sack, 1997), place is more than geography. It is something, the meaning and usefulness of which is continuously created in social relations and networks, that is, in meetings and flows between people and objects. This is something which has gained increasing response within social as well as within human sciences (Ekman and Hultman, 2007). To put it differently, place is culturally defined (Casey, 1993, p. 33).

The political geographer John Agnew (1987) has outlined three fundamental aspects of place as a '*meaningful location*':

1. Location.
2. Locale.
3. Sense of place.

'*Location*' has to do with fixed objective co-ordinates on the Earth's surface (or in the Earth's case a specific location vis-à-vis other planets and the sun). By '*locale*', Agnew means material setting for social relations – the actual shape of place within which people conduct their lives as individuals. By '*sense of place*', Agnew refers to the subjective and emotional attachments people have to place. Place can vary in size from being very large (e.g. the Earth, universe or nation), mid-sized (e.g. cities, communities and neighbourhoods), smaller (e.g. homes or rooms) or very small (e.g. objects of various kinds) (Altman and Low, 1992). It may even be something completely imaginary as *Utopia*. A place can be called a 'room for activities' (Massey, 1995b) or an 'arena' (Berglund and Johansson, 2008). 'Home' is an 'exemplary kind of place' (Cresswell, 2004, p. 115).

One concept that frequently appears alongside place in geography texts is 'landscape'. In most definitions of landscape, however, the viewer is outside of it. Places, on the other hand, are very much things to be inside of (Cresswell, 2004, p. 10). Another concept of interest here is 'region', which became very much a part of common sense during the twentieth century (Curry, 2002, p. 511).

Some views on 'space' and 'place' over the years:

- For Aristotle place was '*prior to all things*'. To be, for Aristotle, was to be in place (Casey, 1993, p. 14). Aristotle's view on place was dominant for more than 1500 years.
- Descartes identified space with matter. To him, place was also a subordinate feature of matter and space (Casey, 1997, pp. 152–6).
- In Motte and Cajori (1934, pp. 6–7) we can read that Newton claimed that 'absolute space, in its own nature, without relations to anything external, remains always similar and immovable' and that 'place is a part of space which a body takes up, and is according to space, either absolute or relative'. According to Newton, places do not exist on their own; they exist in name only. Newton's ideas of absolute space became very dominant for several hundred years. His contemporary 'competitor', Leibniz, trying to promote the idea of a relative space, never had a chance (Casey, 1997).
- The increasing obsession with infinite space from the thirteenth century onward, due to the dominant position of the Catholic church in the Western world at that time and supported by Newton's theories, had the predictable effect of putting place into the shadows (Casey, 1997). The subordination of place to space culminated in the seventeenth century (Casey, 1993). Renaissance thinkers remained capable of equating space

with place and vice versa. However, space eventually took over. From the end of the eighteenth century, place was virtually excluded from the scientific discourse (Rämö, 2004, p. 854). It did not come back, and then in full force, until mid-twentieth century.

- Kant tried to demonstrate that space, as well as time, are conditions under which sense perceptions operate (Jammer, 1982). To him, space was no longer situated in the physical world but in subjectivity of the human mind (Casey, 1997). Space was not something 'out there', but existed as a sort of mental structuring (Curry, 2002).

- According to Curry (2002), two opposing intellectual movements, one deconstructive and one constructive, gave rise to the recasting of thinking of space and, above all, place were coming up during the latter part of the twentieth century. The first of these, the deconstructive, is perhaps most clearly seen in the work of Heidegger. According to him, everything in the world could and should be an object of empirical inquiry. Place is the same as authentic experience, according to Heidegger (Cresswell, 2004, p. 22). Another body of work that took a deconstructive tack toward the concept of space was the later work of Wittgenstein. Words, including 'space' and 'place', only have meanings within the contexts of the individuals and groups that use them, in particular situations and particular places (Curry, 2002).

- Before 1960, place was seen idiographically and space was seen nomothetically. However, from the 1970s, constructive notions of place, which were as universal and theoretically ambitious as approaches to space had been, became more and more common. Some attempts in this direction existed previously, for instance Jacobs (1961), who discusses the notion that in social planning one needs to look both at the everyday activities of people who live and work in urban neighbourhoods and to attend to them as places constructed through these everyday activities, and Hall (1959), who pointed to the ways in which people interact with one another when in close proximity. More central to constructive attempts to move place to the centre of scientific inquiry, however, were geographers like Tuan (1974, 1977), Relph (1976) and Buttimer and Seamon (1980). One element in this movement was a desire to rethink the role of people (and bodies) in the construction of places. Examples of such contributors are the post-structuralist Foucault, the phenomenologist Merleau-Ponty, the historian de Certeau and the Marxist-architect Lefebvre.

- Foucault's historical inquiries reveal an alertness to space, or, more precisely, to the way in which spatial relations – the distribution and arrangement of people, activities and buildings – are always deeply implicated in the historical processes under study (Philo, 2000). He claimed in one interview (Foucault, 1980, p. 149), that 'the history of powers' would at one and the same time amount to a history 'written of space'.

- Merleau-Ponty is claiming that places we inhabit are known by the bodies we live. We cannot be implaced without being embodied. Conversely, to be embodied is to be capable of implacement (Casey, 1997). He teaches us that the human body is never without a place or that place is never without body; he also shows that the lived body is itself a place. Its very movement constitutes place, brings it into being (ibid.).

- De Certeau may seem to have a kind of opposite understanding of space and place to what is the most common one. To him, place is an empty grid over which practice occurs while space is what is created by practice (Cresswell, 2004). While we have to use the rules and structures of language to make sense, the same applies to place. As we live in places that become pre-structured, those places are not operational without practice in them. He stresses that tactics operate through a sense of timing (movements) whereas strategies operate through place (fixation) (Hjorth, 2004).

- Lefebvre presents a theory that 'urban revolution' was supplanting an 'industrial revolution' and that this urban revolution was somehow a 'spatial revolution' as well (Merrifield, 2000). He talks about construction of space through a spatial triad: representations of space (also called firstspace – empirically measurable and mappable phenomena), representational space (secondspace – the domain of representations and image, a felt and cared for centre of meaning) and spatial practices (thirdspace – the lived world, which is practiced and lived rather than being material/conceived or mental/perceived) (ibid., Cresswell, 2004).

- There is a close interconnection between the technologies available for communication and representation and the ways in which space and place are conceptualized. The modern region was in important ways a product of new technologies like the printing press, modern transport and the breakthrough of statistics in social life (Curry, 2002, pp. 508–9).

- A genuine rediscovery of place, alongside space, in most of the social sciences today is obvious (Casey, 1997), like in the course of history (for instance, Foucault), in the natural world (for instance, Berry), in the political realm (for instance, Lefebvre), in gender relations and sexual difference (for instance, Irigaray), in the production of poetic imagination (for instance, Bachelard), in geographic experience and reality (for instance, Tuan), in the sociology of the city (for instance, Arendt), in nomadism (for instance, Deleuze and Guattari), in architecture (for instance, Derrida) and in religion (for instance, Nancy). We can see it in economics (for instance, Krugman) and there are examples where space and place are used in business studies in general (for instance, Rämö) as in entrepreneurship in particular (for instance, Hjorth).

It is possible to have a similar discussion about time. Places are never finished, but are constantly being performed (Thrift, 1996). Whereabout is always whenabout (Casey, 1993). The old Greeks separated *chora* (space) from *topos* (place, or rather, region), but also *chronos* (dated time) from *kairos* (valued time). Rämö (2000, 2004) makes a four-field classification out of this of obvious relevance to entrepreneurship. Being aware of the difficulties to separate time from space and place, however, I still do not discuss separate concepts and perceptions of time explicitly in this book (it would lead too far). One excuse for this 'neglect' is possibly that in modern and post-modern times we are so inured to the primacy of time that we rarely question the dogma that time is the first of all things. This modern obsession with time may have blinded us to the presence of place in our lives (Casey, 1993).

In this book, I use the concepts of 'space' and 'place' the same way Hudson (2001) does. To him, 'space' is an economic evaluation of a situation based on its capacity for profit, with 'place' is a societal situation based on meaning. Spaces are therefore valued predominantly through the lens of production and consumption based on supply and demand, use of factors of production and operations on markets. Places, on the other hand, are situations of meaningful societal life where people live and learn; they are situations of socialization and cultural acquisition. Places are made up of a complex system of societal relations. They create a distinct culture, have meaning and build up identities (ibid.). Thus, while space is the situation of enterprise, place is the situation of societal life. Occasionally, situations thrive both as spaces for profitable business and as places with a rich societal fabric. Under these circumstances, the situation appears to combine the best of economic and societal life (Florida, 2003). In such situations, there is a synergistic relationship between space and place (Johnstone and Lionais, 2004).

Using the concepts of space and place when analysing entrepreneurship can have several advantages according to Hjorth (2004), including:

1. It brings into focus an often-neglected but basic element of everyday life.
2. Power becomes naturally included in our studies, which is something rarely happening as part of entrepreneurship research.

Paradoxically, place has been even more important in our modern society with increased mobility (Ekman and Hultman, 2007, p. 21). Today we can witness a multitude of what might be referred to as 'non-places', like airports and other temporary dwellings, which Augé (1995) sees as different from genuine (what he refers to as 'anthropological') places. Our view on place has importance for such important issues today as migration, cases of refugees and asylum.

Examples of *space factors* influencing entrepreneurship are:

- Degree of organizing.
- Start of separate departments for business development.
- Market growth.
- Possibilities to act freely and across borders.

Examples of *place factors* influencing entrepreneurship are:

- Raw models
- Leadership
- Existing networks and social capital
- Possibilities to get a place where it can be done

Examples of factors *which neither have to do with space nor place*:

- Personal qualities like need for achievement, self-reliance, courage and risk management.

It seems like place is more important to public entrepreneurs than space. Compare concepts like public places, homes and work places with concepts like expansion space and budget space.

More about entrepreneurship, space and place can be read in Bjerke and Rämö (2011).

Discussing entrepreneurship in terms of space or place has some *similarities* with trying to explain entrepreneurship versus trying to understand it.

Summary and conclusion

This chapter has discussed in more detail three philosophical and theoretical foundations, which have been of importance when writing this book, that is, differences between behaving and acting, between explaining and understanding and between space and place.

Think 11.1 Is philosophy really of any importance when you try to understand what entrepreneurship is all about?

Think 11.2 Give examples of entrepreneurship as behaviour and as action.

Think 11.3 Why might it be difficult to combine explaining and understanding entrepreneurship?

Think 11.4 What characterizes an entrepreneurial place?

CH 11 – CASE STUDY

From UN's Declaration of Human Rights (1948)

Article 1: All human beings are born free and equal in dignity and rights. They are endowed with reason and conscience and should act towards one another in a spirit of brotherhood.

Article 2: Everyone is entitled to all the rights and freedoms set forth in this Declaration, without distinction of any kind, such as race, colour, sex, language, religion, political or other opinion, national or social origin, property, birth or other status. Furthermore, no distinction shall be made on the basis of the political, jurisdictional or international status of the country or territory to which a person belongs, whether it be independent, trust, non-self-governing or under any other limitation of sovereignty.

Article 3: Everyone has the right to life, liberty and security of person.

Article 4: No one shall be held in slavery or servitude; slavery and the slave trade shall be prohibited in all their forms.

Article 5: No one shall be subjected to torture or to cruel, inhuman or degrading treatment or punishment.

Article 6: Everyone has the right to recognition everywhere as a person before the law.

Article 7: All are equal before the law and are entitled without any discrimination to equal protection of the law. All are entitled to equal protection against any discrimination in violation of this Declaration and against any incitement to such discrimination.

Article 8: Everyone has the right to an effective remedy by the competent national tribunals for acts violating the fundamental rights granted him by the constitution or by law.

Article 9: No one shall be subjected to arbitrary arrest, detention or exile.

Article 10: Everyone is entitled in full equality to a fair and public hearing by an independent and impartial tribunal, in the determination of his rights and obligations and of any criminal charge against him.

 DISCUSSION QUESTION

Do you see anything entrepreneurial in this text?

To access the teacher's manual that accompanies this book, please use the following link:

http://goo.gl/DXQas.

References

Ackerman, P.L. and L.G. Humphreys (1990), 'Individual differences theory in industrial and organizational psychology', in M.D. Dunnette and L.M. Hough (eds), *Handbook of Industrial and Organizational Psychology*, Vol. 1, (2nd edition), Palo Alto, CA: Consulting Psychology Press.

Ács, Z.J. (2002), *Innovation and the Growth of Cities*, Cheltenham, UK and Northampton, MA, USA: Edward Elgar Publishing.

Ács, Z.J. and L. Szerb (2011), *Global Entrepreneurship & Development Index 2011*, Cheltenham, UK and Northampton, MA, USA: Edward Elgar Publishing.

Agnew, J. (1987), *The United States in the World Economy*, Cambridge: Cambridge University Press.

Ahl, H. (2002), *The Making of the Female Entrepreneur – A Discourse Analysis of Research Texts on Women's Entrepreneurship*, doctoral dissertation, Jönköping International Business School (JIBS), Sweden.

Ajzen, I. (1991), 'The theory of planned behaviour', *Organizational Behavior and Human Decision Processes*, **50**, 179–211.

Alberti, F. (1999), 'Entrepreneurship education: scope and theory', in C. Salvato, P. Davidsson and A. Persson (eds), *Entrepreneurial Knowledge and Learning, Conceptual Advances and Directions for Future Research*, JIBS Research Reports No. 1999-6, Jönköping: Jönköping International Business School (JIBS), Sweden.

Aldrich, H.E. and D. Whetten (1981), 'Organisation-sets, action-sets, and networks: Making the most of simplicity', in P. Nystrom and W. Starbuck (eds), *Handbook of Organizational Design*, Volume One, New York: Oxford University Press.

Aldrich, H.E. and C. Zimmer (1986), 'Entrepreneurship through social networks', in D.L. Sexton and R.W. Wilson (eds), *The Art and Science of Entrepreneurship*, Cambridge, MA: Ballinger.

Allen, K.R. (2010), *New Venture Creation*, International edition (5th edition), Mason, OH: South- Western.

Altman, I. and S.M. Low (1992) (eds), *Place Attachment*, New York and London: Plenum Press.

Alvord, S., D. Brown and C. Letts (2002), 'Social entrepreneurship and social transformation: an exploratory study', Working Paper No. 15, available from *Social Science Research Network Electronic Paper Collection*, Hauser Center for Nonprofit Organizations.

Amin, A. and N. Thrift (1994), 'Living in the global', in A. Amin and N. Thrift (eds), *Globalization, Institutions and Regional Development in Europe*, Oxford: Oxford University Press.

Amin, A., A. Cameron and R. Hudson (2002), *Placing the Social Economy*, London: Routledge.

Andersen, B.R. (1984), 'Rationality and irrationality of the Nordic welfare state', *Journal of the American Academy of Arts and Sciences*, Winter, 109–39.

Anderson, A.R. and S.L. Jack (2002), 'The articulation of social capital entrepreneurial networks: a glue or a lubricant?', *Entrepreneurship and Regional Development*, July–Sept, 193–210.

Apel, K.-O. (1984), *Understanding and Explanation*, Cambridge, MA: The MIT Press.

Arbnor, I. and L. Andersson (1977), *Att förstå sociala system* [To understand social systems], Lund, Sweden: Studentlitteratur.

Arbnor, I. and B. Bjerke (1994), *Företagsekonomisk metodlära* [Business Administration methodology], Lund, Sweden: Studentlitteratur.

Arbnor, I. and B. Bjerke (2009), *Methodology for Creating Business Knowledge* (3rd edition), London: Sage.

Arbnor, I., S.-E. Borglund and T. Liljedahl (1980), *Osynligt ockuperad* [Invisibly occupied], Lund, Sweden: Studentlitteratur.

Arvonen, J. (1989), *Att leda via idéer* [To lead via ideas], Lund, Sweden: Studentlitteratur.

At-Twaijri, M.I. (1989a), 'Saudi approach to business', unpublished research report, King Fahd University of Petroleum and Minerals, Saudi Arabia.

At-Twaijri, M.I. (1989b), 'Three practical cultural styles of strategic management perspectives', unpublished research report, King Fahd University of Petroleum and Minerals, Saudi Arabia.

Audretsch, D.B. and R. Thurik (1999), 'Capitalism and democracy in the 21st century: from the managed to the entrepreneurial economy', *Journal of Evolutionary Economics*, **10**, 17–34.

Augé, M. (1995), *Non-Places: Introduction to an Anthropology of Supermodernity*, London: Verso.

Auster, E. (1990), 'The interorganizational environment: network theory, tools, and applications', in F. Williams and D. Gibson (eds), *Technology Transfer: A Communication Perspective*, London: Sage.

Baker, T. and R.E. Nelson (2005), 'Creating something from nothing: resource construction through entrepreneurial bricolage', *Administrative Science Quarterly*, **50**, 329–66.

Baker, T., E. Gedjlovic and M. Lubatkin (2005), 'A framework for comparing entrepreneurship processes across nations', *Journal of Business Studies*, **36**, 492–504.

Bandura, A. (1995), 'Perceived self-efficacy', in A.S.R. Manstead and M. Hewstone (eds), *The Blackwell Encyclopedia of Social Psychology*, Oxford: Blackwell Publishers Ltd.

Banks, J. (1972), *The Sociology of Social Movements*, London: MacMillan.

Barabási, A.-L. (2002), *Linked: The New Science of Networks*, New York: Perseus Publishing.

Barke, M. and K. Harrop (1994), 'Selling the industrial town: identity, image and illusion', in J.R. Gold and S.V. Ward (eds), *Place Promotion: The Use of Publicity and Marketing to Sell Towns and Regions*, Chichester, UK: John Wiley & Sons.

BarNir, A. and K. Smith (2002), 'Interfirm alliances in the small business: the role of social networks', *Journal of Small Business Management*, **40**(3), 219–32.

Baron, R.A. (1998), 'Cognitive mechanisms in entrepreneurship: why and when entrepreneurs think differently than other people', *Journal of Business Venturing*, **12**, 275–94.

Baron, R.A. and S.A. Shane (2008), *Entrepreneurship. A Process Perspective* (2nd edition), Mason, OH: Thomson.

Barreto, H. (1989), *The Entrepreneur in Microeconomic Theory. Disappearance and Explanation*, London and New York: Routledge.

Barringer, B.R. and R.D. Ireland (2006), *Entrepreneurship. Successfully Launching New Ventures*, Upper Saddle River, NJ: Pearson Education.

Bartunek, J.M. (1984), 'Changing interpretive schemes and organizational restructuring: the example of a religious order', *Administrative Science Quarterly*, **28**, 355–72.

Baumol, W.J. (1990), 'Entrepreneurship: productive, unproductive, and destructive', *Journal of Political Economy*, **98**(5), 893–921.

Baumol, W.J. (1993), *Entrepreneurship, Management, and the Structure of Payoffs*, Cambridge, MA: MIT Press.

Baumol, W.J. (2002), *The Free-Market Innovation Machine: Analyzing the Growth Miracle of Capitalism*, Princeton, NJ: Princeton University Press.

Bell, D. (1974), *The Coming of Post-Industrial Society: A Venture in Social Forecasting*, New York: Basic Books.

Bengtsson, L. (2006), *Entreprenörskap och företagande i akademiska miljöer* [Entrepreneurship and enterprising in academic environments], Lund, Sweden: Studentlitteratur.

Benz, M. (2006), 'Entrepreneurship as a non-profit-seeking activity', Institute for Empirical Research in Economics Working Paper no. 243, University of Zurich, Switzerland.

Berger, P.L and T. Luckmann (1966), *The Social Construction of Reality*, Harmondsworth, UK: Penguin.

Berglund, K. and A.W. Johansson (2008), *Arenor för entreprenörskap* [Arenas for entrepreneurship], Stockholm, Sweden: Stiftelsen för Småföretagsforskning.

Berglund, K. and J. Gaddefors (2010), 'Entrepreneurship requires resistance to be mobilized', in F. Bill, B. Bjerke and A.W. Johansson (eds), *(De)mobilizing the Entrepreneurship Discourse. Exploring Entrepreneurial Thinking and Action*, Cheltenham, UK and Northampton, MA, USA: Edward Elgar Publishing.

Beyes, T. (2006), 'City of enterprise, city as prey? On urban entrepreneurial spaces', in C. Steyaert and D. Hjorth (eds), *Entrepreneurship as Social Change*, Cheltenham, UK and Northampton, MA, USA: Edward Elgar Publishing.

Bhave, M.P. (1994), 'A process model of entrepreneurial venture creation', *Journal of Business Venturing*, **9**(3), 223–42.

Bill, F., A. Jansson and L. Olaison (2010), 'The spectacle of entrepreneurship: a duality of flamboyance and activity', in F. Bill, B. Bjerke and A.W. Johansson (eds), *(De)mobilizing the Entrepreneurship Discourse. Exploring Entrepreneurial Thinking and Action*, Cheltenham, UK and Northampton, MA, USA: Edward Elgar Publishing.

Birch, D. (1979), *The Job Generation Process*, Cambridge, MA: MIT Program on Neighborhood and Regional Change.

Birley, S. (1985), 'The role of networks in the entrepreneurial process', *Journal of Business Venturing*, **1**, 107–17.

Birley, S., S. Cromie and A. Myers (1991), 'Entrepreneurial networks: their emergence in Ireland and overseas', *International Small Business Journal*, **9**(4), 56–74.

Bjerke, B. (1989), *Att skapa nya affärer* [To create new business ventures], Lund, Sweden: Studentlitteratur.

Bjerke, B. (1999), *Business Leadership and Culture. National Management Styles in the Global Economy*, Cheltenham, UK and Northampton, MA, USA: Edward Elgar Publishing.

Bjerke, B. (2007), *Understanding Entrepreneurship*, Cheltenham, UK and Northampton, MA, USA: Edward Elgar Publishing.

Bjerke, B. (2010), 'Entrepreneurship, space and place', in F. Bill, B. Bjerke and A.W. Johansson (eds), *(De)mobilizing the Entrepreneurship Discourse. Exploring Entrepreneurial Thinking and Action*, Cheltenham, UK and Northampton, MA, USA: Edward Elgar Publishing.

Bjerke, B. and A.R. Al-Meer (1993), 'Culture's consequences: management in Saudi Arabia', *Leadership & Organization Development Journal*, **14**(2), 30–5.

Bjerke, B. and U. Kazi (1990), 'Saudi Arabia economy and industrial development', unpublished research report, King Fahd University of Petroleum and Minerals, Saudi Arabia.

Bjerke, B. and A.R. Al-Meer (1994), 'A behavioral consciousness view of corporate culture', *The Association of Management 12th Annual International Conference*, Dallas, Texas: Proceeding of the Organizational Studies Group, **12**(1), 174–9.

Bjerke, B. and C. Hultman (2002), *Entrepreneurial Marketing*, Cheltenham, UK and Northampton, MA: USA: Edward Elgar Publishing.

Bjerke, B. and H. Rämö (2011), *Entrepreneurial Imagination – Time, Timing, Space and Place in Business Action*, Cheltenham, UK and Northampton, MA, USA: Edward Elgar Publishing.

Bjerke, B. and M. Karlsson (2013), *Social Entrepreneur. To Act As If and Make a Difference*, Cheltenham, UK and Northampton, MA, USA: Edward Elgar Publishing.

Blackburn, R. and M. Ram (2006), 'Fix or fixation? The contributions and limitations of entrepreneurship and small firms to combating social exclusion', *Entrepreneurship and Regional Development*, **18**, 73–89.

Blomgren, M. and T. Bergman (2005), *EU och Sverige – ett sammanlänkat statsskick* [EU and Sweden – a state government linked together], Malmö, Sweden: Liber Förlag.

Blundel, R.K. and D. Smith (2001), *Business Networking: SMEs and Inter-Firm Collaboration, a Review of the Research Literature with Implication for Policy*, Report to Small Business Services PP03/01, Department of Trade and Industry, Small Business Service, Sheffield.

Boddice, R. (2009), 'Forgotten antecedents: entrepreneurship, ideology and history', in R. Ziegler (ed.), *An Introduction to Social Entrepreneurship*, Cheltenham, UK and Northampton, MA, USA: Edward Elgar Publishing.

Boussevain, J. (1974), *Friends of Friends: Networks, Manipulations and Coalitions*, Oxford: Basil Blackwell.

Bornstein, D. (2004), *How to Change the World. Social Entrepreneurs and the Power of New Ideas*, Oxford: Oxford University Press.

Borzaga, C. and J. Defourney (eds) (2001), *The Emergence of Social Enterprise*, Oxford and New York: Routledge.

Boschee, J. (1998), 'What does it take to be a social entrepreneur?', www.socialentrepreneurs. org./whatdoes.html.

Bosma, N. and R. Harding (2007), *Global Entrepreneurship. GEM 2006 Summary Results*, Babson Park, MA, USA and London, UK: Babson College and London Business School.

Bottomore, T. and R. Nisbet (eds) (1979), *A History of Sociological Analysis*, London: Heinemann.

Boulding, K.E. (1956), 'General systems theory: the skeleton of science', *Management Science*, **2**, 197–208.

Boyd, N. and G.S. Vozikis (1994), 'The influence of self-efficacy on the development of entrepreneurial intentions and actions', *Entrepreneurial Theory and Practice*, Summer, 53–77.

Brenner, N. (1997), 'Global, fragmented, hierarchical: Henri Lefebvre's geographies of globalization', *Public Culture*, **10**(1), 135–67.

Brewster, C., A. Lundmark and L. Holden (1993), *'A Different Tack'. An Analysis of British and Swedish Management Styles*, Lund, Sweden: Chartwell Bratt.

Brickell, P. (2000), *People before Structures: Engaging Communities Effectively in Regeneration*, London: Demos.

Bridge, S., K. O'Neill and S. Cromie (2009), *Understanding Enterprise, Entrepreneurship and Small Business* (3rd edition), New York: Palgrave Macmillan.

Brinckerhoff, P.C. (2000), *Social Entrepreneurship. The Art of Mission-Based Venture Development*, New York, NY: John Wiley & Sons.

Brockhaus, R.H. (1982), 'The psychology of the entrepreneur', in C.A. Kent, D.L. Sexton and K.H. Vesper (eds), *Encyclopedia of Entrepreneurship*, Englewood Cliffs, NJ: Prentice Hall.

Brown, B. and J.E. Butler (1995), 'Competitors as allies: a study of the entrepreneurial networks in the US wine industry', *Journal of Small Business Management*, **33**(3), 57–66.

Buchanan, J.M. (1982), 'The domain of subjective economics: between predictive science and moral philosophy', in I.E. Kirzner (ed.), *Method, Process and Austrian Economics. Essays in the Honour of Ludwig von Mises*, Toronto, Canada: Lexington Books.

Burchell, G., C. Gordon and P. Miller (eds) (1991), *The Foucault Effect: Studies in Governmentality*, Chicago, IL: University of Chicago Press.

Burgess, J. and P. Wood (1988), 'Decoding Docklands: place advertising and the decision-making strategies of the small firm', in J. Eyles and D.M. Smith (eds), *Qualitative Method in Human Geography*, Cambridge: Polity Press.

Burns, P. (2011), *Entrepreneurship and Small Business. Start, Growth and Maturity* (3rd edition), New York: Palgrave Macmillan.

Burt, R.S. (1992), *Structural Holes. The Social Structure of Competition*, Cambridge, MA: Harvard University Press.

Burt, R.S. (1997), 'The contingent value of social capital', *Administrative Science Quarterly*, **42**, 339–65.

Business Week, 1982, 'Europe's new managers. Going global with the US style', *Business Week*, 24 May 1982, 78–82.

Business Week, 1991, 'Hidden Japan', *Business Week*, 26 August, 14–22.

Business Week, 1995, 'Asia's new giants', *Business Week*, 27 November, 30–40.

Business Week, 1997, 'Information anxiety', *Business Week*, 9 June, 52–3.

Buttimer, A. and D. Seamon (eds) (1980), *The Human Experience of Space and Place*, New York: St. Martin's Press.

Böhm-Bawerk, E. (1890–91), 'The Historical vs. The Deductive Method in Political Economy', translated by H. Leonard, *Annals of the American Academy*, Volume 1. (1890–91), Lähde, Finland, available at: http://socserv2.mcmaster.ca/econ/ugcm/3113/pawerk/pohm001.html.

Callon, M. (1986), 'The sociology of an actor-network', in M. Callon, J. Law and A. Rip (eds), *Mapping the Dynamics of Science and Technology*, Basingstoke, UK: MacMillan.

Callon, M. (1999), 'Actor-network theory – the market test', in J. Law and J. Hassard (eds), *Actor Network Theory and After*, Oxford: Blackwell.

Campbell, K. (2004), 'Quilting a feminist map to guide the study of women entrepreneurs', in D. Hjorth and C. Steyaert (eds), *Narrative and Discursive Approaches in Entrepreneurship. A Second Movements in Entrepreneurship Books*, Cheltenham, UK and Northampton, MA: USA: Edward Elgar Publishing.

Cantillon, R. (1755), *Essai sur la nature du commerce en general*, London: Fletcher Gyles.

Carlsson, B. (1992), 'The rise of small business: causes and consequences', in W.J. Adams (ed.), *Singular Europe, Economy and Policy of the European Community After 1992*, Ann Arbor, MI: University of Michigan Press.

Carson, D., S. Cromie, P. McGowan and J. Hill (1995), *Marketing and Entrepreneurship in SMEs*, Hemel Hempstead, UK: Prentice Hall International (UK) Ltd.

Carter, S. and D. Bennett (2006), 'Gender and entrepreneurship', in S. Carter and D. Jones-Evans (eds), *Enterprise and Small Business. Principles, Practice and Policy* (2nd edition), Harlow, UK: Pearson Education Limited.

Casey, E.S. (1993), *Getting Back into Place: toward a Renewed Understanding of the Place-World*, Bloomington, IN: Indiana University Press.

Casey, E.S. (1997), *The Fate of Place: a Philosophical History*, Berkeley, CA: University of California Press.

Casson, M. (1982), *The Entrepreneur. An Economic Theory*, Totowa, NJ: Barnes and Noble Books.

Castells, M. (1998), *Informationsåldern. Ekonomi, samhälle och kultur: Band I: Nätverkssamhällets framväxt* [The information age. Economy, society and culture, Volume I: The rise of the network society], Gothenburg, Sweden: Daidalos.

Chau, T.T. (1991), 'Approaches to succession in East Asian business organizations', *Family Business Review*, **IV**(2), 161–79.

Chell, E. (2001), *Entrepreneurship: Globalization, Innovation and Development*, Stanford, CT: Thomson South-Western.

Chell, E. and S. Baines (2000), 'Networking, entrepreneurship and microbusiness behaviour', *Entrepreneurship and Regional Development*, **12**, 195–215.

Chen, M. (1995), *Asian Management Systems*, London: Routledge.

Cho, A.H. (2006), 'Politics, values and social entrepreneurship: a critical appraisal', in J. Mair, J. Robinson and K. Hockerts (eds), *Social Entrepreneurship*, Hampshire, UK and New York, USA: Palgrave Macmillan.

Choi, Y.B. (1993), *Paradigms and Conventions – Uncertainty, Decision Making and Entrepreneurship*, Chicago: The University of Michigan Press.

Chu, C.-N. (1991), *The Asian Mind Game*, New York: Macmillan Publishing Company.

Ciborra, C.U. (1996), 'The platform organization: Recombining strategies, structures, and surprises', *Organization Science*, 7, 103–18.

Coleman, J.S. (1990), *Foundations of Social Theory*, Cambridge, MA: Harvard University Press.

Conway, S. (1997), 'Informal networks of relationships in successful small firm innovation', in D. Jones-Evans and M. Klofsten (eds), *Technology, Innovation and Enterprise: The European Experience*, Basingstoke, UK: MacMillan.

Conway, S. and O. Jones (2006), 'Networking and the small business', in S. Carter and D. Jones-Evans (eds), *Enterprise and Small Business. Principles, Practice and Policy* (2nd edition), Harlow, UK: Pearson Education.

Conway, S, O. Jones and F. Steward (2001), 'Realising the potential of the social network perspective in innovation studies', in O. Jones, S. Conway and F. Steward (eds), *Social Interaction and Organisational Change: Aston Perspectives on Innovation Networks*, London: Imperial College Press.

Cooke, P. (1989), 'Locality, economic restructuring and world development', in P. Cooke (ed.), *Localities: The Changing Face of Urban Britain*, London: Unwin Hyman.

Cooper, R. and J. Law (1995), 'Organization: distal and proximal views', *Research in the Sociology of Organizations*, 13(1995), 237–74.

Coulter, M. (2001), *Entrepreneurship in Action*, Upper Saddle River, NJ: Prentice Hall.

Cox, K.R. and A. Mair (1988), 'Locality and community in the politics of local economic development', *Annals of the Association of American Geographers*, 78, 307–25.

Cresswell, T. (2004), *Place. A Short Introduction*, Oxford: Blackwell.

Cronon, W. (1992), 'Kennecott journey: the paths out of town', in W. Cronon, W. Miles and J. Gitlin (eds), *Under an Open Sky*, New York: Norton.

Cunningham, J.-B. and J Lischeron (1991), 'Defining entrepreneurship', *Journal of Small Business Management*, 29(1), 43–51.

Curran, J. and R.A. Blackburn (1991), *Paths of Enterprise*, London: Routledge.

Curry, M.R. (2002), 'Discursive displacement and the seminal ambiguity of space and place', in L. Lievrouw and S. Livingstone (eds), *Handbook in New Media*, London: Sage Publications.

Czinkota, M.R., P. Rivoli and I.A. Ronkainen (1994), *International Business* (3rd edition), Orlando, FL: Harcourt Brace & Company.

Dahmén, R. (1950), *Svensk industriell företagsverksamhet* [Swedish industrial business activities], Stockholm, Sweden: Industrins Utredningsinstitut.

Danilda, I. (2001), 'Finns det ett speciellt företagsklimat för kvinnor som driver företag? [Is there a special business climate for women running businesses?], in E. Ekstedt (ed.), *Kunskap och handling för företagande och regional utveckling* [Knowledge and action for enterprising and regional development], Arbetsliv i omvandling, Arbetslivsinstitutet, 4, 2001, 77–97.

Dart, R. (2004), 'The legitimacy of social enterprise', *Non-profit Management & Leadership*, 14(4), 411–24.

Daun, Å. (1989), *Svensk mentalitet* [Swedish mentality], Stockholm, Sweden: Rabén & Sjögren.

Davidsson, P. (1989), *Continued Entrepreneurship and Small Firm Growth*, doctoral dissertation, Handelshögskolan i Stockholm, Sweden.

Davidsson, P. (2003), 'The domain of entrepreneurship research: some suggestions', in

D. Shepherd and J. Katz (eds), *Cognitive Approaches to Entrepreneurship Research*, Amsterdam: Elsevier.

Davidsson, P. (2004), *Researching Entrepreneurship*, New York: Springer.

Davis, C. and L. Hulett (1999), 'Skills needs in the resource-based sectors in Atlantic Canada', report presented at *Skills Development in the Knowledge-Based Economy*, Moncton, Canada, June.

Davoudi, S. (1995), 'Dilemmas of urban governance', in P. Healey et. al. (eds), *Managing Cities: The New Urban Context*, Chichester, UK: Wiley.

Deal, T. and A. Kennedy (1988), *Corporate Cultures*, London: Penguin Books.

de Bruin, A. (2003), 'State entrepreneurship', in A. de Bruin and A. Dupuis (eds), *Entrepreneurship: New Perspectives in a Global Age*, Aldershot, UK: Ashgate Publishing Limited.

de Carolis, M. (1996), 'Toward a phenomenology of opportunities', in P. Virno and M. Hardt (eds), *Radical Thought in Italy*, Minneapolis, MN: University of Minnesota Press.

de Certeau, M. (1984), *The Practice of Everyday Life*, Berkeley, CA: University of California Press.

Dedijer, S. (1991), 'Development & management by intelligence: Japan', School of Economics and Management Lund University Working Paper Series, Institute of Economic Research, 1991/15.

Dees, J.G. (1998), *The Meaning of Social Entrepreneurship*, available at: http://faculty.fuqua.duke.edu/centers/case/files/dees-SE.pdf.

Dees, J.G., J. Emerson and P. Economy (2001), *Enterprising Nonprofits. A Toolkit for Social Entrepreneurs*, New York, NY: John Wiley and Sons.

Dees, J.G., J. Emerson and P. Economy (2002), *Strategic Tools for Social Entrepreneurs. Enhancing the Performance of Your Enterprising Nonprofit*, New York, NY: John Wiley and Sons.

Deetz, S. (1998), 'Discursive formations, strategized subordination and self- surveillance', in A. McKinley and K. Starkey (eds), *Foucault, Management and Organization Theory*, London: Sage.

Defourney, J. (2001), 'Introduction. From third sector to social enterprise', in C. Borzaga and J. Defourney (eds), *The Emergence of Social Enterprise*, Oxford and New York: Routledge.

Defourney, J. (2003), 'A new entrepreneurship in the social economy', available at: www.emes.net/en/recherche/emes/analyse.php.

De Leeuw, E. (1999), 'Healthy cities: Urban social entrepreneurship for health', *Health Promotion International*, **14**(3), 261–9.

Delmar, F. (2006), 'The psychology of the entrepreneur', in S. Carter and D. Jones- Evans (eds), *Enterprise and Small Business. Principles, Practice and Policy* (2nd edition), Harlow, UK: Pearson Education Limited.

Delmar, F. and P. Davidsson (2000), 'Where do they come from? Prevalence and characteristics of nascent entrepreneurs', *Entrepreneurship and Regional Development*, **12**, 1–23.

Dennis, C. (2000), 'Networking for marketing advantage', *Management Decision*, **38**(4), 287–92.

Derrida, J. (2000), *Also ich tot wäre. Ein Interview mit Jacques Derrida* [Consequently, I would be dead. An interview with Jacques Derrida], Vienna: Turia + Kant.

'Det nya näringslivet' [The new industrial sector] (2001), report published by Svenskt Näringsliv.

Dey, P. and C. Steyaert (2010), 'The politics of narrating social entrepreneurship', *Journal of Enterprising Communities*, **4**(1), 85–108.

Dollinger, M.C. (2003), *Entrepreneurship, Strategies and Resources* (3rd edition), Upper Saddle River, NJ: Prentice Hall.

Dosi, G. (1988), 'Sources, procedures and microeconomic effects of innovation', *Journal of Economic Literature*, **36**, 1126–71.

Dreyfus, H.L. and P. Rabinow (eds) (1982), *Michel Foucault – Beyond Structuralism and Hermeneutics*, London: Harvester Wheatsheaf.

Droysen, J.G. (1858 [1897]), *Grundrisse der Historik,* published as *Outline of the Principles of History,* transl. E.B. Andrews, Boston, MA: Ginn & Co.

Drucker, P. (1969), *The Age of Discontinuity: Guidelines to our Changing Society,* London: Heinemann.

Drucker, P. (1985), *Innovation and Entrepreneurship. Practice and Principles,* London: Heinemann.

du Gay, P. (ed.) (1997), *The Production of Culture – Cultures of Production,* London: Sage.

Dunn, K.M., P.M. McGuirk and H.P.M. Winchester (1995), 'Place-making: the social construction of Newcastle', *Australian Geographical Studies,* **33,** 149–66.

Dupuis, A. and A. de Bruin (2003), 'Community entrepreneurship', in A. de Bruin and A. Dupuis (eds), *Entrepreneurship: New Perspectives in a Global Age,* Aldershot, UK: Ashgate Publishing Limited.

Dupuis, A., A. de Bruin and R.D. Cremer (2003), 'Municipal-community entrepreneurship', in A. de Bruin and A. Dupuis (eds), *Entrepreneurship: New Perspectives in a Global Age,* Aldershot, UK: Ashgate Publishing Limited.

Eagly, A.H. and S. Chaiken (1993), *The Psychology of Attitudes,* Fort Worth, TX: Harcourt Brace Jovanovich, Inc.

The Economist (1990), 'A survey of Japanese finance', *The Economist,* 8 December, Supplement.

The Economist (1993), 'A survey of the Japanese economy', 6 March, *The Economist,* Supplement.

The Economist (1995), 'How to conquer China (and the world) with instant noodles', *The Economist,* 17 June, 27–8.

The Economist (1996a), 'A survey of business in Asia', *The Economist,* 23 November, Supplement.

The Economist (1996b), 'A survey of business in Europe', *The Economist,* 9 March, Supplement.

The Economist (1996c), 'Fissiparous fortunes and family feuds', *The Economist,* 30 November, 69–70.

The Economist (1997), 'And never the twain shall meet . . .', *The Economist,* 29 March, 73–4.

The Economist (1998), 'Entrepreneurs in order', *The Economist,* 14 March, 63–5.

The Economist (2000), 'The new economy. Untangling e-economics', *The Economist,* 23 September, Supplement.

The Economist (2001), 'The next society. A survey of the near future', *The Economist,* 3 November, Supplement.

Edquist, C. and M. McKelvey (1998), 'High R&D intensity without high tech products: a Swedish paradox?', in K. Nielsen and B. Johnsen (eds), *Institutions and Economic Change: New Perspectives on Markets, Firms and Technology,* Cheltenham, UK and Northampton, MA, USA: Edward Elgar Publishing.

Ehrlich, S. and R. King (1994), 'Feminist meanings and the (de)politization of the lexicon', *Language in Society,* **23,** 59–76.

Eisenschitz, A. and J. Gough (1993), *The Politics of Local Economic Development,* London: Macmillan.

Ekman, R. and J. Hultman (eds) (2007), *Plats som produkt* [Place as product], Lund, Sweden: Studentlitteratur.

Eliasson, G. (1987), *Technological Competition and Trade in the Experimentally Organized Economy,* Research Report No. 32, Stockholm, Sweden: Industrins Utredningsinstitut.

Emerson, J. (1999), 'Social return on investment: exploring aspects of social creation', *REDF box set,* 2, Chapter 8, San Francisco: Roberts Enterprise Development Foundation.

Emerson, J. and F. Twersky (1996), *New Social Entrepreneurs: The Success, Challenges and Lessons of Non-Profit Enterprise Creation,* San Francisco, CA: Roberts Enterprise Development Foundation.

EOS Gallup (2004), 'Flash 160 "Entrepreneurship"', survey for Directorate General Enterprise – European Commission, Brussels: EOS Gallop.

Eriksson, K. and M. Ådahl (2000), 'Finns det en ny ekonomi och kommer den till Europa?' [Is there a new economy and will it come to Europe?], *Penning- och Valutapolitik*, Nr. 1, Stockholm, Sweden: Sveriges Riksbank.

Evers, A. (1998), 'Soziales Engagement. Zwischen Selbstverwirklung und Bürgerpflicht' [Social involvement. Between self-realization and citizen duty], *Transit*, **15**, 186–200.

Evers, A. (2001), 'The significance of social capital in the multiple goal and resources structure of social enterprises', in C. Borzaga and J. Defourney (eds), *The Emergence of Social Enterprise*, Oxford and New York: Routledge.

Fafchamps, M. (2000), 'Ethnicity and credit in African manufacturing', *Journal of Development Economics*, **61**, 205–35.

Favreau, L. (2000), 'The social economy and globalization: an overview', in J. Defourney, P. Develtere and B. Foneneau (eds), *Social Economy North and South*, Belgium: Katholieke Universiteit Leuvren and Universited de Liege.

Fay, B. (1996), *Contemporary Philosophy of Social Science*, Oxford: Blackwell Publishers.

Fayolle, A., P. Kyrö and J. Ulijn (eds) (2005), *Entrepreneurship Research in Europe. Outcomes and Perspectives*, Cheltenham, UK and Northampton, MA, USA: Edward Elgar Publishing.

Ferguson, M. (1980), *The Acquarian Conspiracy*, Los Angeles, CA: Jeremy P. Tarcher.

Ferraro, G.P. (1994), *The Cultural Dimension of International Business* (2nd edition), Englewood Cliffs, NJ: Prentice Hall.

Filion, L.J. (1997), 'Le champ de l'entrepreneuriat: historique, evolution, tendances' [The entrepreneurial champions: history, evolution, tendencies], *Cahier de researche* no. 97.01, HTC Montreal.

Flax, J. (1987), 'Postmodernism and gender relations in feminist theory', *SIGNS*, **12**(4), 621–43.

Flora, J.L. (1998), 'Social capital and communities of place', *Rural Sociology*, **63**, 481–506.

Florida, R. (2002), *The Rise of the Creative Class*, New York, NY: Basic Books.

Florida, R. (2003), 'Cities and the venture class', *City & Community*, **2**, 1, March, 3–19.

Forbes, D.P. (2005), 'Are some entrepreneurs more overconfident than others?', *Journal of Business Venturing*, **20**, 623–40.

Forss, K., D. Hawk and G. Hedlund (1984), 'Cultural differences – Swedishness in legislation, multinational corporations and aid administration', Institute of International Business, Handelshögskolan i Stockholm.

Foucault, M. (1980), 'The eye of power: conversation with J.-P. Barou and M. Perrot', in C. Gordon (ed.), *Power/Knowledge: Selected Interviews and Other Writings, 1972–1977, by Michel Foucault*, Hemel Hempstead, UK: Harvester Press.

Foucault, M. (1991), 'Governmentality', in G. Burchell, C. Gordon and P. Miller (eds), *The Foucault Effect*, London: Harvester Wheatsheaf.

Foucault, M. (1997), 'What is enlightenment?', in P. Rabinow (ed.), *Michel Foucault. Ethics, Subjectivity and Truth*, New York: The New Press.

Franco, A. and K. Winqvist (2002), 'The entrepreneurial gap between women and men', *Statistics in Focus*, Population and Social Conditions Theme 3, **11**/2002, Brussels: Eurostat.

Freel, M. (2000), 'External linkages and product innovation in small manufacturing firms', *Entrepreneurship and Regional Development*, **12**, 245–66.

Frykman, J. (1987), 'Bryt upp! Förändring som livsprojekt' [Break up! Change as life-project], paper presented at a symposium on *The Swedish Model's Cultural Face*, Umeå University, January, 14–6.

Fyall, A. and B. Garrod (2005), *Tourism Marketing: A Collaborative Approach. Aspects of Tourism 18*, Clevedon, UK: Channel View Publications.

Gadamer, H.G. (1960 [1997]), *Wahrheit und Methode* [Truth and Method], Gothenburg, Sweden: Daidalos.

Gaglio, C.M. (1997), 'Opportunity recognition: Review, critique and suggested research directions', in J. Katz and R.H. Brockhaus (eds), *Advances in Entrepreneurship, Firm Emergence and Growth*, Greenwich, CT: JAI Press.

Gaglio, C.M. and J.A. Katz (2001), 'The psychological basis of opportunity identification: entrepreneurial alertness', *Small Business Economics*, **16**, 95–111.

Gartner, W.B. (1988), 'Who is the entrepreneur? is the wrong question', *American Journal of Small Business*, **12**(4), 11–32.

Gartner, W.B. (2007), 'Entrepreneurial narrative and a science of the imagination', *Journal of Business Venturing*, **22**(5), 613–27.

Gartner, W.B. and N.M. Carter (2003), 'Entrepreneurial behavior and firm organizing processes', in Z.J. Ács and D.B. Audretsch (eds), *Handbook of Entrepreneurship*, Dordrecht, the Netherlands: Kluwer.

Gartner, W.B., B.J. Bird and J.A. Starr (1992), 'Acting as if: differentiating entrepreneurial from organizational behavior', *Entrepreneurship Theory and Practice*, **16**, Spring, 13–30.

Garud, R., A. Kumaraswamy and P. Nayyar (1998), 'Real options of fool's gold. Perspective makes the difference', *Academy of Management Review*, **3**(2), 212–14.

Gatewood, E., C. Brush, N. Carter, P. Greene and M. Hart (2003), *Women Entrepreneurs, Their Ventures, and the Venture Capital Industry: An Annotated Bibliography*, Report 2003:1, Stockholm, Sweden: Esbri.

Gawell, M. (2009), 'Samhällsentreprenörskap för en global utveckling' [Social entrepreneurship for a global development], in M. Gawell, B. Johannisson and M. Lundqvist (eds), *Samhällets entreprenörer* [The societal entrepreneurs], Stockholm: KK-stiftelsen.

Gawell, M., B. Johannisson and M. Lundqvist (eds) (2009), *Samhällets entreprenörer* [The societal entrepreneurs], Stockholm: KK-stiftelsen.

Geertz, C. (1973), *The Interpretation of Cultures*, New York: Basic.

Gibson, D. (1991), *Technology Companies and Global Markets: Programs, Policies and Strategies to Accelerate Innovation and Entrepreneurship*, Lanham, MD: Rowman and Littlefield.

Gioia, D.A. (1986), 'Symbols, scripts and sensemaking: creating meaning in organizational experience', in H.P. Sims and D.A. Gioia (eds), *The Thinking Organization*, San Francisco, CA: Jossey-Bass Publishers.

Girndt, H. (1967), *Das soziale Handeln als Grundkategorie Erfahrungswissenschaftlicher Soziologie* [The social negotiation as basic category in experience-based sociology], Tübingen, Germany: J.C.B. Mohr (Paul Siebeck).

Global Entrepreneurship Monitor. Executive Report, 2007.

Gorz, A. (1999), *Reclaiming Work*, Cambridge: Polity Press.

Gottdiener, M. (1987), *The Decline in Urban Politics*, Beverly Hills, CA: Sage.

Graham, S. (1995), 'The city economy', in P. Healey, S. Cameron, S. Davoudi, S. Graham and A. Madani-Pour (eds), *Managing Cities: The New Urban Context*, Chichester, UK: John Wiley.

Grant, A. (1998), 'Entrepreneurship – the major academic discipline for the business education curriculum for the 21st century', in M.G. Scott, P. Rosa and H. Klandt (eds), *Educating Entrepreneurs for Wealth Creation*, Burlington, VT, USA: Ashgate.

Grenier, P. (2009), 'Social entrepreneurship in the UK: from rhetoric to reality?', in R. Ziegler (ed.), *An Introduction to Social Entrepreneurship*, Cheltenham, UK and Northampton, MA, USA: Edward Elgar Publishing.

Guinchard, C.G. (ed.) (1997), *Swedish Planning: Towards Sustainable Development*, Gävle, Sweden: Swedish Society for Town and Country Planning.

Gunnered Berg, N. (1997), 'Gender, place and entrepreneurship', *Entrepreneurship and Regional Development*, **9**, 259–68.

Habermas, J. (1984), *The Theory of Communicative Action*, Cambridge: Polity Press.

Habermas, J. (1996), *Between Facts and Norms*, Cambridge, MA: MIT Press.

Hacking, I. (1983), *Representing and Intervening: Introductory Topics in the Philosophy of Natural Science*, Cambridge: Cambridge University Press.

Hall, E.T. (1959), *The Silent Language*, New York: Doubleday.

Hall, T. (1992), 'Art and image: public art as symbol in urban regeneration', Working Paper no. 61: School of Geography, University of Birmingham.

Hall, T. (1998), 'Introduction', in T. Hall and P. Hubbard (eds), *The Entrepreneurial City*, Chichester, UK: John Wiley & Sons Ltd.

Hall, T. (2005), *Urban Geography* (3rd edition), London: Routledge.

Hamilton, B.H. (2000), 'Does entrepreneurship pay? An empirical analysis of the returns to self-employment', *Journal of Political Economy*, **108**, 604–31.

Hardt, M. (2002), *Gilles Deleuze. An Apprenticeship of Philosophy*, Minneapolis, MN: University of Minnesota Press.

Hardt, M. and A. Negri (2004), *Multitude, War and Democracy in the Age of Empire*, London: Harvard University Press.

Harris, P.R. and R.T. Moran (1987), *Managing Cultural Differences* (2nd Edition), Houston, Texas: Gulf Publishing Company.

Harvey, D. (1989), 'From managerialism to entrepreneurialism: the transformance of governance to late capitalism', *Geografiska Annaler*, 71B, 3-17.

Hatten, T. (2003), *Small Business Management* (2nd edition), Boston and New York: Houghton Mifflin Company.

Haughton, G. (1998), 'Principles and practice of community economic development', *Regional Studies*, **32**(9), 872–7.

Hayek, F.A. (1945), 'The use of knowledge in society', *American Economic Review*, **35**(4), 519–30.

Healey, P. (1997), *Collaborative Planning: Shaping Places in Fragmented Societies*, Houndmills and London: MacMillan Press.

Hébert, R.F and A.N. Link (1982), *The Entrepreneur. Mainstream Views and Radical Critique*, New York: Praeger.

Hébert, R.F and A.N. Link (1989), 'In search of the meaning of entrepreneurship', *Small Business Economics*, **1**(1), 39–49.

Henrekson, M. and N. Rosenberg (2000), *Akademiskt entreprenörskap. Universitet och näringsliv i samverkan* [Academic entrepreneurship. University and industry in co-operation], Stockholm, Sweden: SNS Förlag.

Henton, D., J. Melville and K. Walesh (1997), *Grassroots Leaders for a New Economy. How Civic Entrepreneurs are Building Prosperous Communities*, San Francisco, CA: Jossey-Bass.

Herbert, D.T. and C.J. Thomas (1997), *Cities in Space. City as Place* (3rd edition), London: David Fulton Publishers.

Hill, J. and L.T. Wright (2001), 'A qualitative research agenda for small to medium-sized enterprises', *Marketing Intelligence & Planning*, **19**(6), 432–43.

Hisrich, R.D. and C.G. Brush (1986), *The Woman Entrepreneur: Starting, Financing and Managing a Successful New Business*, Lexington, MA: Lexington Books.

Hisrich, R.D. and M.P. Peters (1992), *Entrepreneurship* (2nd edition), Homewood, IL: Richard D. Irwin.

Hite, J. and W. Hesterley (2001), 'The evolution of firm networks: from emergence to early growth of the firm', *Strategic Management Journal*, **22**(3), 275–86.

Hjorth, D. (2004), 'Creating space for play/invention – concepts of space and organizational entrepreneurship', *Entrepreneurship and Regional Development*, **16**, September, 413–32.

Hjorth, D. (2009), 'Entrepreneurship, sociality and art: re-imagining the public', in R. Ziegler (ed.), *An Introduction to Social Entrepreneurship*, Cheltenham, UK and Northampton, MA, USA: Edward Elgar Publishing.

Hjorth, D. and B. Johannisson (1998), 'Entreprenörskap som skapelseprocess och ideologi' [Entrepreneurship as creative process and ideology], in B. Czarniawska (ed.), *Organisationsteori på svenska* [Organization theory in Swedish], Malmö, Sweden: Liber Ekonomi.

Hjorth, D. and B. Johannisson (2000), 'Training for enrepreneurship: playing and language games: an inquiry into the Swedish education system', SIRE, Växjö University.

Hjorth, D. and B. Johannisson (2003), 'Conceptualising the opening phase of regional development as the enactment of "collective identity"', *Concepts and Transformations*, **8**, 69–92.

Hjorth, D. and C. Steyaert (2003), 'Entrepreneurship beyond (a new) economy: creative swarms and pathological zones', in C. Steyaert and D. Hjorth (eds), *New Movements in Entrepreneurship*, Cheltenham, UK and Northampton, MA, USA: Edward Elgar Publishing.

Hjorth, D. and C. Steyaert (eds) (2004), *Narrative and Discursive Approaches in Entrepreneurship. A Second Movements in Entrepreneurship Books*, Cheltenham, UK and Northampton, MA, USA: Edward Elgar Publishing.

Hjorth, D. and B. Bjerke (2006), 'Public entrepreneurship: moving from social/consumer to public/citizen', in C. Steyaert and D. Hjorth (eds), *Entrepreneurship as Social Change*, Cheltenham, UK and Northampton, USA: Edward Elgar Publishing.

Hjorth, D. and C. Steyaert (eds) (2009), *The Politics and Aesthetics of Entrepreneurship. A Fourth Movements in Entrepreneurship Book*, Cheltenham, UK and Northampton, MA, USA: Edward Elgar Publishing.

Hoang, H. and B. Antoncic (2003), 'Network-based research in entrepreneurship. A critical review', *Journal of Business Venturing*, **18**, 165–87.

Hodgetts, R.M. and F. Luthans (1991), *International Management*, Singapore: McGraw-Hill.

Hofstede, G. (1984), *Culture's Consequences* (2nd Edition), Beverly Hills, CA: Sage Publications.

Hofstede, G. and M.H. Bond (1988), 'The Confucian connection. From cultural roots to economic growth', *Organization Dynamics*, Spring, 5–21.

Hoggart, K. (1991), *People, Power and Place: Perspectives on Anglo-American Politics*, London: Routledge.

Holgersson, C. (1998), 'Den nödvändiga periferin' [The necessary periphery], in A. Wahl, C. Holgersson and P. Höök (eds), *Ironi & Sexualitet. Om ledarskap och kön* [Irony & sexuality. About leadership and gender], Stockholm, Sweden: Carlssons.

Holmberg, I., M. Salzer-Mörling and L. Strannegård (2002), 'Epilogue: stuck in the future?', in I. Holmberg, M. Salzer-Mörling and L. Strannegård (eds), *Stuck in the Future? Tracing the 'New Economy'*, Stockholm, Sweden: Bookhouse Publishing.

Holmquist, C. (1996), 'The female entrepreneur – woman and/or entrepreneur', in B. Nutek (ed.), *Aspects of Women's Entrepreneurship*, 87–112.

Holmquist, C. (1997), 'The other side of the coin – or another coin? – Women's entrepreneurship as a complement or alternative', *Entrepreneurship and Regional Development*, **9**, 179–82.

Holmquist, C. (2002), 'Integration mellan genus- och entreprenörskapsteori' [Integration between gender and entrepreneurship theory], in C. Holmquist and E. Sundin (eds), *Företagerskan – Om kvinnor och entreprenörskap* [The woman entrepreneur – about women and entrepreneurship], Stockholm, Sweden: SNS Förlag.

Holmquist, C. and E. Sundin (eds) (2002), *Företagerskan. Om kvinnor och entreprenörskap*, [The woman entrepreneur – about women and entrepreneurship], Stockholm, Sweden: SNS Förlag.

Hoon-Halbauer, S.K. (1994), *Management of Sino-Foreign Joint Ventures*, Lund, Sweden: Lund University Press.

Hubbard, P. and T. Hall (1998), 'The entrepreneurial city and the "new urban politics"', in T. Hall and P. Hubbard (eds), *The Entrepreneurial City*, Chichester, UK: John Wiley & Sons.

Hudson, R. (2000), *Production, Places and Environment: Changing Perspectives in Economic Geography*, Harlow, UK: Prentice Hall.

Hudson, R. (2001), *Producing Places*, London: Guildford Press.

Humes, S. (1993), *Managing the Multinational*, Harlow, UK: Prentice Hall.

Ireland, R.D., M.A. Hitt and D.G. Sirmon (2003). 'A model of strategic management', *Journal of Management*, **29**, 963–89.

Jacob, F. (1977), 'Evolution and tinkering', *Science*, **196**, 1161–6.

Jacobs, J. (1961), *The Death and Life of Great American Cities*, New York: Random House.

Jammer, M. (1982), *Concepts of Space. The History of Theories of Space in Physics* (3rd, enlarged edition), New York: Dover Publications, Inc.

'Jämställdhet för tillväxt' [Equality for growth] (2011), **entré**, 1, Stockholm, Sweden: Esbri.

Jansson, H. (1987), *Affärskulturer och relationer i Sydostasien* [Business cultures and relationships in South East Asia], Stockholm, Sweden: Marknadstekniskt Centrum, No. 29.

Jarillo, J. (1989), 'Entrepreneurship and growth: the strategic use of external resources', *Journal of Business Venturing*, **4**(2), 133–47.

Javefors Grauers, E. (2000), 'Familjeföretagande ur ett genusperspektiv – exemplet ICA' [Family business out of a gender perspective – the example ICA], in B. Gandemo (ed.), *Familjeföretag och familjeföretagande* [Family businesses and family enterprising], FSF 2000, 6, Örebro, Sweden: Forum för Småföretagsforskning.

Javefors Grauers, E. (2002), *Profession, genus och företagarpar – en studie av advokater och köpmän* [Profession, gender and enterprising couples – a study of lawyers and traders], doctoral dissertation, Linköpings University, Sweden.

Jessop, B. (1994), 'Post-Fordism and the state', in A. Amin (ed.), *Post-Fordism*, Oxford: Blackwell.

Jessop, B. (1996), 'The entrepreneurial city: re-imaging localities, re-designing economic governance or re-structuring capital', paper presented at the *Annual Conference of the Institute of British Geographers*, University of Strathclyde.

Jessop, B. (1997), 'The governance of complexity of governance: preliminary remarks on some problems and limits of economic guidance', in A. Amin and J. Hausner (eds), *Beyond Markets and Hierarchy. Third Way Approaches to Transformation*, Aldershot, UK: Edward Edgar.

Johannisson, B. (2000), 'Networking and entrepreneurial growth', in D.L. Sexton and H. Landström (eds), *The Blackwell Handbook of Entrepreneurship*, Oxford: Blackwell Publishers Ltd.

Johannisson, B. (2005), *Entreprenörskapets väsen* [The essence of entrepreneurship], Lund, Sweden: Studentlitteratur.

Johannisson, B. and R. Peterson (1984), 'The personal networks of entrepreneurs', paper presented at the *Third Canadian Conference of the International Council for Small Business*, Toronto, 23–25 May.

Johannisson, B. and A. Nilsson (1989), 'Community entrepreneurs: networking for local development', *Entrepreneurship and Regional Development*, **1**, 3–19.

Johansson, A.W. (2010), 'Innovation, creativity and imitation', in F. Bill, B. Bjerke and A.W. Johansson (eds), *(De)mobilizing the Entrepreneurship Discourse. Exploring Entrepreneurial Thinking and Action*, Cheltenham, UK and Northampton, MA, USA: Edward Elgar Publishing.

Johnson, C. (1988), 'Japanese-style management in America', *California Management Review*, Summer, 34–45.

Johnstone, H. and R. Haddow (2003), 'Industrial decline and high technology renewal in Cape

Breton: exploring the limits of the possible', in D. Wolfe (ed.), *Clusters Old and New: The Transition to a Knowledge Economy in Canada's Regions*, Kingston, Quebec: McGill-Queen's University Press.

Johnstone, H. and D. Lionais (1999), 'Identifying equity gaps in a depleted local economy', paper presented at the *Canadian Council for Entrepreneurship and Small Business Annual Conference*, Banff, Alberta, Canada, November.

Johnstone, H. and D. Lionais (2000), 'Using Pareto distributions to better characterize equity gaps and improve estimates of informal venture capital', paper presented at the *Frontiers of Entrepreneurship Research Conference 2000*, Kauffman Center for Entrepreneurship Leadership, Babson College, Wellesley, MA.

Johnstone, H. and D. Lionais (2004), 'Depleted communities and community business entrepreneurship: revaluing space through place', *Entrepreneurship and Regional Development*, **16**, May, 217–33.

Jones, C. and A. Spicer (2009), *Unmasking the Entrepreneur*, Cheltenham, UK and Northampton, MA, USA: Edward Elgar Publishing.

Jones, O., C. Carduso and M. Beckinsale (1997), 'Mature SMEs and technological innovation: entrepreneurial networks in the UK and Portugal', *International Journal of Innovation Management*, **1**(3), 201–27.

Jonung, L. (2000), 'Den nya ekonomin i ett historiskt perspektiv utifrån debatten och litteraturen' [The new economy in a historical perspective from the point of view of public debate and literature], *Ekonomisk Debatt*, **28**(6), 561–6.

Judd, D. and R.L. Ready (1986), 'Entrepreneurial cities and the new politics of economic development', in G.E. Peterson and C.W. Lewis (eds), *Reagan and the Cities*, Washington DC: Urban Institute Press.

Kanter, R.M. (1983), *The Change Masters: Innovation and Entrepreneurship in the American Corporation*, New York: Simon and Schuster.

Katz, D. and R.L. Kahn (1978), *The Social Psychology of Organizations* (2nd edition), New York: Wiley.

Katz, J.A. (1998), 'A brief history of tertiary entrepreneurship education in the United States', paper presented at *the Entrepreneurship Education Workshop*, Stockholm.

Kawasaki, K. (1984), *Negotiating with the Japanese*, Tokyo: JETRO.

Kelley, M. and H. Brooks (1991), 'External learning opportunities and the diffusion of process innovations to small firms: the case of programmable automation', *Technological Forecasting and Social Change*, **39**, 103–25.

Kelly, K. (1998), *Den nya ekonomin. 10 strategier för en uppkopplad värld* [The new economy. 10 strategies for a connected world], Stockholm, Sweden: Timbro.

Kenney, M. (1986), 'Schumpeterian innovation and entrepreneurs in capitalism: a case study of the US bio-technology industry', *Research Policy*, **15**, 21–31.

Kickul, J., M.D. Griffiths and L. Gundry (2010), 'Innovating for social impact: is bricolage the catalyst for change?', in A. Fayolle and H. Matlay (eds), *Handbook of Research on Social Entrepreneurship*, Cheltenham, UK and Northampton, MA, USA: Edward Elgar Publishing.

Kilkenny, M., L. Nalbarte and T. Besser (1999), 'Reciprocated community support and small town-small business sector', *Entrepreneurship and Regional Development*, **11**, 231–46.

Kirlin, J.J. and D.R. Marshall (1988), 'Urban governance and the new politics of entrepreneurship', in M. McGeary and I. Lynn (eds), *Urban Change and Poverty*, Washington DC: National Academic Press.

Kirzner, I.M. (1973), *Competition and Entrepreneurship*, Chicago, IL: University of Chicago Press.

Kirzner, I.M. (1979), *Perception, Opportunity, and Profit*, Chicago, IL: University of Chicago Press.

Klausen, A.M. (1984), *Den norske vaeremåten. Antropologisk sökelys på norsk kultur* [The Norwegian way to be. Anthropological view on Norwegian culture], Oslo, Norway: Cappelen.

Knight, F.H. (1916), *Risk, Uncertainty and Profit*, New York: Houghton Mifflin.

Knorr-Cetina, K. (1981), *The Manufacture of Knowledge: An Essay on the Constructivist and Contextual Nature of Science*, Oxford: Pergamon Press.

Kobayashi, Y. (1990), 'A message to American managers', *Economic Eye*, Spring, 1–8.

Koontz, H. and H. Weihrich (1988) (Sixth Edition), *Management*, New York: Harper and Row.

Krashinsky, M. (1998), *Does Auspice Matter? The Case of Day for Children in Canada*, New Haven and London: Yale University Press.

Kreiner, K. and M. Schultz (1993), 'Informal collaboration in R&D: the formation of networks across organizations', *Organization Studies*, **14**(2), 189–209.

Kroll, L. (1998), 'Entrepreneur moms', *Forbes*, May 18, 84–91.

Kuhn, T. (1962), *The Structure of Scientific Revolution*, Chicago, IL: University of Chicago Press.

Kuratko, D.F. and R. M. Hodgetts (2004), *Entrepreneurship. Theory, Process, Practice* (6th edition), Stanford, CT: Thomson South-Western.

Landström, H. (2005) (Third Edition), *Entreprenörskapets rötter* [The roots of entrepreneurship], Lund, Sweden: Studentlitteratur.

Landström, H. and M. Löwegren (red) (2009), *Entreprenörskap och företagsetablering. Från idé till verklighet* [Entrepreneurship and establishing of businesses. From idea to reality], Lund, Sweden: Studentlitteratur.

Lanzara, G.F. (1999), 'Between transient constructs and persistent structures: Designing systems in action', *Journal of Strategic Information Systems*, **8**, 331–49.

Lasserre, P. and H. Schütte (1995), *Strategies for Asia Pacific*, London: Macmillan Press Ltd.

Latour, B. (1993), *We Have Never Been Modern*, Boston, MA: Harvard University Press.

Latour, B. and S. Wolgar (1979), *Laboratory Life: The Social Construction of Scientific Facts*, Beverley Hills, CA: Sage.

Laville, J.-L. and M. Nyssens (2001), 'Towards a socio-economic approach', in C. Borzaga and J. Defourney (eds), *The Emergence of Social Enterprise*, Oxford and New York: Routledge.

Lawrence, P. and T. Spybey (1986), *Management and Society in Sweden*, London: Routledge & Kegan Paul.

Leadbeater, C. (1997), *The Rise of the Social Entrepreneur*, London: Demos.

Leana, C.R. and Van Buren, H.J. (1999), 'Organizational social capital and employment practices', *Academy of Management Review*, **24**, 538–54.

Lechner, C. and M. Dowling (2003), 'Firm networks: external relationships as sources for the growth and competitiveness of entrepreneurial firms', *Entrepreneurship and Regional Development*, **15**(1), 1–26.

Leitner, H. (1990), 'Cities in pursuit of economic growth: the local state as entrepreneur', *Public Geography Quarterly*, **9**, 146–70.

Leitner, H and E. Sheppard (1998), 'Economic uncertainty, inter-urban competition and the efficacy of entrepreneurialism', in T. Hall and P. Hubbard (eds), *The Entrepreneurial City*, Chichester, UK: John Wiley & Sons Ltd.

Lévi-Strauss, C. (1966), *The Savage Mind*, Chicago, IL: The University of Chicago Press.

Liedman, S.-E. (2002), *Ett oändligt äventyr* [A never-ending adventure], Stockholm, Sweden: Albert Bonniers Förlag.

Liedman, S.-E. (2004), *Tankens lätthet, tingens tyngd, om frihet* [The lightness of thought, the heaviness of things, about freedom], Stockholm, Sweden: Albert Bonniers Förlag.

Light, I. and S.J. Gold (2000), *Ethnic Economics*, London: Academic Press.

Limlingan, V.S. (1986), *The Overseas Chinese in ASEAN: Business Strategies and Management Practices*, Manila, Philippines: Vita Development Corporation.

Lindgren, M. (2000), *Kvinnor i friskolor – Om kön, entreprenörskap och profession i identitetskapandet* [Women in non-public schools – about gender and profession in creating identity], FSF 2000, 3, report from the FEM-gruppen, Örebro, Sweden: Forum för Småföretagsforskning.

Lindgren, M. (2009), 'Gransöverskridande entreprenörskapsforskning: entreprenörskap som process, projekt och emancipation' [Transgressing entrepreneurship research: entrepreneurship as process, project and emancipation], in C. Holmquist (ed.), *Entreprenörskap på riktigt* [Entrepreneurship for real], Lund, Sweden: Studentlitteratur.

Lindgren, M. and J. Packendorff (2007), *Konstruktion av entreprenörskap. Teori, praktik och interaktion* [Construction of entrepreneurship. Theory, practice and interaction], Stockholm, Sweden: Forum för Småföretagsforskning.

Lindkvist, L. (1988), *A Passionate Search for Nordisk Management*, Copenhagen, Denmark: Institute for Organisation og Arbejdssociologi, August.

Ljungbo, K. (2010), *Language as a Leading Light to Business Cultural Insight*, doctoral dissertation, Department of Business Administration, Stockholm University, Sweden.

Locke, E.A. (1991), 'The motivation sequence, the motivation hub and motivation core', *Organizational Behavior and Human Decision Processes*, **50**, 288–99.

Low, M.B. (2001), 'The adolescence of entrepreneurship research: specification of purpose', *Entrepreneurship Theory and Practice*, **25**(4), 17–25.

Lundqvist, M. (2009), 'Den tekniska högskolan på den samhällsentreprenöriella arenan' [The technological academic institution on the social entrepreneurial arena], in M. Gawell, B. Johannisson and M. Lundqvist (eds), *Samhällets entreprenörer* [The societal entrepreneurs], Stockholm, Sweden: KK-stiftelsen.

MacKinnon, D., A. Cumbers and K. Chapman (2002), 'Learning, innovation and regional development: a critical appraisal of recent debates', *Progress in Human Geography*, **26**(3), 293–311.

MacMillan, I.C. and Katz, J.A. (1992), 'Idiosyncratic milieus of entrepreneurial research: the need for comprehensive theories', *The Journal of Business Venturing*, **7**(1), 1–8.

Magnusson, E. (1996), 'Jag har faktiskt aldrig lidit av att vara kvinna' [I have never suffered from being a woman, if fact], *Kvinnovetenskaplig tidskrift*, **17**(1), 30–46.

Maravelias, C. (2009), 'Freedom, opportunism and entrepreneurialism in post-bureaucratic organizations', in D. Hjorth and C. Steyaert (eds), *The Politics and Aesthetics of Entrepreneurship. A Fourth Movements in Entrepreneurship Book*, Cheltenham, UK and Northampton, MA, USA: Edward Elgar Publishing.

Mariotti, S. and C. Glackin (2010), *Entrepreneurship* (2nd edition), Upper Saddle River, NJ: Prentice Hall.

Martin, F. and M. Thompson (2010), *Social Enterprise. Developing Sustainable Businesses*, Hampshire, UK: Palgrave Macmillan.

Martin, L.H., H. Guttmann and P.H. Hutton (1988), *Technologies of the Self – A Seminar with Michel Foucault*, Amherst, MA: University of Massachusetts Press.

Massey, D. (1995a), *Spatial Divisions of Labour: Social Structures and the Geography of Production*, London: Macmillan.

Massey, D. (1995b), 'The conceptualization of place', in D. Massey and P. Jess (eds), *A Place in the World*, Oxford: Oxford University Press.

Mawson, A. (2008), *The Social Entrepreneur: Making Communities Work*, London: Atlantic Books.

Maxmin, J. and S. Zuboff (2002), *The Support Economy*, New York: Viking Penguin.

Mayer, M. (1995), 'Urban governance in the post-Fordist city', in P. Healey, S. Cameron, S. Davoudi, S. Graham and A. Madani-Pour (eds), *Managing Cities: The New Urban Context*, Chichester, UK: Wiley.

McClelland, D. (1961), *The Achieving Society*, Princeton, NJ: D. van Nostrand.

McMillan, J.C. (1985) (Second Revised Edition), *The Japanese Industrial System*, New York: Walter de Gruyter.

Menger, C. (1871), *Principles of Economics*, translated by J. Dingwall and B.F. Housesits, New York: New York University Press (1981).

Merrifield, A. (2000), 'Henri Lefebvre. A socialist in space', in M. Crag and N. Thrift (eds), *Thinking Space*, London and New York: Routledge.

Miles, M. (1997), *Art, Space and the City*, London: Routledge.

Miner, A.S., P. Bassoff and C. Moorman (2001), 'Organizational improvisation and learning. A field study', *Administrative Science Quarterly*, **46**, 304–37.

Mollenkopf, J.H. (1983), *The Contested City*, Princeton, NJ: Princeton University Press.

Moore, F.G. (1982), *Management in Organizations*, New York: John Wiley & Sons, Inc.

Moore, H. (2002), 'Building the social economy', available at: www.fathom.com/feature/35515/.

Moran, R.T. (1988), *Venturing Abroad in Asia*, Maidenhead, UK: McGraw-Hill.

Morita, A. (1986), *Made in Japan*, New York: Dolton.

Mort, G., J. Weerawardena and K. Carnegie (2003), 'Social entrepreneurship: towards conceptualization', *Nonprofit and Voluntary Sector Marketing*, **8**(1), 76–88.

Motte, A. and F. Cajori (1934), *Sir Isaac Newton's Mathematical Principles of Natural Philosophy and his System of the World*, Berkeley, CA: University of California Press.

Mulgan, G. (2006), 'Cultivating the other invisible hand of social entrepreneurship: comparative advantage, public policy, and future research priorities', in A. Nicholls (ed.), *Social Entrepreneurship: New Models of Sustainable Social Change*, Oxford: Oxford University Press.

Mulgan, G. (2007), *Ready or Not? Taking Innovation in the Public Sector Seriously*, London: NESTA.

Mulholland, K. (1996), 'Entrepreneurialism, masculinities and the self-made man', in D. Collinson and J. Hearn (eds), *Men as Managers, Managers as Men: Critical Perspectives on Men, Masculinities and Management*, London: Sage.

Muna, F.A. (1980), *The Arab Executive*, London: McMillan.

Murdoch, J. (2008), 'Inhuman/nonhuman/human: actor–network theory and the prospects for the nondualistic and symmetrical perspective on nature and society', in C. Philo (ed.), *Theory and Methods. Contemporary Foundations of Space and Place*, Hampshire, UK, and Burlington, VT, USA: Ashgate. Reprinted from Murdoch, J. (1997), *Environment and Planning D: Society and Space*, **15**, 731–56.

Murphy, K.M., A. Schleifer and R.W. Vishny (1991), 'The allocation of talent: implications for growth', *Quarterly Journal of Economics*, **106**(2), 503–30.

Murray, R. (2009), *Danger and Opportunity. Crisis and the New Social Economy*, London: National Endowment for Science, Technology and the Art.

Nadler, L. (1984), 'What Japan learned from the US – that we forgot to remember', *California Management Review*, **XXVI**(4), 46–61.

Nahapiet, J. and S. Ghoshal (1998), 'Social capital, intellectual capital and the organizational advantage', *Academy of Management Review*, **23**, 242–67.

Naisbitt, J. (1995), *Megatrends Asia*, London: Nicholas Brealey Publishing.

Naisbitt, J., N. Naisbitt and D. Philips (2001), *High Tech High Touch: Our Accelerating Search for Meaning*, London: Nicholas Brealey Publishing.

Namiki, N. and S.P. Sethi (1988), 'Japan', in R. Nath (ed.), *Comparative Management. A Regional View*, Cambridge, MA: Ballinger Publishing Company.

Neergaard, H. and J.P. Ulhøi (eds) (2007), *Handbook of Qualitative Research in Entrepreneurship*, Cheltenham, UK and Northampton, MA, USA: Edward Elgar Publishing.

New Economics Foundation (2004), *Social Return on Investment: Valuing What Matters*, London: New Economics Foundation.

Newman, J. (2001), *Modernising Governance: New Labour, Policy and Society*, London: Sage.

Nicholls, A. (2006), 'Social entrepreneurship', in S. Carter and D. Jones-Evans (eds), *Enterprise and Small Business. Principles, Practice and Policy* (2nd edition), Harlow, UK: Pearson Education.

Nicholls, A. (2010), 'The legitimacy of social entrepreneurship: reflexive isomorphism in a pre-paradigmatic field', *Entrepreneurship Theory and Practice*, July, 611–33.

Nilsson, N. (2003), *Entreprenörens blick* [The entrepreneur's look], doctoral dissertation, Department of Business Administration, doctoral dissertation, Gothenburg University, Denmark.

Nilsson, P. (2004), Konstruktioner i entreprenörskapstext' [Constructions in entrepreneurship text], in D. Ericsson, (ed.), *Det oavsedda entreprenörskapet* [The unintended entrepreneurship], Lund, Sweden: Academia Adacta.

Nordfors, D, J. Sandred and C. Wessner (eds) (2003), *Commercialization of Academic Research Results*, Forum VFI:2003:1, Vinnova, Sweden.

Normann, R. (2001), *Reframing Business: When the Map changes the Landscape*, New York, NY: John Wiley & Sons.

Office of the Deputy Prime Minister (ODPM) 2003: 'Business-led regeneration of deprived areas: a review of the evidence base', Research Report, Neighbourhood Renewal Unit, Office of the Deputy Prime Minister, London.

O'Gorman, C. (2006), 'Strategy and the small business', in S. Carter and D. Jones- Evans (eds), *Enterprise and Small Business. Principles, Practice and Policy* (2nd Edition), Harlow, UK: Pearson Education.

Ohmae, K. (1982), *The Mind of a Strategist*, New York: Penguin Books.

Öhrström, B. (2005), 'Urban och ekonomisk utveckling. Platsbaserade strategier i den postindustriella staden' [Urban and economic development. Place-based strategies in the post-industrial city], in O. Sernhede and T. Johansson (eds), *Storstadens omvandlingar. Postindustrialism, globalisering och migration. Göteborg och Malmö* [Transformations of the big city. Postindustrialism, globalization and migration. Göteborg and Malmö], Gothenburg, Sweden: Daidalos.

Oinas, P. (1999), 'Voices and silences: the problem of access to embeddedness', *Geoforum*, **30**, 351–61.

Osborne, D. and T. Gaebler (1992), *Reinventing Government: How the Entrepreneurial Spirit is Transforming the Public Sector*, Reading, MA: Addison-Wesley.

Ostgaard, T.A. and S. Birley (1994), 'Personal networks and firm competitive strategy: a strategic or coincidental match?', *Journal of Business Venturing*, **9**, 281–305.

Painter, J. (1998), 'Entrepreneurs are made, not born: learning and urban regimes in the production of entrepreneurial cities', in T. Hall and P. Hubbard (eds), *The Entrepreneurial City*, Chichester, UK: John Wiley & Sons.

Paredo, A.M. and J.J. Chrisman (2006), 'Toward a theory of community-based enterprise', *Academy of Management Review*, **31**(2), 309–28.

Parker, S.C. (2004), *The Economics of Self-employment and Entrepreneurship*, Cambridge: Cambridge University Press.

Parkinson, C. and C. Howorth (2008), 'The language of social entrepreneurs', *Entrepreneurship and Regional Development*, **20**, 285–309.

Pascale, R. and A. Athos (1982), *Japansk företagsledning* [Japanese management], Malmö, Sweden: LiberFörlag.

Paton, R. (2003), *Managing and Measuring Social Enterprises*, London: Sage.

Peck, J. (1995), 'Moving and shaking: business elites, state localism and urban privatism', *Progress in Human Geography*, **19**, 16–46.

Penrose, E.G. (1959), *The Theory of the Growth of the Firm*, New York: Wiley.

Pereira, A.A. (2004), 'State entrepreneurship and regional development. Singapore's industrial parks in Batam and Suzhou', *Entrepreneurship and Regional Development*, **16**, March, 129–44.

Peters, T. (1989), *Thriving on Chaos*, London: Pan Books Ltd.

Peters, T. (1994a), *The Pursuit of WOW! Every person's guide to topsy-turvy times*, London, Sydney and Auckland: Pan Books.

Peters, T. (1994b), *The Tom Peters Seminar. Crazy Times Call for Crazy Organizations*, London, Sydney and Auckland: Pan Books.

Peters, T. and R. Waterman (1982), *In Search of Excellence*, London: Harper and Row.

Petersen, A., I. Barns, J. Dudley and P. Harris (1999), *Poststructuralism, Citizenship and Social Policy*, London: Routledge.

Pettersson, K. (2004), 'Masculine entrepreneurship: the Gnosjö discourse in a feministic perspective', in D. Hjorth and C. Steyaert (eds), *Narrative and Discursive Approaches in Entrepreneurship*, Cheltenham, UK and Northampton, MA, USA: Edward Elgar Publishing.

Phillips-Martinsson, J. (1992) (Revised edition), *Svenskarna som andra ser dem* [Swedes as other people see them], Lund, Sweden: Studentlitteratur.

Philo, C. (2000), 'Foucault's geography', in M. Crang and N. Thrift (eds), *Thinking Space*, London and New York: Routledge.

Pinchot III, G. (1985), *Intrapreneuring*, New York: Harper & Row.

Piore, M.J. and C.F. Sabel (1984), *The Second Industrial Divide. Possibilities for Prosperity*, New York: Basic Books.

Porter, M. (1998), 'The Adam Smith address: location, clusters, and the "New" microeconomics of competition', *Business Economics*, January, 7–13.

Portes, A. and J. Sensenbrenner (1993), 'Embeddedness and immigration: notes on the social determinants', *American Journal of Sociology*, **98**, 1320–50.

Powell, W.W. and L. Smith-Doerr (1994), 'Networks and economic life', in N. Smelser and R. Swedberg (eds), *Handbook of Economic Sociology*, Princeton, NJ: Princeton University Press.

Preston, O. (1987), 'Freedom and bureaucracy', *American Journal of Political Science*, **31**(4), 773–95.

Putnam, R.D., R. Leonardi and R.Y. Nanetti (1993), *Making Democracry Work. Civic Traditions in Modern Italy*, Princeton, NJ: Princeton University Press.

Ram, M., C. Barrett and T. Jones (2006), 'Ethnicity and enterprise', in S. Carter and D. Jones-Evans (eds), *Enterprise and Small Business* (2nd edition), London: Pearson Education.

Rämö, H. (2000), *The Nexus of Time and Place in Economical Operations*, doctoral dissertation, Department of Business Administration, Stockholm University, Sweden.

Rämö. H. (2004), 'Spatio-temporal notions and organized environmental issues: an axiology of action', *Organization*, **11**(6), 849–72.

Ranson, S., B. Hinings and R. Greenwood (1980), 'The structuring of organizational structures', *Administrative Science Quarterly*, **25**, March, 1–17.

Redding, S.G. (1993), *The Spirit of Chinese Capitalism*, Berlin: Walter de Gruyter.

Rehn, A. and S. Taalas (2004), 'Acquaintances and connections: *Blat*, the Soviet Union and mundane entrepreneurship', *Entrepreneurship and Regional Development*, **16**, May, 235–50.

Relph, E. (1976), *Place and Placelessness*, London: Pion.

Renard, M.-C. (2002), 'Fair trade quality, market and conventions', *Journal of Rural Studies*, **19**, 87–96.

Rizzo, M.J. (1982), 'Mises and Lakatos: A reformulation of Austrian methodology', in I.E. Kirzner (ed.), *Method, Process and Austrian Economics*, Toronto: Lexington Books.

Rogers, E. and D. Kincaid (1981), *Communication Networks*, New York: Free Press.

Rohwer, J. (1995), *Asia Rising*, Singapore: Butterworth: Heinemann Asia.

Rose, N. (1999), *Powers of Freedom. Reframing Political Thought*, Cambridge: Cambridge University Press.

Rothwell, R. (1991), 'External networking and innovation in small and medium-sized manufacturing firms in Europe', *Technovation*, **11**(2), 93–111.

Rowan, D. (1997), 'Lastword: glossary for the 90s', *Guardian*, Guardian Weekend, 15 February, T67.

Sack, R. (1997), *Homo Geographicus*, Baltimore, MD: Johns Hopkins University Press.

Sahlin, N.-E. (2001), *Kreativitetens filosofi* [The philosophy of creativity], Nora: Bokförlaget Nya Doxa.

Sallivan, J. and I. Nonaka (1988), 'Culture and strategic issue categorization theory', *Management International Journal*, **28**(3), 6–10.

Salomon, L.M. and H.K. Anheier (1994), *The Emerging Sector Revisited: An Overview*, Baltimore, MD: John Hopkins Institute for Policy Studies.

Salomon, L.M. and H.K. Anheier (1997), 'The civil society sector', *Society*, **34**(2), 60–5.

Samovar, L.A., R.E. Porter and N.C. Jain (1981), *Understanding Intercultural Communication*, Belmont, CA: Wadsworth Publishing Company.

Sánchez, A.A., A.R. Bañón and P.S. Vivaracho (2010), 'Contextual factors favouring entrepreneurship initiative in Spain', in J. Bonnet, D.G.P. De Lema and H. Van Auken (eds), *The Entrepreneurial Society. How to Fill the Gap Between Knowledge and Innovation*, Cheltenham, UK and Northampton, USA: Edward Elgar Publishing.

Sanner, L. (1997), *Trust between Entrepreneurs and External Actors. Sensemaking in organizing new business ventures*, doctoral dissertation, Department of Business Administration, Gothenburg University, Sweden.

Sarasvathy, S. (2001), 'Causation and effectuation: toward a theoretical shift from economic inevitability to entrepreneurial contingency', *Academy of Management Review*, **26**(2), 243–63.

Savage, M. and A. Warde (1993), *Urban Sociology, Capitalism and Modernity*, Basingstoke, UK: Macmillan.

Savitch, H.V. and P. Kantor (1995), 'City business: an international perspective on marketplace politics', *International Journal of Urban and Regional Studies*, **19**, 495–512.

Say, J.B. (1855), *A Treatise on Political Economy* (4th edition), Philadelphia, PA: Lippincott and Grambo & Co.

Scarborough, N.M., D.L. Wilson and T.W. Zimmerer (2009) (Ninth Edition), *Effective Small Business Management. An Entrepreneurial Approach*, Upper Saddle River, NJ: Pearson International Edition.

Schon, D.A. (1983), *The Reflective Practitioner: How Professionals Think in Action*, New York: Basic Books, Inc.

Schreier, J. (1973), *The Female Entrepreneur: A Pilot Study*, Milwaukee, WI: Center for Venture Management.

Schumpeter, J.A. (1934), *The Theory of Economic Development*, Cambridge, MA: Harvard University Press.

Schutz, A. (1962), *Collected Papers*, Vol. I, ed. and intr. M. Natanson, Haag: Martinus Nijhoff.

Schutz, A. (1967), *The Phenomenology of the Social World*, Evanston, IN: Northwestern University Press.

Schwartz, E.B. (1976), 'Entrepreneurship: a new female frontier', *Journal of Contemporary Business*, Winter, 47–76.

Schwind, H.F. and R.B. Peterson (1985), 'Shifting personal values in the Japanese management system', *International Studies of Management and Organization*, Summer, 60–74.

Scott, M.G., R. Rosa and H. Klandt (1998), 'Educating entrepreneurs for wealth creation', in

M.G. Scott, P. Rosa and H. Klandt (eds), *Educating Entrepreneurs for Wealth Creation*, Burlington, VT: Ashgate.

Scott, W.R. (1998), *Organizations: Rational, Natural, and Open Systems* (4th edition), Upper Saddle River, NJ: Prentice Hall.

Seagrave, S. (1996), *Lords of the Rim*, London: Corgi Books.

Sen, A. (1999), *Development as Freedom*, Oxford: Oxford University Press.

Sennett, R. (1998), *The Corrosion of Character: The Personal Consequence of Work in the New Capitalism*, New York: W.W. Norton and Company.

Sernhede, O. and T. Johansson (eds) (2005), *Storstadens omvandlingar. Postindustrialism, globalisering och migration. Göteborg och Malmö* [Transformations of the big city. Postindustrialism, globalization and migration. Göteborg and Malmö], Gothenburg, Sweden: Daidalos.

Sexton, D.L. and N.B. Bowman-Upton (1991), *Entrepreneurship. Creativity and Growth*, New York: Macmillan Publishing Company.

Shane, S. (2003), *A General Theory of Entrepreneurship: The Individual–Opportunity Nexus*, Cheltenham, UK and Northampton, MA, USA: Edward Elgar Publishing.

Shapero, A. and L. Sokol (1982), 'The social dimension of entrepreneurship', in C.A. Kent, D.L. Sexton and K.H. Vesper (eds), *Encyclopedia of Entrepreneurship*, Englewood Cliffs, NJ: Prentice Hall.

Shapin, S. (1995), 'Here and everywhere: sociology of scientific knowledge', *Annual Review of Sociology*, **21**, 289–321.

Sharpe, L.J. (1976), 'The role and functions of local government in modern Britain', in Layfield Report, *The Relationship between General and Local Government*, London: HMSO.

Shaw, E. (1997), 'The real networks of small firms', in D. Deakins, P. Jennings and C. Mason (eds), *Small Firms: Entrepreneurship in the 1990s*, London: Paul Chapman Publishing.

Shaw, E. (1998), 'Social networks: their impact on the innovative behaviour of small service firms', *International Journal of Innovation Management*, **2**(2), 201–22.

Sitaram, K.S. and R.T. Cogdell (1976), *Foundations of Intercultural Communication*, Columbus, OH: Charles E. Merrill.

Sjögren, A. (1985), 'Förhållandet till barnen visar kulturskillnader' [The relationship to the children shows cultural differences], *Invandrare & Minoriteter*, Nr. 4–5.

Skloot, E. (1995), *The Nonprofit Entrepreneur*, New York: Foundation Center.

Small Business Service (SBS) 2004, *SME Statistics*, available at: http://www.sbs.gov.uk/smes.

Smircich, I. and C. Stubbart (1985), 'Strategic management in an enacted world', *Academy of Management Review*, **10**(4), 724–36.

Smith, A. (1776), *The Wealth of Nations*, New York: Cosino, Inc.

Snyder, M. and N. Cantor (1998), 'Understanding personality and social behaviour: a functionalist strategy', in D.T. Gilbert, S.T. Fiska and G. Lindzey (eds), *The Handbook of Social Psychology* (4th edition), Vol. 1, Boston, MA: The McGraw-Hill Companies, Inc.

Soja, E.W. (1996), *Thirdspace. Journeys to Los Angeles and Other Real-and-Imagined Places*, Oxford: Blackwell.

Spilling, O.R. and N. Gunnered Berg (2000), 'Gender and small business management: the case of Norway in the 1990s', *International Small Business Journal*, **18**(2), 38–59.

Spinosa, C., F. Flores and H. Dreyfus (1997), *Disclosing New Worlds*, Cambridge, MA: MIT Press.

Stacey, R.D. (1996), *Complexity and Creativity in Organizations*, San Francisco, CA: Berret-Koehler.

Stam, E. and B. Nooteboom (2011), 'Entrepreneurship, innovation and institution', in D.B. Audretsch, O. Falck, S. Heblich and A. Lederer (eds), *Handbook of Research on Innovation and Entrepreneurship*, Cheltenham, UK and Northampton, MA, USA: Edward Elgar Publishing.

Steinberg, M. and S. Åkerblom (1992), 'Swedish leadership in Singapore: a cross-functional feasibility study', student essay, Handelshögskolan i Stockholm, Stockholm.

Stevenson, H.H. and S. Harmeling (1990), 'Entrepreneurial management's need for a more "chaotic" theory', *Journal of Business Venturing*, **5**, 1–14.

Stevenson, H.H. and J.C. Jarillo (1990), 'A paradigm for entrepreneurship: entrepreneurial management', *Strategic Management Journal*, **11**, 17–27.

Steyaert, C. (1997), 'A qualitative methodology for process studies of entrepreneurship. Creating local knowledge through stories', *International Studies of Management and Organization*, **27**(3), 13–33.

Steyaert, C. (2000), 'Entre-concepts: conceiving entrepreneurship', paper presented at *the RENT-conference XIV*, Prague.

Steyaert, C. (2004), 'The prosaic of entrepreneurship', in D. Hjorth and C. Steyaert (eds), *Narrative and Discursive Approaches to Entrepreneurship. A Second Movements in Entrepreneurship Books*, Cheltenham, UK and Northampton, USA: Edward Elgar Publishing.

Steyaert, C. (2005), 'Entrepreneurship in between what? On the "frontier" as a discourse of entrepreneurship research', *International Journal of Entrepreneurship and Small Business*, **2**(1), 2–16.

Steyaert, C. (2007), '"Entrepreneuring" as a conceptual attractor? A view of process theories in 20 years of entrepreneurship studies', *Entrepreneurship and Regional Development*, **19**(6), 453–77.

Steyaert, C. and D. Hjorth (eds) (2003), *New Movements in Entrepreneurship*, Cheltenham, UK and Northampton, MA, USA: Edward Elgar Publishing.

Steyaert, C. and J. Katz (2004), 'Reclaiming the space of entrepreneurship in society: geographical, discursive and social dimensions', *Entrepreneurship and Regional Development*, **16**, May, 179–96.

Steyaert, C. and D. Hjorth (eds) (2006), *Entrepreneurship as Social Change. A Third Movements in Entrepreneurship Book*, Cheltenham, UK and Northampton, MA, USA: Edward Elgar Publishing.

Storey, D. (1980), *Job Creation and Small Firms Policy in Britain*, Centre for Environmental Studies.

Storper, M. (1997), *The Regional World. Territorial Development in a Global Economy*, New York: The Guilford Press.

Sundin, E. (1988), 'Osynliggörandet av kvinnor – exempel företagare' [Invisualizing women – the example of business enterpriser], *Kvinnovetenskaplig Tidskrift*, **1**, 3–15.

Sundin, E. (2009), 'Det dolda samhällsentreprenörskapet – omsorgsmotiv i småföretag' [Hidden social entrepreneurship – the caring motive in small businesses], in M. Gawell, B. Johannisson and M. Lundqvist (eds), *Samhällets entreprenörer* [The societal entrepreneurs], Stockholm, Sweden: KK-stiftelsen.

Sundin, E. and C. Holmquist (1989), *Kvinnor som företagare – osynlighet, mångfald, anpassning, en studie* [Women as business enterprisers – invisibility, variety, adaptation, a study], Malmö, Sweden: Liber.

Sundin, E. and C. Holmquist (eds) (2002), *Företagerskan – Om kvinnor och entreprenörskap* [The woman entrepreneur – about women and entrepreneurship], Stockholm, Sweden: SNS Förlag.

Söderman, S. (1983), *Japan och industriell marknadsföring* [Japan and industrial marketing], Lund, Sweden: Studentlitteratur.

Taylor, M. (2003), *Public Policy in the Community*, Basingstoke and New York: Palgrave Macmillan.

Thake, S. and S. Zadek (1997), *Practical People, Noble Causes: How to Support Community-based Social Entrepreneurs*, London: New Economics Foundation.

Thompson, J. (2002), 'The world of the social entrepreneur', *International Journal of Public Sector Management*, **15**(5), 412–31.

Thompson, J., G. Alvy and A. Lees (2000), 'Social entrepreneurship: a new look at the people and the potential', *Management Decision*, **38**(5), 328–38.

Thornton, P.H. (1999), 'The sociology of entrepreneurship', *Annual Review of Sociology*, **25**, 19–46.

Thrift, N.J. (1996), *Spatial Formations*, London and Thousand Oaks, CA: Sage.

Thurik, A.R. and Van Dijk (1998), 'Entrepreneurship: visies en benaderingen' [Entrepreneurship: points of views and approaches], in D.P. Scherjon and A.R. Thurik (eds), *Handboek ondernemers en adviseurs in het MKB* [Handbook for enterprisers of and advisors to SMEs], Dordrecht, the Netherlands: Kluwer Bedrijfsinformatie.

Tichy, N.M., N.L. Tushman and C. Forbrun (1979), 'Social network analysis for organisations', *Academy of Management Review*, **4**(4), 507–19.

Timmons, J.A. (1999), *New Venture Creation. Entrepreneurship for the 21st Century* (5th edition), New York: Irwin McGraw-Hill.

Toffler, A. (1980), *The Third Wave*, London: Collins.

Tomasson, R.F. (1970), *Sweden: Prototype of Modern Society*, New York: Random House.

Tornikoski, E. (1999), 'Entrepreneurship through constructivist lenses: visionary entrepreneurship process – a conceptual development', licentiate thesis, *Management and Organization*, Vaasa University, Finland.

Townley, B. (1995), '"Know thyself": self-awareness, self-formation and managing', *Organization*, **2**(2), 271–89.

Trompenaars, F. (1995), *Riding the Waves of Culture*, London: Nicholas Brealey Publishing.

Tuan, Y.-F. (1974), *Topophilia: a Study of Environmental Perception, Attitudes, and Values*, Englewood Cliffs, NJ: Prentice Hall.

Tuan, Y.-F. (1977), *Space and Place. The Perspective of Experience*, Minneapolis and London: The University of Minnesota Press.

Vasi, I.B. (2009), 'New heroes, old theories? Toward a sociological perspective on social entrepreneurship', in R. Ziegler (ed.), *An Introduction to Social Entrepreneurship*, Cheltenham, UK and Northampton, MA, USA: Edward Elgar Publishing.

Venkataraman, S. (1997), 'The distinctive domain of entrepreneurship research', in J.A. Katz and R. Brockhaus (eds), *Advances in Entrepreneurship, Firm Emergence and Growth*, Vol. 3, Greenwich, CT: JAI Press.

Vestrum, I.K. and O.J. Borch (2006), 'Dynamics of entrepreneurship culture', paper presented at *ESU2006 Conference* at University of Tampere in Hämeenlinna, Finland.

Virno, P. (1996), 'The ambivalence of disenchantment', in P. Virno and M. Hardt (eds), *Radical Thought in Italy*, Minneapolis, MN: University of Minneapolis Press.

von Mises, L. (1949), *Human-action. A Treatise on Economics*, New Haven, CT: Yale University Press.

von Mises, L. (1981), *Epistemological Problems of Economics*, transl. by G. Riesman, New York: New York University Press (originally published in German in 1933).

von Wright, G. H. (1971), *Explanation and Understanding*, London: Routledge & Kegan Paul.

Waterman, R.H. (1982), 'The seven elements of strategic fit', *Journal of Business Strategy*, **2**(3), 69–73.

Watkins, J. and D. Watkins (1984), 'The female entrepreneur: background and determinants of business choice: some British data', *International Small Business Journal*, **2**(4), 21–31.

Watson, J.B. (1970), *Behaviorism*, New York: Norton.

Watson, S. (1991), 'Gilding the smokestacks: the new symbolic representations of deindustrialised regions', *Environment and Planning D: Society and Space*, **9**, 59–70.

Weber, M. (1975) (2nd Edition), *Makt og byråkrati* [Power and bureaucracy], Oslo, Norway: Gyldendal Norsk Förlag.

Wee, C.H., K.S. Lee and W.H. Bamwang (1991), *Sun Tzu: War and Management*, Singapore: Addison-Wesley Publishing Company.

Weick, K.E. (1993), 'The collapse of sensemaking in organizations: The Mann Gulch disaster', *Administrative Science Quarterly*, **38**, 628–52.

Wei-Skillern, J., J.E. Austin, H. Leonard and H. Stevenson (2007), *Entrepreneurship in the Social Sector*, London, UK and Thousand Oaks, CA, USA: Sage Publications.

Weiskopf, R. and C. Steyaert (2009), 'Metamorphoses in entrepreneurship studies: towards an affirmative politics of entrepreneuring', in D. Hjorth and C. Steyaert (eds), *The Politics and Aesthetics of Entrepreneurship. A Fourth Movements in Entrepreneurship Book*, Cheltenham, UK and Northampton, MA, USA: Edward Elgar Publishing.

Westerdahl, H. (2001), *Business and Community*, Gothenburg, Sweden: Bokförlaget BAS.

Westlund, H. (2001), 'Social economy and the case of Sweden', *Uddevalla Symposium 2001. Regional Economies in Transition*, Vänersborg, Sweden.

Westlund, H. and S. Westerdahl (1997), *Contribution of the Social Economy to Local Employment*, Östersund/Stockholm, Sweden: Institutet för social ekonomi/Koopi.

Westlund, H. and R. Bolton (2003), 'Local social capital and entrepreneurship', *Small Business Economics*, **21**, 77–113.

Wickham, P.A. (2006), *Strategic Entrepreneurship* (4th edition), Harlow, UK: Pearson Education Limited.

Wiklund, J. (1998), *Small Firm Growth and Performance*, JIBS Dissertation Series No. 003, Jönköping International Business School.

Wilkinson, J. (1997), 'A new paradigm for economic analysis? Recent convergences of French social science and an exploration of the convention theory approach with a consideration of its application to the analysis of the agro-food sector', *Economy and Society*, **26**(3), 305–39.

Winch, P. (1958), *The Idea of a Social Science and its Relation to Philosophy*, London: Routledge and Kegan Paul.

Winnicott, D.W. (1971), *Playing and Reality*, Harmondsworth: Penguin.

Wong, S. (1995), 'Business networks, cultural values and the state of Hong Kong and Singapore', in R.A. Brown (ed.), *Chinese Business Enterprise in Asia*, London: Routledge.

Wood, M. (2005), 'The fallacy of misplaced leadership', *Journal of Management Studies*, **42**(6), 1101–21.

Yang, B. (1991), *The Ugly Chinaman and the Crisis of Chinese Culture*, St. Leonards, Australia: Allen & Unwin.

Zerbinati, S. and V. Soutaris (2005), 'Entrepreneurship in the public sector: a framework of analysis in European local governments', *Entrepreneurship and Regional Development*, **1**, 3–19.

Ziegler, R. (ed.) (2009), *An Introduction to Social Entrepreneurship*, Cheltenham, UK and Northampton, MA, USA: Edward Elgar Publishing.

Zimmerer, T.W. and N.M. Scarborough (2005) (Fourth Edition), *Essentials of Entrepreneurship and Small Business Management*, Upper Saddle River, NJ: Prentice Hall.

Index